# TRAINING WITH NLP

The key to the success of any individual or organisation is
continuous learning. This intensely practical book shows you how
to both learn and train more effectively than ever before. It is
destined to become required reading for anyone who trains
anyone else on any subject.

*Brian Tracey, author of* Maximum Achievement

*Training with NLP* is a comprehensive guide to major training
requirements for the 21st century by two authors who are models
of the future training manager – a highly recommended read.

*Tony Buzan, author of* Use your Head *and*
The Mind Map Book – Radiant Thinking

**BY THE SAME AUTHORS:**
Introducing NLP

# TRAINING WITH NLP

## SKILLS FOR MANAGERS, TRAINERS AND COMMUNICATORS

Joseph O'Connor
and John Seymour

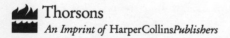
Thorsons
*An Imprint of* HarperCollins*Publishers*

Thorsons
An Imprint of HarperCollins*Publishers*
77-85 Fulham Palace Road
Hammersmith, London W6 8JB
1160 Battery Street
San Francisco, California 94111–1213

Published by Thorsons 1994
10 9 8 7 6 5 4 3 2 1

Joseph O'Connor and John Seymour assert the moral right to
be identified as the authors of this work

'Mind Map' is a registered trade mark

A catalogue record for this book
is available from the British Library

ISBN 0 72252853 1

Typeset by Harper Phototypesetters Limited,
Northampton, England

Illustrations by Jennie Dooge

Printed in Great Britain by
Mackays of Chatham, Kent

FOR THOSE WHO DEVOTE THEIR LIVES TO
CREATING A BETTER WORLD BY EMPOWERING OTHERS.

# CONTENTS

PART FOUR − EVALUATION

APPENDICES

# FOREWORD

## A Natural Selection

Over the years many books have been published about Neuro-Linguistic Programming. Some books have been skillful and successfully presented. They have developed new processes and frameworks in the field of communication. Other books have merely been a rehash of the same material. Every now and again, a book comes along that expresses the utilization of NLP at several levels. *Training with NLP* by O'Connor and Seymour uses skillful modelling techniques to outline the process of training.

I felt this book was very close to the thought processes and levels of interaction I employ in training. Perhaps even more important is the fact that the book is written in 'English' and is not full of NLP jargon. The consequence of this translation is that more people have access to the set of patterns called NLP without having to learn the NLP language. Those of us involved in NLP who share a vision of touching the world in many areas have to recognize the importance of reaching business management leadership and education.

I believe this book is a natural selection for anyone in the training or teaching arena. Thank you Joseph O'Connor and John Seymour for your modelling and clear presentation.

*Judith DeLozier*
*Co-Developer of NLP*

# ACKNOWLEDGEMENTS

We would like to thank our many friends and teachers who have helped and inspired us and made this book possible: Tony Coughlan for his work on universal access; and trainers at John Seymour Associates, Michael Neill and Peter McNab.

To Ravi Lander and Neil McKee, our thanks for the Mind Maps®.

Especial thanks to Annie Dalton. Thank you to Liz Puttick and Elizabeth Hutchins, our editors at Thorsons.

Many thanks to Bob Janes, Brian Van der Horst and Steve Andreas for reading the manuscript and making helpful suggestions. We owe a debt to all our original trainers, particularly John Grinder and Robert Dilts.

Finally, deservably and inevitably, to the many thousands of students of courses that we have both given in a wide variety of settings: health, education, business and public NLP seminars.

*Joseph O'Connor and John Seymour*
*September 1993*

# INTRODUCTION

If a man begin with certainties he shall end in doubts, but if he will be content to begin with doubts he shall end in certainties.

*Francis Bacon, 1605*

This book has two themes: the challenge that faces trainers; and how to meet it. Many trainers are threatened by changes in business organisation and advances in technology. As time passes many more will be. It is becoming clear that other resources, particularly computer-aided learning, are more cost-effective at passing on skills and knowledge in many situations. Training is being pushed from its comfortable niche and has yet to find its place in the new order.

To meet this challenge, trainers will need to be very effective in the areas they choose to work in. They will increasingly need the skills that have been traditionally associated with organisational consultants to make their training more effective at the *organisational* level. They will also need the best possible presentation and training skills available to be effective at the *individual* level.

**Part One** provides a broad overview of training and the evolutionary moves that are currently taking place:

- *Why* training is changing – the organisational changes taking place and the emergence of learning organisations that empower and develop their people.
- *What* is changing – our understanding of competence-based standards and the learning processes that underlie them.
- *How* to increase training skills – part of the answer is to model the strategies of outstanding performers for learning, communication skills and the practical means to develop the most

effective training skills. Neuro-Linguistic Programming is the discipline with the knowledge to model complex skills. Competence is no longer enough in the training world.

In **Part Two** we look at the skills of designing training and presentations, also trainers' beliefs, values and identity, an area neglected in most training books.

**Part Three** explores the interactive skills of live delivery. At its best, training can provide the six criteria for an optimal experience for an individual. It has the learning of skills, concrete goals, it provides feedback, lets the person feel in control, facilitates concentration and involvement and is distinct from the everyday world. This section is based round three important training skills:

- Look after your own emotional state. The better your state, the better the training.
- Make your primary outcome to keep the trainees in a good learning state. This is more important than any teaching you give them.
- Teach to the conscious and unconscious minds of the trainees. In other words, have them leave the training room knowing more and having more skills than they know they have or noticed they learned.

**Part Four** completes the training cycle by focusing on evaluation and training development.

Each part is self-contained, so you can dip into any sections that interest you, in any order. You can speed read the book and reread interesting sections afterwards. At the same time, the book has a coherence and an interweaving of themes in the way a musical piece uses the same thematic material, even though it may be divided into several movements.

There is a difference in writing styles in the four main parts. This is deliberate. We have attempted to make the style congruent with the area we are exploring.

For those of you that like to notice difference, here is what this book is NOT. It is not an academic treatise, although it is well founded on current research. Nor does it put forward one approach to training, except insofar as training is driven by the learning needs of those you train and train for. It is not an expert's view of organisational change and development, it is a *trainer's* perspective. It is not primarily a book of presentation skills, although there are many useful ones here.

To avoid gender bias and keep a simple writing style, we have used 'he' or 'she' equally and randomly throughout the book to reflect the fact that trainers and trainees may be male or female.

Unlike a training, this book has only words. Thank you for bringing your imagination to enliven our words.

## Mind Maps®

Here is the first of six Mind Maps that you will find in this book. This one summarises the whole book. The next one summarises the first chapter and the remaining ones summarise the four main parts of the book. We invite you to make your own as you read through to help you organise and remember the key material.

If you want to know more about Mind Mapping, read Tony Buzan's *The Mind Map Book – Radiant Thinking* (details in the Bibliography).

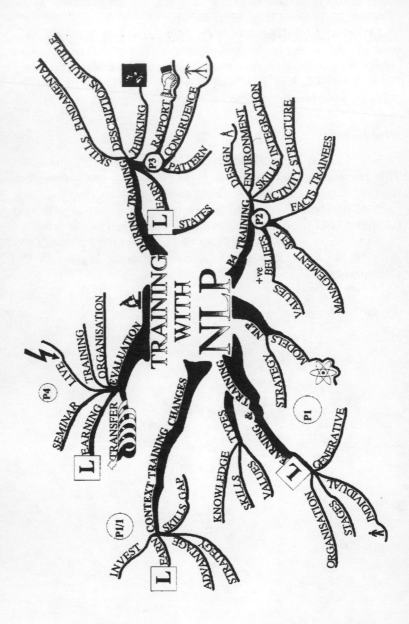

# PART ONE

# THE CHALLENGE TO TRAINERS

# THE CHANGING CONTEXT OF TRAINING

I

May you live in interesting times.

*Ancient Chinese curse*

Training is in trouble. It faces an increasing challenge to justify its effectiveness in the face of massive changes in business organisation and advances in technology. For businesses seeking to improve their performance and develop their people, training is only one choice among many. At the same time, there are unprecedented opportunities for skilled trainers who can not only ride, but also drive the changes that are happening. The choice is to seize the day or be left behind.

Training is big business. In 1987 it was a £33 billion a year business in the UK. Employers spent £18 billion, of which £6 billion went to on-the-job training, individuals spent £8 billion and the government £7 billion. The industry consists of further and higher education providers as well as almost 3,000 providers in the private sector. It is hard to know how many people are employed in the training and development area, but a quarter of a million would be a reasonable guess. To these you can add managers, experts and part-time trainers who are expected to train others as part of their job.

To maintain its place, training must be effective – and be seen to be effective. Public trainings, for example, are under pressure from the increasing number of distance learning packages as well as interactive computer-based learning tools and the trainer needs excellent live presentation skills to be successful. In organisations, where the majority of training takes place, the days of training being seen as 'a good thing' in itself are going fast. Training has to justify itself – and it can. Training can be one of the most effective (and cost-effective) ways of passing on skills and a powerful force in organisational development.

*Competitive advantage*

Ideally training leads to better performance at an individual, work and organisational level, and this will be translated into a competitive advantage for the organisation.

A company can seek competitive advantage in three main areas. First, it can use the best and most up-to-date technology. However, although technology is easily purchased and readily available, it can be outdated in a matter of months. Secondly, it can use the most efficient systems of working and delivery – but so can its competitors.

Thirdly, there is the quality of its people. Smart people will make the most of smart machines, find smart ways of using them and invent smarter ones still. And be able to do it consistently. 'The ability to learn faster than your competitors may be the only sustainable competitive advantage' is a widely circulated quote from Arie De Geus, head of planning for Royal Dutch/Shell. Organisations are coming to act on this and are investing more in their people. One way of doing this is with effective training.


## THE LEARNING ORGANISATION


. . . the most successful corporation of the 1990s will be something called a learning organisation.

*Fortune* magazine


A learning organisation is one which recognises the importance of the people within it, supports their full development and creates a context in which they can learn. This new kind of business organisation is possible because we are natural learners, despite a formal education system that often hinders our natural learning abilities. It is also swimming against the tide, for the culture that we live in is not a natural learning culture.

The learning organisation is a fundamental innovation. It is as different from our present organisations as these are from a medieval village. The purpose, the values and the ways of working and thinking are all different. Being part of a group of people who trust each other and share a common goal, where you can use your strengths and have others cover your weaknesses, is a rewarding experience. It is surprising what such a group can accomplish.

The learning organisation and its creative culture is possible, yet hard to create at will. It cannot be imposed, it has to be grown organically at every level. We are still seeking the disciplines and development pathways that will enable us to achieve it effectively.

The learning organisation may seem idealistic and hard to implement, but look at the example of the Brazilian company Semco, as described in the book *Maverick!* by Ricardo Semler. *Maverick!* tells of one company's response to ferocious competition from the Far East. Workers at Semco fix their own working days, many are encouraged to work from home, the assembly line has been abandoned, a quarter of employees fix their own salaries and soon everybody will. The workers decide how much of the profits to share and how much to invest. They also vote regularly on the performance of their boss. Managers who underperform fade away or are squeezed out. This is a company that takes empowerment seriously. And one that is being taken seriously, as 150 of the Fortune top 500 companies in the USA have visited it to see what is happening. They would not have bothered unless Semco was successful – and it is. It has experienced a sevenfold rise in productivity and a fivefold increase in profits after allowing for inflation. Learning organisations would have remained as just a nice idea if they were not so effective in the market-place.

## The qualities of the learning organisation

Peter Senge, director of the systems thinking and organisational learning programme at the Sloan School of Management, Massachusetts Institute of Technology (MIT), outlines the qualities of a learning organisation in his excellent book, *The Fifth Discipline – the Art and Practice of the Learning Organisation*

Senge's unique contribution comes from the computer modelling of dynamic systems that MIT has excelled in since the pioneering work of Jay Forester in the 1970s. Senge identifies five key disciplines that are needed to create a learning organisation. The fifth discipline of the title is *systemic thinking*, very different from our traditional linear thought process. Thinking systemically about an organisation means looking at the connection of its parts and seeing a process of change rather than separated snapshots. Important consequences of decisions are often not connected to the original cause because causes and effects are separated by time and place. This is as true in companies as it is in medicine and weather forecasting. Systemic thinking can show how a company structure can create problems and how the consequences of executive decisions show up elsewhere in the system, sometimes coming back to create the very problem they were designed to alleviate. Learning how to think systemically is an essential skill for management if companies are to learn at the organisational level. Organisational learning is different from individual learning, because it involves changes in the operating systems and structures of the organisation itself.

Peter Senge's other four disciplines of the learning organisation are: building shared vision, team learning, mental models and personal mastery. Building shared vision is the process of creating an organisational purpose and identity that inspires and motivates all of the members of the organisation. Team learning is how people can form effective teams. Mental models are the unconscious beliefs of individuals and groups that shape their behaviour and decisions. All of us have beliefs that limit our effectiveness. This discipline is about learning how to surface these limiting beliefs and change them into more empowering ones, leading to better decisions and actions. Finally, there is personal mastery. This is not about dominance. It is about mastery in the sense of the master craftsman or woman who has a lifelong commitment to improving their skills. It is personal because it is part of personal development. No one else can do it for you. The motivation and satisfaction both come from within.

All of Senge's disciplines involve learning thinking skills, acting effectively and continuously improving what we do. This is a trainer's territory. And yet, if we are to deliver results, more of us will need the skills of the best of us. We need to make these skills explicit and to create ways of rapidly transferring them.

## DEALING WITH CHANGE

Organisations need to equip people for change. Performance management systems are implemented to manage the changes, often with management coaching schemes. These help individuals to cope with change and to broaden their skills base, usually within a range of defined competencies. Interpersonal skills are important; task-oriented behaviour is no longer enough. Managers need to manage people as well as information. Communication and relationship skills are critical if mentoring and coaching schemes are to work and bring out the best in people. Training is needed to update existing skills and, more importantly, to learn new ones, for technology has cut through existing job structures, destroying many and creating some new ones. People are retraining for totally new jobs or to operate new technologies. No longer can a person expect to do one job for the whole of his life. Instead individuals will need a range of skills, which Charles Handy, in his book the *Age of Unreason*, calls a 'portfolio' of different jobs and skills.

## The skills gap

The education system is too slow to respond to changes, let alone the increasing pace of current changes. It teaches a curriculum that was relevant to the last generation and can never catch up, because it has to be designed long before it is implemented. By the time it gets used, the world has moved on. This means the education system does not train people in current skills and knowledge. There is a gap. For example, senior managers now in their forties were educated at a time when computer studies did not exist and the enormous spread of personal computers was only a gleam in the eyes of the inhabitants of Silicon Valley. Many have little training in understanding the role and potential of computers. It is only in the last few years that there have been people on the job market who were exposed to computers in their primary school.

## Training in the learning organisation

What role do trainers have in creating and maintaining a learning organisation? Training is an inherent part of the working culture and environment in a learning organisation. Training is one way of helping people learn to improve and so is regarded as a continuing investment rather than an expense. It is part of the strategy of the learning organisation to invest in people. Communication skills and interpersonal skills are important in any organisation and these are areas where live training is the most effective choice.

The opportunities for trainers are great, though training will become an increasingly central aspect of company policy if, and only if, trainers deliver the necessary results. Yet as trainers learn the skills to train more effectively, they will be able to demonstrate more clearly that good training is one of the most cost-effective investments possible.

## THE CHANGING CONTEXT OF TRAINING

### *Key Points*

THE CHALLENGE TO TRAINING
- Training is facing challenges from advances in technology and changes in business culture and organisation. There are new opportunities – and dangers – for trainers.
- Training needs to be effective and efficient and seen to be so.
- Businesses seek a competitive edge in three areas:
    1. The newest technology.
    2. The best business systems.
    3. The skills of their people.

LEARNING ORGANISATIONS
- The ability to learn faster than competitors may be the only sustainable competitive advantage.
- Many companies are becoming 'learning organisations'. A learning organisation seeks to:
    empower its people
    continuously improve itself and its people
    learn at every level from corporate to individual
    be responsive to customer needs
    support the full development of each person within the company
    create a learning culture

CREATING A LEARNING ORGANISATION
- It is not yet clear how to implement the learning organisation and its learning culture.
- Peter Senge has identified five disciplines needed to create a learning organisation:
    1. Systemic thinking: thinking in relationship and long-term consequences rather than short-term linear cause and effect.
    2. Building shared vision: creating organisational purpose and identity.

3. Team learning.
4. Mental models: surfacing the unconscious beliefs of individuals and groups that shape all behaviour and decisions.
5. Personal mastery: a commitment to continually improving skills at work.

- People need skills to deal with change.
- There is always a skills gap between the educational curriculum and the knowledge and skills actually needed. Training fills this gap.
- Training is an important and cost-effective way of creating and maintaining a learning organisation, provided it makes the most of the resources available and trainers are skilled enough to deliver the desired results.

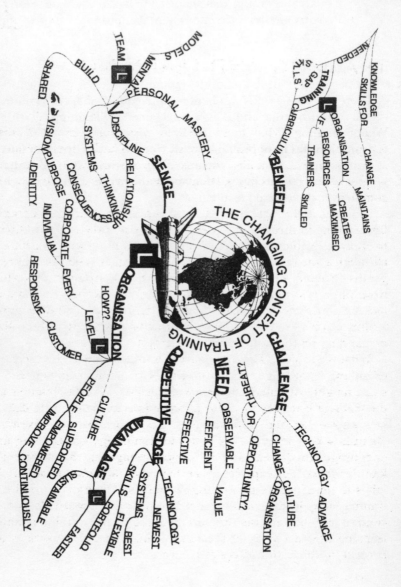

# 2

# TRAINING AND LEARNING

What is training? What does it mean to you? What does it do? This is a question you have probably asked yourself and it does not have a 'right' answer. Training means different things to different people. Because training is about human learning, the field is as complex as we are.

Training is the process that amplifies, and provides a context for, learning in three main areas. First there is knowledge and how to apply it. Problem solving is an example of this kind of learning, although some rate it a skill. The second category is skills learning. Hands-on experience is essential for the development of skills, from physical ones, such as touch typing, to interpersonal ones, like training. The last area is learning at the level of values and attitudes. This kind of training is probably the most technically demanding on the trainer and the hardest to evaluate.

What is learning? The dictionary tells us learning is 'the process of getting knowledge, skills or abilities by study, experience or being taught'. Although the *process* of learning is hard to pin down, the *results* of learning are clear: improved performance, new skills, new knowledge and new attitudes. The more we can discover about how people learn, the better we can design our training to encourage this. Learning is about *change* in the trainees' knowledge, skill or experience. Perhaps the trainer's fundamental job is to demonstrate that change is possible. There is a trend in training away from teacher-centred courses and towards learner-centred events because they are more effective. Training and learning are two sides of the same coin. The trainer creates a context in which individuals can learn.

## Types of training

Training embraces a whole spectrum of possibilities. Most training takes place in an organisational framework. There is vocational training and experiential training in the workplace. Our main focus in this book is on group training and learning. This is the domain of trainers, training courses, seminars and workshops. Group training, if done well, is one of the most cost-effective ways of delivering the skills needed for continuous improvement in an organisation.

There is training for work, initiated and maintained by the organisation for its people as part of their professional development, and individuals also take training courses for personal development.

Individuals learn in the live training experience. If it is a public training they take the new knowledge and skills back to their lives. In an organisation, the trainees take the new knowledge and skills back to their workplace. The results of effective training lead to improved job performance. Improved job performance leads to an improvement in organisational performance. Training is part of the way that an organisation learns. There is a pattern and a parallel between how individuals and how organisations learn.

## ORGANISATIONAL LEARNING

At the organisational level, the actual training event is part of a wider cycle of how organisations learn and develop. The cycle begins with identifying and establishing outcomes for the training. There is the training event itself, the systematic process to impart knowledge, skills, attitudes and changes in behaviour. This is followed by an evaluation process to establish how far the outcomes have been met.

### The training cycle
1. Identifying training needs at three different levels: the needs of the organisation as a whole; the needs of each of the different jobs in the workforce; and the needs of each individual in the workforce. This is the Training Needs Analysis (TNA).
2. Setting outcomes for the training in terms of skills, values and attitudes, knowledge and resources. This is done by assessing present skill levels and identifying desired ones.
3. Designing training to meet needs and outcomes.
4. The live training process.

5. Evaluating the effectiveness of the training in achieving its goals and using the results to refine the training cycle.

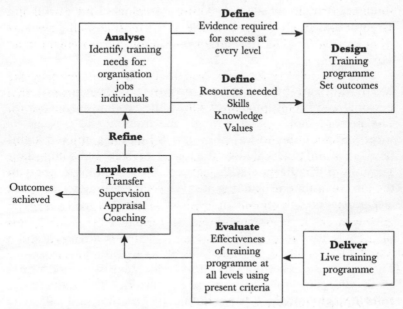

*Figure 1.1 The training cycle*

## The organisation

From the organisation's point of view, the purpose of training is to make it more effective and successful by improving the combined performance of the individuals in it. The end evaluation will be based on whether the training has increased organisational effectiveness, and one evidence of this may be increased profits. The organisation wants training to deliver skills to the people who need them, when they need them and at an acceptable cost, so the whole process is cost-effective. Training from this viewpoint is part of organisational development.

## The job

Within the organisation there will be specific jobs and tasks to be done. Ideally, the Training Needs Analysis determines which jobs need to be targeted for improved performance and, once identified, how specifically they need to improve and how you can measure the improvement. Managers need to be actively involved in this process. There will be an evaluation at the end of the training for each specific task. This is a counsel of perfection and very effective when followed through.

## The individual trainee

Nearly everyone has a need for growth and development at a personal and professional level. Often the two are not separated. The person who is going through the training will evaluate its success in a number of ways: how much he or she enjoyed it and how useful and practical he or she found it. There is the important question of whether the skills learned in the training transfer to the job environment. Training at this level is learning for personal and professional development.

## The trainer

The trainer is the key person in the cycle. He or she works with a group of people for the purpose of learning. The trainer may come into an organisation, give a 'one off' training and walk away or, at the other extreme, be fully involved at the organisational level. In this case, he or she needs a set of specialised skills to design, deliver and evaluate the training. The trainer has a personal viewpoint, and if the training is to be an effective part of the overall system and not an isolated event, also needs to appreciate and be involved with the other viewpoints.

The trainer has the demanding job of dovetailing the organisational and individual needs. A good trainer in an organisational setting needs to know the field well and have the skills to pass it on to groups of people. This needs specialised knowledge, presentation skills, an understanding of individual and group learning and group dynamics. Finally, if that was not enough, he or she also needs the skills of an organisational consultant to be involved in the Training Needs Analysis and to consult with line managers to analyse job performance. The trainer also needs to be able to evaluate the results of the training at the levels of individual, work and organisational performance. Training in an organisation will be effective if it is a fully integrated part of the training cycle.

## Continuous improvement

Organisational learning involves continuous improvement and here the ideas of the Total Quality Movement (TQM) have spread widely. The single most influential person in this field is Dr W. Edwards Deming, the American trainer and consultant who first introduced these ideas to the Japanese in the post-war years. Such has been his influence that in Japan the annual Deming Prize is probably the most coveted national business award.

Deming formulated a total philosophy of continuously improving every process of planning, production and service for business. TQM aims to create an organisational learning culture by building quality into the business process, instituting modern methods of training and undertaking a vigorous programme of education. A stated aim is to drive out fear from the organisation, because frightened people can neither work well nor be empowered. Gone are the days immortalised in the quote attributed to Samuel Goldwyn: 'I don't want any yes-men around me, I want everyone to tell me the truth even if it costs them their job.' The Deming philosophy also calls for the elimination of sales targets, commissions and such competitive markers as annual merit ratings. The argument for these measures is that structural problems in the job cause most individual failures and if these are outside any individual's control then any merit rewards are arbitrary and counterproductive.

Building a learning organisation by continuous improvement needs to start with clear leadership and an overall shared vision. TQM has often been seized as a panacea and imposed on an organisation from the top. The results have been disappointing. Deming is very clear that unless the TQM philosophy is *applied at the top*, and is seen to be, it will have little effect.

## INDIVIDUAL LEARNING

### Standards and competence

There can be no organisational learning without individual learning and one goal of training is the continuously improving performance of the individual. Improved performance comes from gaining new skills or developing existing ones.

In order to define what constitutes an improved performance

level, standards are needed. These may be measured quantitively, for example on an assembly line as number of items produced per hour, however it is far from easy to define standards in a field of interpersonal skills.

In the United Kingdom the system of National Vocational Qualifications (NVQ) and Scottish Vocational Qualifications (SVQ) was instituted as a set of competency-based standards to facilitate more effective learning skills in all major industries. Competence is the ability to carry out a task to a defined standard. The NVQ approach is to take skills and break them down into small elements, with standards of performance attached. Levels of skill can then be assessed as a composite of elements. A trainer can look at the skill in finer and finer detail and see the standards of competence required and the criteria by which they will be judged.

The NVQ structure is dealt with at greater length in the appendix on page 266. It is relevant to trainers in two ways. First, as a structured task analysis and a way of thinking about assessing competence in the areas they train. More and more training is being linked to appropriate NVQ standards. Secondly, it provides a map of competencies for training itself, defined by the Training and Development Lead Body (TDLB) in the UK, and so attempts to answer the interesting question, 'What makes a competent trainer?'

## Motivation

For people to learn new skills regardless of their organisational role, a number of conditions must be met. First, they must want to learn the skills. They must see them as meaningful and worthwhile for themselves. Learning needs motivation. Sending people on courses to learn skills that somebody else thinks they need to learn does not work. Unfortunately this still happens in many businesses (and is almost universal in education until the age of 16). A better idea is to offer people a choice of courses and clear benefits for attending them. Training goals are what the trainers want the trainees to know and do. Learning goals are what the trainees want to know and do. The actual training will be a mix and a dovetailing of these two goals for the purpose of learning.

## Four stages of learning

Learning a skill tends to fall into four general stages. As you read on, think how learning a skill, such as driving, fits into this framework. The first stage is known as *unconscious incompetence*. Not only do you not know what to do, you have no experience of it either. This is the 'ignorance is bliss' stage. To a child, car driving is a mystery.

The second stage is *conscious incompetence*. You start to do it and soon find out the problems. At this point, it takes all your conscious attention. Although this stage is uncomfortable, it is also the stage when you are learning the most. Because it is uncomfortable, it is important that trainers fully support learners and let them know this discomfort is evidence of learning. If the unconscious competence stage is too long or too uncomfortable, learners may become discouraged, hence the importance of dividing the skill into manageable chunks.

Next you reach the stage of *conscious competence*. You can do it, but it takes attention and concentration.

Finally, there is *unconscious competence*. The skill becomes a smooth series of habits and your conscious mind is free to listen to the radio, look at the scenery or have a conversation while you drive.

## CREATING AN ENVIRONMENT FOR LEARNING

Trainees must have the chance to learn the skills. This raises the question of how we learn. The trainer's idea of what learning is, and how it happens, will strongly influence the design and presentation of the training course. If you think back to the important things you have learned in your life, you will probably find you did not consciously put them all together piece by piece. Your experiences and knowledge came together as new insights without you 'trying' to make it happen. Our conscious mind is very much the tip of the iceberg. Most of our thought processes are unconscious, we only become aware of the results. This is hardly surprising, for our conscious attention is limited to between five and nine pieces of information. What is important is how we piece together information and the connections we make.

Given that much learning is unconscious, the question becomes how to create an environment that maximises the opportunities for learning, an environment that is open and safe to explore and experiment, where people are free to be themselves; an environment where trainees have responsibility for their own learning, as they are increasingly taking responsibility for their personal and professional development.

As training deals mostly with adult learning, we need to look at the adult learning process. As we mature, our need and ability to be self-directed learners grows, along with our ability to use experience for learning and to organise our own learning around our life problems. Adults will not tolerate the passive experience of learning content that is so great a part of the formal education process, unless there is an explicit contract to do so and the benefits are made clear. Adults tend to provide more of their own motivation and to take their standards more from themselves than from the outside. They tend to need less support than children. There is also a strong drive to own the learning. Adults will have a varied experience to draw on as a resource in learning. Any training needs to utilise this.

## The learning cycle

There is a cycle of learning that can be applied at an organisational and an individual level. You start from a present state, say a level of skill or performance. You have an outcome or desired state in mind, an increased level of performance. You need criteria and evidence about what you need to see, hear and feel that will let you know you have reached the desired state. You then make a comparison between what you have and what you want. This shows you a gap, so you do something, training, reading or learning in some way, to reduce the gap. Then you compare again and you continue acting until you have reached the desired state according to your criteria and evidence. After this you identify the next learning outcome.

At an individual level we can refine the model by using the further cycle that was formalised by David Kolb in the mid-1970s from his work on learning styles.

1. Learning starts from a concrete experience.
2. The individual thinks about the experience and gathers information.
3. The learner begins to generalise and internalise what happened in the experience.
4. Finally there is a test phase where the new ideas are tested.

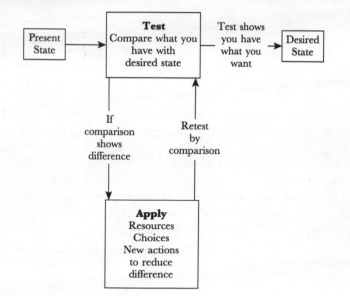

*Figure 1.2 The learning cycle*

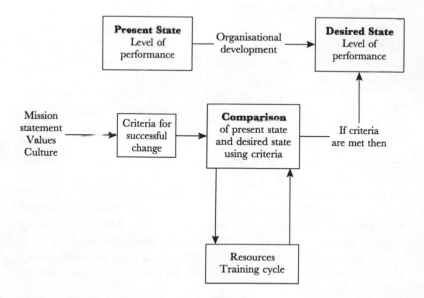

*Figure 1.3 Organisational learning cycle*

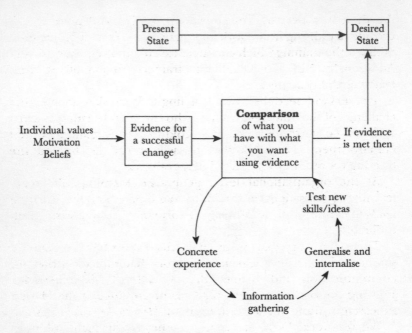

*Figure 1.4 Individual learning cycle*

The nice thing about this model is that it is recursive. Each cycle can have another cycle within it like a nest of Russian dolls. This means that one model can be widely applied.

### Generative learning

These simple learning cycles are only a first step. Just as they have cycles within them, so they are part of a wider cycle: *generative learning* or learning to learn. Now the trainer can come into her own if she can pass on these skills. Generative learning actually improves the whole cycle, making it faster and more effective. Education at school usually stops at the first level of learning: remembering facts or skills. We are not generally taught how to learn. We are told to remember, but not how to remember. This is the difference between giving a person a fish and teaching him how to fish.

Neuro-Linguistic Programming (NLP) has its place in this book because it is about learning how to learn, about how to use what you know to learn more and faster. This makes NLP invaluable for the trainer in her roles of consultant, analyst and presenter. It provides a unifying framework and many powerful communication skills for the training which can increase effectiveness dramatically. Additionally, NLP is invaluable to trainees for amplifying their learning ability in any area.

Trainers will need their own learning to learn skills to meet the challenge of the times and trainers who can train learning to learn skills will be worth their weight in gold to every organisation that employs them. The work they do will spread far beyond the training room. They will never be out of work.

At the organisational level, generative learning will create learning organisations, at the individual level generative learning leads to continuously improving performance and increasing self-fulfilment.

There is a story that neatly illustrates the difference between simple and generative learning. Gregory Bateson, the writer on communication and systems theory, tells of his experience studying the communication patterns of dolphins at the Marine Research Institute in Hawaii in his book *Steps to the Ecology of Mind*.

Bateson worked with the trainers as they taught the dolphins to perform for the public shows. The process started with a naïve dolphin. On the first day, when the dolphin did something unusual, such as jumping out from the water, the trainer blew a whistle and threw the dolphin a fish as a reward. Every time the dolphin behaved that way, the trainer would blow the whistle and throw the dolphin a fish. Very soon the dolphin learned that this behaviour guaranteed a fish; it repeated it more and more and expected a reward each time.

The next day the dolphin would come out and do its jump, expecting a fish. No fish. The dolphin would repeat its jump fruitlessly for some time, then in annoyance do something else such as rolling over. The trainer would then blow the whistle and throw the dolphin a fish. When the dolphin repeated this new trick in this session, it was rewarded with fish. No fish for yesterday's trick, only for something new.

This pattern was repeated for 14 days. The dolphin would come out and do the trick it had learned the day before, to no avail. Often it would throw in some of the tricks from days back, just to check out the rules. But it was only rewarded when it did something new. This was probably very frustrating for the dolphin. On the fifteenth day however, it suddenly appeared to learn the rules of the game. It went wild and put on an amazing show, including eight new unusual forms of behaviour, four of which had never been observed in the species before. The dolphin seemed to understand not only how to generate new behaviour, but the rules about how and when to generate it. Dolphins are clever.

One last detail: during the 14 days Bateson saw the trainer throwing unearned fish to the dolphin outside the training situation. Bateson was curious and questioned this. The trainer replied, 'Oh that. It's to keep on friendly terms, of course. After all, if we do not have a good relationship, he is not going to bother about learning anything.'

---

## TRAINING AND LEARNING

### *Key Points*

TRAINING AND LEARNING
- Training is the process that amplifies and provides a context for learning in three main areas:
  knowledge and how to apply it
  skills
  values and attitudes
- Learning is the process of getting knowledge, skills or abilities by study, experience or being taught.
- Training and learning are two sides of the same process. The trainer creates a context where individuals can learn.
- The more we can discover about the learning process, the better we can design training courses and the more effective they will be.

TYPES OF TRAINING
- Training covers many possibilities:
  vocational training, experiential training in the workplace
  group training courses, seminars and workshops
- Group training, if done well, is one of the most cost-effective way of delivering the skills needed for continuous improvement in an organisation.

THE TRAINING CYCLE

- Individual and organisational learning are different expressions of a common underlying pattern.
- In an organisation, the training cycle involves:
  identifying needs and defining the criteria with which to judge improvement
  setting learning outcomes in terms of skills, values and knowledge
  designing training to meet needs and objectives
  the training/learning event
  evaluating the results and using them to improve the process
- This training cycle can be looked at from three levels:
  1. The organisation: organisational development.
  2. The job: task effectiveness.
  3. The trainee: individual improvement and satisfaction.
- The trainer brings the levels together.

TQM

- Deming's ideas of TQM aim to create a learning culture in an organisation. TQM focuses more on improving the system than on individual achievement.

S/NVQS

- The system of National and Scottish Vocational Qualifications (S/NVQs) was instituted as a set of competency-based standards to facilitate more effective skills learning in all major industries.
- The Training and Development Lead Body sets national standards and administers S/NVQs for trainers.

MEANINGFUL TRAINING

- The trainees must want to attend the training. They must see what they are learning as meaningful and worthwhile for themselves.
- Training goals are what the trainers want the trainees to know and do. Learning goals are what the trainees want to know and do. The actual training needs to dovetail these two goals.

STAGES OF LEARNING

- There are four stages of learning:
  1. Unconscious in competence
  2. Conscious incompetence

3. Conscious competence
4. Unconscious competence
- Much learning is at the unconscious level.
- Learning is strongly influenced by our emotional state. The trainer needs to be able to create a safe environment where trainees can take responsibility for their learning.

ADULT LEARNING
- Adults are self-directed learners. They will not tolerate passive learning without responsibility.
- Adults have many varied experiences to share and utilise in a training.

SIMPLE LEARNING CYCLE
- There is a learning cycle that involves:
    1. Knowing your present state
    2. Knowing your desired state
    3. Knowing the evidence for arrival at your desired state
    4. Values and criteria about the learning
    5. Acting to reduce the difference between present and desired state
    6. Continuing round the cycle until you have evidence that you have reached your goal

GENERATIVE LEARNING
- Generative learning is learning to learn and creates continuous improvement and self-fulfilment for individuals.
- Generative learning is needed to create a learning organisation.
- Neuro-Linguistic Programming (NLP) is a method of generative learning.
- Trainers who can train learning to learn skills will have the greatest influence and success.

# NEURO-LINGUISTIC PROGRAMMING (NLP)

## Modelling behaviour

There are presenters, teachers, trainers and facilitators who are truly outstanding at what they do. If you have had the experience of being with one of these people, you will know what an impact they can make on your life. NLP is the study of how people excel in any field and how to teach these patterns to others, so they too can get the same results. This process is called *modelling*.

The field of NLP covers not only modelling but also the models that are created. These patterns, skills and techniques are being used increasingly in counselling, education and business for more effective communication, accelerated learning, and personal and professional development. NLP bypasses *why* some people excel, for the idea of inborn talent leads nowhere. Instead NLP focuses on *how* they excel and how to teach others to excel using these patterns.

## Thinking, language and behaviour

NLP is about our subject experience: how we think about our values and beliefs, and how we create our emotional states. As such it is the key to experiential training. With NLP we can create experiences that link with beliefs and create emotional states. Our beliefs and emotional states generate our behaviour. With NLP we can discover how we create our subjective world.

The title Neuro-Linguistic Programming gives the three areas that NLP has brought together:

- 'Neuro' refers to our neurology, our thinking processes.
- 'Linguistic' is language, how we use it and how we are influenced by it.

- 'Programming' refers to the patterns of our behaviour and the goals we set.

So NLP relates our words, thoughts and behaviour to our goals. Programming is a computer metaphor, but the way it is used here is not the old artificial intelligence model of computers, but the neural network model. NLP is a systemic and eclectic generative psychology that looks at the relations and influences of the different parts of our personality. It is not a linear model of behaviour. Behaviourism is the psychology of artificial intelligence where stimulus leads to response in a straight line.

## What, why, how

In order to model outstanding people we need to explore *what* they do: their behaviour, actions and physiology. We need to find out *why* they do it: the empowering beliefs and values behind the behaviour. Skills are consistent actions backed and supported by beliefs. We also need to know *how* they do it; their thinking process and mental strategies.

### Neurological levels

Learning can happen at different levels. This model was developed by the American NLP trainer Robert Dilts.

- The first level is the *environment:* the context, our surroundings and the other people we relate to.
- The second level is *behaviour:* the specific actions we carry out.
- The third level is skills and *capabilities:* what we can do.
- The fourth level is *beliefs and values:* what we believe and what matters to us.
- Next there is our *identity:* our basic sense of self, core values and mission in life.
- Additionally, most people have something *beyond* themselves to which they relate (spiritual).

Applying this to training, a statement

- at the *environment level* would be: 'It's easy to train with top class resources and a supportive department.'
- at the *behaviour level:* 'You wrote clearly on the flip chart in that training.'

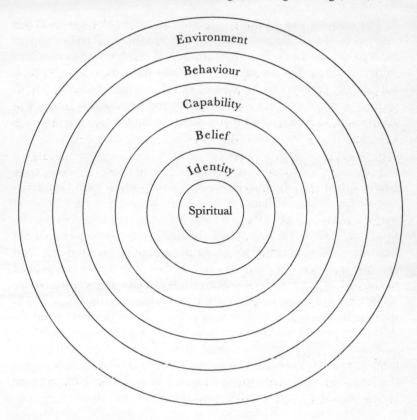

*Figure 1.5 Neurological levels*

- *capability level:* 'You have developed some impressive skills.'
- *belief level:* 'Having fun makes learning easier.'
- *identity level:* 'You are a good trainer.'

Many courses and books on training concentrate on the environmental level: how to lay out the room and what resources to use. Some books on presentation skills focus on the behavioural level of what you do to present the material. What is often missed are the higher levels: how the skills work and what beliefs and values empower and amplify them. Skills will not flow without empowering beliefs and values to back them up. Your beliefs and values also strongly affect your thoughts and your emotional state. Performance anxiety can wreck a presentation, regardless of how competent the performer may be normally.

The training you do that flows from your sense of self and your mission in life will be powerful and congruent. NLP training gives tools to change not only behaviour and skills, but also beliefs and values, an area traditional training finds hard to influence. NLP particularly focuses on the area of skills: how beliefs connect with actions. One of our main motivations for writing this book is to address this imbalance and focus on these higher levels of training.

## Models of language

NLP originated in the mid-1970s in America when John Grinder, a linguist, and Richard Bandler, a student of computer science and mathematics, started to model excellent communicators in the field of psychotherapy. They initially explored patterns of language and questions to generate a model of language that became known as the Meta Model: the art of using language itself to clarify language. ('Meta' comes from the Greek, meaning above or beyond.) Miscommunication usually happens because words mean different things to different people. If you doubt this, ask 10 different people what the words 'training', 'competence' or 'learning' mean. Sometimes the differences are slight and do not matter. At other times they matter a great deal. The Meta Model is the art of asking key questions to find out what words mean to an individual. This gets you high quality, specific information.

The reverse of the Meta Model was called the Milton Model, after Milton Erickson, the world-renowned hypnotherapist. This is the art of using artfully vague language to give people the freedom to make their own meaning of the words you say.

Trainers need both skills. Sometimes you need to be very specific, for example, when you give instructions. Often you need to ask a trainee good questions to clarify for yourself (and often for him), what exactly he means. Unless you can do this, you will end up answering the question you thought he meant, rather than the question he thought he meant. On other occasions you will want to talk in general, so each person can fill in just the particular experience that fits for them.

## Inner experience

From their early work on language, it became clear to John and Richard that language was itself a representation of something

*Visualisation*

*Visual constructed images*

*Visual remembered images*

*Constructed sounds*

*Remembered sounds*

*Kinesthetic*
*(Feelings and bodily*
*sensations)*

*Auditory Digital*
*(Internal dialogue)*

*NB. This is as you look at another person*

*Figure 1.6 Eye movement patterns*

deeper. The words we use and how we use them is based on our individual experience. What is inner experience made up of? Their first clues came from noticing curious sentences like: 'I see what you are saying' and wondering whether they could be taken as literally true. Could inner experience be made from internal representations of sensory experience?

John and Richard became fascinated by what people were actually doing when they were thinking. They were not the first to notice the eye movement patterns we make when thinking, but they were the first to link them systematically to thinking and language. When people visualise they are more likely to defocus and look straight ahead or look up to the right or left. When they talk to themselves internally, referred to as internal dialogue, they are more likely to look down and to their left. When they are aware of feelings, they are more likely to look down and to their right. So how we are thinking is mirrored in our body by the way we are moving our eyes.

### Internal senses

Our inner world of experience is made up of feelings, sounds and images, just like the outer one. As we differ in how we use our senses on the outside, so we will also differ in the way we think. Some people may talk to themselves a great deal, others think more in pictures, others in feeling or sounds. We know what thinking is for ourselves and may have assumed that it is the same for everyone else, but we are all unique.

NLP is sometimes defined as 'the structure of subjective experience' – how we create our own unique world for ourselves in the way we think, feel, see and hear. Our beliefs and interests also condition what we notice, what we pay attention to and what we ignore. Now that you know about eye movements, you may notice people doing them all the time. They were before, it is just that you did not pay attention to them.

Our way of thinking is also reflected in our language. Some people will describe their perspective on events, the bright future they see for themselves. Others may listen carefully and tune in to the same wavelength. Yet others will want to get a good grasp of what you do, so they can feel comfortable. It is reasonable to suppose the first person's words reflect mental pictures, the second is describing the sounds they hear mentally and the third is getting in touch with their feelings.

The obvious training application here is to vary your own language to include different ways of saying the same thing, so the visualisers can see what you are saying, the auditory people can hear you loud and clear and the feeling people will get to grips with your material.

## Mental strategies

A strategy is an ordered sequence of thoughts resulting in an ordered sequence of actions. For example, people have strategies for motivation, buying, decision making, writing and learning. Strategies will involve different ways of thinking: in pictures, in sounds and in feelings. Different tasks need different ways of thinking. For example a strategy for designing a building is likely to involve a lot of visualisation. A strategy for composing music will have more internal hearing. Different thinking strategies will have definite sequences of images, sounds and feelings, and the exact form of each may be important.

Try this experiment. Make a picture of a training that you have taken. If you think you cannot make these pictures, just imagine for a moment that you could.

Make it bright, moving and in colour. . .
Now darken the picture, take out the colour and make it still...
How does that change your reaction to the memory?

In the same way you can change the volume or direction of internal sounds or voices. These qualities of the internal pictures, sounds and feelings are known as *submodalities* in NLP.

Different people have different strategies for learning. Once you have NLP modelling skills, you can find out how people learn, suggest possible improvements and design learning strategies for them. This makes learning generative – they learn how to learn.

## Conscious and unconscious learning

In NLP, something is conscious when it is in present moment awareness, as these words are, right now. Everything else, not in present moment awareness, is unconscious. You use conscious attention in learning, yet you are most skilful when you act unconsciously, using streamlined practice or habits. This is why it is hard for people to tell you consciously you how they do things well. They have forgotten the learning stages. In the same way it is hard to see how a building was constructed once the scaffolding has been dismantled. One of the qualities of being able to do something well is precisely the fact that you do not have to think about it.

With NLP modelling skills it is now possible for you to uncover these invisible successful learning strategies from words and body language, so that others may benefit.

## Communication skills

Good communication stems from good rapport and appreciating the unique reality of the other person. Rapport can be achieved by tuning in your body language, tonality and words to those of the other person.

Given initial rapport, NLP has a simple model at the heart of good communication:

1. Know what you want, your goal or outcome in any situation, so there is a purpose to the communication.
2. Be alert to the responses you are getting. Keep your attention outwards to see, hear and feel how the other people are responding.
3. Have the flexibility to keep changing what you do or say until you get what you want.

This model of Outcome Acuity Flexibility is quite different from what often happens in stuck situations: doing the same thing – and when it does not work, doing it harder.

## Different perspectives

One powerful way of being flexible in your thinking is to take different perspectives. For example, with training, there is the organisational view of training, there is training for a particular job and also what training means to the individual. Depending on your focus, there will be different ideas and priorities to consider. The more viewpoints you can have, the richer the information you have and the easier it becomes to find the most useful move to make next. In NLP this is known as *multiple description*.

There are three basic viewpoints, three ways of looking at any communication:

1. There is your own reality. What you think as an individual from your personal experience. This is known as *first position*.
2. Then there is what it looks like from another person's point of view: this is *second position*. Many people are uncomfortable with this, thinking that understanding and agreement are the same, i.e. that if you look at something from another's view, you have to agree with it. However, although you need to understand another's point of view, you do not need to agree with it. Unless you understand it you will not know if you agree with it anyway.
3. Lastly there is what is called the *third position* or *metaposition*. This is the systemic view that looks at the relationship from the outside.

Here is a training example. A trainee asks a question. From your point of view (first position), the answer is so obvious you wonder why on earth he bothered. If you take a moment to imagine yourself in his shoes (second position) you notice there is a key point which he must have missed to ask the question. So you answer that key point. Then you mentally step back from yourself (third position) and notice that he is satisfied with your answer and that you have enhanced rapport with the group.

This is a necessarily brief overview of NLP, enough we hope, to introduce some basic concepts and indicate the potential. NLP supplies the missing link in creating the learning organisation. It explores mental models by way of strategies and beliefs, and mastery through modelling. It links with S/NVQ competencies by exploring how to develop skills through modelling and strategies. It is also a rich source of skills for trainers, created by modelling skilled trainers and communicators. We will develop the practical applications for training in the main part of the book.

---

## NEURO-LINGUISTIC PROGRAMMING (NLP)

### *Key Points*

NLP
- NLP is about modelling: studying, understanding and transferring the skills of top performers in any field.
- NLP relates our words, thoughts and behaviour to our goals and purpose.

NLP MODELS

- A complete model consists of beliefs, actions and mental strategies.
- Learning can be thought of at different neurological levels:
  environment
  behaviour
  skills and capabilities
  beliefs and values
  identity or mission
- NLP originated in America in the mid-1970s when John Grinder and Richard Bandler modelled outstanding communicators.
- NLP has developed two language models:
  The Meta Model: how to ask key questions to move from the words to the deep structure of the experience that underlies them.
  The Milton Model; how to use words in artfully vague ways to cover all possible individual meanings.
- Words and body language are linked to the way we think.
- There are three main ways of thinking:
  images (visual)
  sounds/words (auditory)
  and feelings (kinesthetic)

STRATEGIES

- A mental strategy consists of:
  the ways of thinking: visual, auditory or kinesthetic
  the qualities of these internal pictures, sounds or feelings (submodalities)
  the sequence of these thoughts
- Modelling and strategies give you 'learning to learn' skills.
- Most learning and skill takes place at the unconscious level.

COMMUNICATION

- The simple model of good communication involves:
  knowing your outcome
  being sensitive to feedback
  being flexible and having a number of different ways of achieving the outcome

PERSPECTIVE

- Taking different perspectives is a key analytical and communication skill:

    first position is your own reality

    second position is another's reality

    third position is the systemic overview of both
- The more perspectives you have, the more valuable information you get.

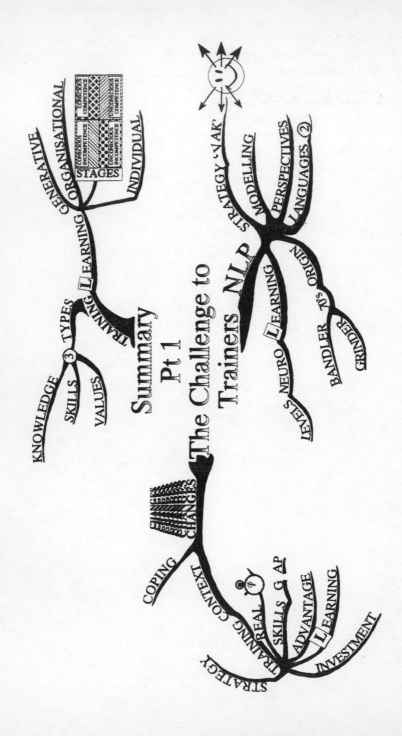

Summary
Pt 1

The Challenge to Trainers

# BEFORE TRAINING

## OVERVIEW

Any activity in the hands of a skilled performer looks easy. Perhaps you have switched on the television in the middle of an athletics programme and seen the runners toiling round the track. One of the best indications of the eventual winner is the one who is making running look easy and is expending the least effort. Apparent ease and simplicity is the hallmark of a good performer. This is true in any field – athletics, the performing arts, sports, public speaking, teaching or managing. Training is no exception. While this ease is the outward sign of mastery in many different areas, it masks the time, work and discipline that has gone into the preparation. The better the practice and preparation, the easier the task. Effort alone on the day is not enough and practising inefficient moves just makes those inefficient moves easier.

This overview will highlight 11 important areas in preparing a training to make it easier, more enjoyable and successful. Each area has a chapter to itself in this part of the book.

1. *Training outcomes*

   Preparing training starts with setting outcomes. What do you want to achieve for the group? What do you want to achieve for yourself? If you are working within an organisation you will want a training brief based on the Training Needs Analysis, with the outcomes clearly identified and prioritised. Think before you start about how you will know you have achieved them. Outcomes need to be thought through from all points of view – trainer, trainees and the organisational sponsor, if there is one.

2. *The trainees*

   You will want to know about the people you will be training

and their needs. Do they know each other? What is their level of morale and motivation? What are their existing skill levels? What are their expectations?

3.  *Design principles*

    The content and structure of the training needs to be mapped out, understood and sometimes memorised. You want the best design to achieve the training outcomes, and still be flexible enough to allow for improvisation, space and experimentation. Designing training is a learnable skill at every level, from the individual exercises to the total structure.

4.  *Designing for learning*

    This section looks at design more from the trainees' point of view to increase the amount of learning.

5.  *Designing the design*

    This introduces the Disney strategy, a creative strategy that you can apply to any aspect of designing.

6.  *Activity structures*

    This describes the main structured activities you can use, such as role playing and case studies, to achieve your outcomes.

7.  *Exercise design*

    As well as using existing structured activities, you need a range of ways of designing your own experiential exercises for learning skills. This is covered here.

8.  *Presentation skills*

    Once the content and structure of the training is decided, there is the important skill of putting it across. Two different trainers can present the same material and yet the group experience of the training – and the outcomes it achieves – can be profoundly different. This section is about integrating presentation skills to enhance your natural individual style.

9.  *Beliefs and values*

    Training goes deeper than what you do and where you do it. Your beliefs and values as a trainer will affect the training. For your best performance, you want your training outcomes to be in alignment with your values and beliefs. Empowering beliefs empower you. Limiting beliefs limit you. Values are what is important to you.

10. *Self-management*
Finally, and perhaps the most important of all, there are the skills of taking care of your own emotional and physical state. It is important to get them well in place before you train. Your skills will flow from a good emotional state, while a poor state will make them inaccessible.

11. *The training environment*
The practicalities of training and the suitability of the training environment are important to give trainer and trainees a secure basis. The layout of the room, the facilities for the comfort of the trainer and participants, and the range of equipment and materials that you will be using all need to be checked in advance.

With these skills and principles you will be equally ready to present a topic for half an hour to a small group or an experiential training to a large group for several days.

---

## PART TWO OVERVIEW

### *Key Points*

There are 11 important areas in preparing a training.

1. Training outcomes
2. The trainees
3. Design principles
4 Designing for learning
5. Designing the design
6. Activity structures
7. Exercise design
8. Presentation skills
9. Beliefs and values
10. Self-management
11. The training environment

---

# 4

# TRAINING OUTCOMES

However experienced a trainer you are, the first question to ask yourself is: 'What do I want to achieve in this training?' Without clear outcomes you have nowhere to go. The outcomes are the centre of your design and the structure of the training will be built round them. You cannot build round a vacuum. This is why the quality of the Training Needs Analysis is so important: it gives you outcomes to aim for. At the other end of training, follow-up evaluation will demonstrate the results you have achieved.

There are two main types of outcome:

1. End outcomes. These are *what* you want to achieve.
2. Process outcomes. These are *how* you want to achieve the end outcomes.

There are four distinctions here:

- The trainer's end outcomes for the trainees: what he wants them to achieve.
- The trainer's process outcomes for the trainees: how he wants them to achieve these outcomes. (These are covered by the training design, see pages 58–62.)
- The trainer's end outcome for himself: what he wants to get from the training.
- The trainer's process outcomes. (These are covered later in the section on self-management, see pages 113–17.)

### End outcomes for the trainees

These outcomes are about what the trainees will learn, achieve or be able to do, not about what the trainers wish to accomplish.

For example: '*Participants will learn the difference between open and closed questions and to identify the appropriate time to ask each type'* is a well expressed training outcome.

'*The trainer will teach the difference between open and closed questions and how to identify the appropriate time to ask each type'* is a very different outcome, and does not specify that anyone will learn anything. Teaching does not automatically imply learning, contrary to the rather naïve view of our educational system which assumes that if a subject is on the curriculum and being taught, then the students will learn it and if they do not, then it is their fault. Training challenges many of the assumptions of the formal educational system.

To set achievable outcomes, follow these guidelines:

1. *Outcomes need to be stated in the positive.*
   Specify what you want the participants to achieve, or learn, and the knowledge and skill they will go away with. Do not set outcomes about what they will *not* be doing, what they will *stop* doing, or what they will *not* take away with them. You cannot learn how not to do something. Remedial training is about what to do instead of existing problems. So if you find a negative outcome that contains what you do not want, turn it round by asking: 'What do I want instead?'

2. *The trainer has to be an active party in realising the outcomes.*
   The object of training is learning and although the outcomes will be stated in terms of what the participants will learn, your training plan will be centred around what you do. You cannot depend on others or fortuitous circumstances. Plan what you will do directly to influence people.

3. *Think of the outcomes as specifically as possible in terms of who, what, when, where and how long.*
   Many of these will be clear already. You will have information about the trainees, the location and time. The time-scale of the training will set clear limits, as will the number and existing skills of trainees. It is futile to expect to teach a total approach to sales communication in a two-hour class. The most common reason for trainers failing to meet their outcomes is because they overestimate what can be done in a limited time.

4. *The outcomes need to be measurable in behavioural terms.*
   There has to be evidence that the outcome has been achieved, or the training is meaningless. This evidence comes from what

you see, hear and feel the trainees doing. For example, evidence for the skill of asking open and closed questions might take the form of a role-playing exercise where the operator alternates between asking open and closed questions. The observer of the exercise would watch, check and give feedback to the operator. The trainees could then discuss the effect of the two types of questions, both as interviewer and interviewee.

Behavioural evidence for a skill can be brought down to specific competency standards and into the whole National Vocational Qualifications (NVQ) arena. First, skills can be broken down into specific competencies that are measurable in a trainee's behaviour. For example leadership is a very high level skill and will consist of such skills as team building, coaching, openly confronting problems and asking high quality questions. Secondly, the skills and competencies themselves are not all or nothing achievements, but will have standards of performance attached to them. Standards of performance are laid down to achieve certain designated levels of competence in a skill. These levels will also specify certain conditions for success, in terms of numbers, resources used or time taken.

Companies who commission trainings may provide specific standards to be met from their TQM programme or the training may take place under the NVQ competency standards. Standards imply a set competency level and evidence that it is met. These guidelines will specify the training outcomes and focus them quite precisely, providing specific qualitative evidences that the trainer needs to see, hear or feel to assess the training objectives and ensure that outcomes have been met.

This whole area of evidence and evaluation is important from individual trainee to organisational level and is dealt with in detail in Part Four.

5. *Adequate resources.*
These resources will include your own skills, tapes, books, colleagues, designs and feedback from previous trainings, and the training environment aids you have at the training.

6. *Check consequences.*
We may formulate outcomes really well but miss what *else* can happen. For example, if you are teaching psychotherapeutic techniques, make sure that there are sufficient safeguards built in. If you are teaching the precise use of language, make sure

that the participants do not go off and alienate their friends and lovers by asking awkward questions that are not appropriate in those relationships. Think from the participants' viewpoint how they will perceive the skills. In what situation will they use the skill? When will they use it? Are their occasions when it would not be right to use it?

### Review from different perspectives

View the training outcomes from three main perspectives: your view as trainer, the trainees' view and that of the sponsoring organisation, if there is one. Once *you* are clear, put yourself in the place of the trainee. What is it like from their viewpoint? Then take the organisational position if you are working in-house. Review the Training Needs Analysis and be ready to evaluate the outcomes in terms of cost-effectiveness.

### Size of outcomes

The whole outcome setting process will leave you with a number of outcomes of varying degrees of size. Often it is easiest to start at high level outcomes and then develop a series of smaller outcomes, each nested inside others like a Russian doll.

Your final design will enable you to achieve them. Separating the outcomes initially does not imply they have to be addressed individually or sequentially in the training.

For example, the trainer's overall outcome might be that participants learn to get rapport with customers. This can be broken down into a series of smaller outcomes:

- Participants will learn to match body posture with others.
- Participants will learn to match voice tone and volume with others.
- Participants will learn to pick out key words in the other person's communication and use these words in a reply.

This last outcome might be broken down in turn:

- words to do with seeing (visual)
- words to do with hearing (auditory)
- words to do with acting (kinesthetic)

Once the outcomes are specified, you can start to design a series of exercises to achieve them.

### Prioritise outcomes

Having mapped the course outcomes, you need to put them in order. Training outcomes can be put into three classes:

* First, there is the information or skills that the participants *must* know as a result of the training.
* Secondly, there are the skills or information that the participants *should* know.
* Lastly there are the skills and information that the participants *could* know as a result of the course. This last class of outcomes give you some flexibility, so it will not be a disaster if time pressure or other unforeseen circumstances prevents them being covered in the training.

## TRAINING OUTCOMES

### *Key Points*

* Training starts by setting outcomes for both trainer and trainee.
* There are two types of outcome:
    end outcomes (what is achieved)
    process outcomes (how it is achieved)
* End outcomes for trainees need to be expressed in terms of what trainees will learn.
* Outcomes need to meet certain guidelines to be achievable:
    expressed in the positive
    under the trainer's control
    specific in terms of who, what, where, when and how long
    sensory specific behavioural evidence: what the trainer will see, hear and feel that lets her know the outcome has been reached
    resources are adequate
    possible negative consequences have been checked
    reviewed from three different perspectives: the trainer's, the trainees' and the organisation's
    evaluated – look at the size of the outcomes and how you will prioritise and sequence them

# THE TRAINEES

## Group size and composition

People come into training with diverse wants, needs, outcomes and expectations and some of these may shape your design. If you are running a public seminar, then the trainees may come from many different backgrounds, united by a common interest in your subject. You can use the seminar enrolment forms to find out their occupations and interests. The extent of the press and marketing arrangements will also determine how broad a range of people you attract. Your training may be in-house for a company, in which case you will have a good idea of the group before you begin.

The size of the group is important and will affect your design. A small group will probably have more discussion and people sharing experiences. You will be able to devote more time to individual coaching. In a large group, people are less likely to talk personally and ask questions, unless you have good rapport. The size of the group will also affect what exercises you can do.

## Level of training

The training will be pitched at a particular level of knowledge and skill from introductory to advanced. You can find out how familiar the trainees are with the subject material beforehand or, as the training starts, by asking round the group. If the training is a general one, some people may struggle and need extra coaching, while the experienced trainees may need extra tasks and challenges. A wide spread on an in-house training suggests that the training has not been well targeted.

## Group dynamics

Another question you might consider is how well the trainees know each other. This will affect group rapport and group dynamics. A group who all hail from the same company are likely to find it difficult to complain openly about work. It also makes a big difference whether the training is voluntary or compulsory. Trainings where attendance is required will have a different atmosphere and some trainees may be ambivalent or resentful. Do not try to ignore this. Put it into the open from the start, by saying something like, 'I know you have not had a choice about attending this training. Let's put that to one side for the moment and find out how we can make the most of our time together.' This acknowledges group concerns and takes you out of the conspiracy that made them come.

## Gender

When the group is all one sex, specific concerns are more likely to surface. For example, a communication skills training will bring out different issues for women than it will for men and the trainer needs to be prepared. Issues such as sexual harassment, how to manage in a predominantly male environment and being seen as aggressive or nurturing are likely to surface. The age, marital status and ethnic group of trainees may also influence your design and the way you conduct the training.

## Anti-discriminatory practice

There are many ways that discrimination towards minority groups can surface in training and it would be fruitless to attempt an exhaustive list. There are many fine books on equal opportunities awareness and anti-discriminatory practice. Our personal position, which is reflected in our training, is that everyone is equally valuable and deserving. And everyone is different. The difference is to be valued. To treat someone less well because you perceive them as different or because they belong to a different group from the one you identify with is unworthy. Everyone deserves every opportunity to learn and develop in their own time and in their own way and to fully appreciate their difference.

Care is needed over clumsy language. Put yourself in the other person's place to understand how your words could be construed. This is all part of genuinely welcoming people and appreciating their world. Politically correct language may be useful in certain circumstances, but it can also sound phony and convoluted and be very annoying. As a rule, groups like to know where you stand and will pay attention to actions rather than words. Politically correct language about minority groups is no use if you are seen to treat them disdainfully. Be congruent, so that what you say and what you do give the same message. Any incongruence between your words and actions will leak out and the group will spot the puddles.

Any remark or action by a participant that demeans another, whether of a minority or not, needs to be taken seriously, although the meaning will depend on context and the relationship between the people. Some remarks can be highly insulting in one context and a joke in another. How you deal with such issues can be a difficult choice, especially if the perpetrator says they are a joke and the recipient is offended. You might utilise such a remark in the group as an example of a particular pattern of language that causes offence. You might let the person know privately that his behaviour was not acceptable. If a participant persists you might take him aside and tell him that if he continues you will ask him to leave the training. This is the last resort. A direct challenge in front of the group may be effective but can easily start an emotional maelstrom. Arguments are rarely constructive, for prejudices are not reasonable and so cannot be changed by reason alone.

## Trainees' beliefs

This brings us on to the issue of how far the belief systems of the trainees affect the training. A person's response to new experiences is influenced by her social, ethnic, religious and political identity. Respect the belief systems of the trainees. Unless the training is on beliefs, you have no right to try to change beliefs or persuasions. In some of our introductory seminars we have a box at the entrance next to the coat stand and invite trainees to leave their beliefs metaphorically at the door together with their (real) hats and coats. We promise them the beliefs will be perfectly safe there and can be collected again if required, unchanged, at the end of the seminar.

## THE TRAINEES

### *Key Points*

- Training design will be influenced by:
    group wants, needs, outcomes and expectations
    size of group
    familiarity with material
    gender
    compulsory or voluntary attendance
- Anti-discriminatory practice is important.
- Respect individual beliefs.

# DESIGN PRINCIPLES

## CONTENT AND PROCESS

A trainer manages two interwoven parts of a training. The first is the seminar content to achieve the end outcome for the trainees. The trainer has skills and knowledge in a particular field and gives information as clearly and concisely as possible. He will also be clarifying the information for the trainees, presenting it from different angles. He will give examples, elaborate and synthesise ideas. He will demonstrate certain skills that are part of the content of the seminar and he will be an influential role-model.

The content of the training will cover three main areas:

*Knowledge.* The ideas the group will learn and remember. These are likely to be put over by lectures, handouts, slides and videos.

*Skills.* The practical capabilities that form the core of most trainings.

*Values and attitudes.* The underlying ideas behind the skills and knowledge.

Secondly, the trainer manages the process of the seminar: how the knowledge, skills and values are put over. The trainer must make sure there is adequate time to meet the goals of the training. He evaluates the progress of the trainees on an ongoing basis. He may need negotiation skills to resolve differences between trainees or between trainees and himself.

He needs facilitation skills to ensure all the trainees who wish to speak are heard. Sometimes he does this directly by intervening to stop some people talking or actively encouraging others to have their say. More often his involvement is indirect – as a model, he creates a permissive, empowering atmosphere. He creates the culture of the training by the rules he explicitly lays down and those he implicitly creates as a role-model.

The trainer tracks the group throughout the training. He may ask outright how they are doing and he will be picking up clues from the questions they ask. He will notice when they are flagging and need a break or are getting bored with a topic and need to move on. These tracking skills are all part of the process of a training.

## Design principles

Process outcomes are how you achieve the end outcomes for the trainees; in other words, the design of the training. What sort of design do you want? Given the content of the training, what are the overall qualities of a good design? The main principle is keeping yourself and the group in a good learning state.

One of the best ways to do this is to make the training fun and engaging. Learning is creative and exciting, although trainees may have fixed ideas built from their schooldays that learning is hard work and a serious business. This is a belief they will be happy to lose.

Another way to keep a good learning state is to design the training to include a set of varied experiences. Vary the length of the exercises. Most important, vary the medium of communication. Vary the structures you use – role play, case studies and brainstorming, for example. Vary the focus of the structures towards mental, physical, emotional or spiritual aspects. Finally, vary the methods so there is a mix of group, interpersonal and individual activities. We will consider all these variations in detail.

## Time frames

Time is an important issue. It takes some practice and experience to judge how long it will take to convey skills and knowledge to a group. Even experienced trainers can go wildly wrong with a highly vocal and argumentative group. Sometimes, if the training is dealing with emotional areas like counselling, important issues are touched on in passing and need to be resolved at the time.

Build in flexibility. Allow some time for slippage when planning; material is unlikely to take the exact time you allow. Keep your outcomes in mind and have extra material ready or the self-confidence of being able to design a new time-filling exercise on the spot that fits into the flow of the training and reinforces the training outcomes. On other occasions some material will be squeezed out. You may need to modify your outcomes slightly or add new ones depending on what issues the trainees bring to the training. They may be more important in the circumstances than the prepared training outcomes. Be willing to improvise and depart from your plan to bring the group back to a good learning state if you see they are getting tired, bored or listless.

## Breaks

Breaks are just as much part of the training as any other element. Everyone needs them for refreshment and they provide a natural punctuation to the flow of the day, separating different material and exercises. Breaks are also directly under the trainer's control. They are part of the learning cycle and an essential part of keeping the group in a good learning state.

You can also break informally at any time. There is the free-for-all-break, where you essentially tell the group to relax and do what they like for five minutes to recharge their batteries. There is the physical break, where you can use rhythmic clapping exercises, Kinesiology exercises and informal physical stretching. Thirdly, there is the relaxation or trance break. Here you suggest everyone gets comfortable and you essentially lead them through a guided visualisation, finishing with suggestions that they come back to the room feeling refreshed and invigorated. This is not a good idea after lunch, when the natural dip in energy levels can lead to people falling asleep. Sleep is not the best learning state.

Something to take into account is that there is a basic natural physiological rhythm to our day governed by our automatic and endrocine systems. This Break–Rest–Activity–Cycle (BRAC) lasts about 90 to 120 minutes and is a deep part of our daily living. This cycle is even seen when we are asleep, in the patterns of dreams alternating with deep sleep. In practice, every one-and-a-half to two hours we need a break if we are continue to function well. Two hours is the limit for a work cycle and this is independent of the mix of activity that goes on within that time to keep the group interested and engaged. A good rule to follow is to break formally every hour and a half maximum.

Breaks are also essential to ensure good recall of material. Research has shown overwhelmingly that recall falls drastically after about 50 minutes to an hour. A 10-minute break at the end of an hour vastly improves group recall. Trainees also need time to integrate material that they are learning. If the group is clamouring for a break then you have left it too late. It is usually better to leave people wanting more than tired out. Break at a high point if you can, for then recall will be good and, what is more, it will be recall of good experiences. Recall is strongest at the beginning and end of a learning session, so place important material immediately after a break.

What applies to the group also goes for the trainer. The trainer needs a break too!

## Sequence

Sequence the material to serve your outcome: what is the best path to get them from where they are to where you want them to be? Every journey starts with a single step, as the saying goes, and every training has an introduction, however short, followed by the body of the training, when most of the work is done, and finally an ending, where the group can integrate what they have learned and bring the training to a natural conclusion. Training is a bit like a sandwich – although the filling is the important bit, it falls apart without the bread to keep it together.

The beginning of the training basically introduces the trainer and lets the trainees get to know each other. He sets expectations, deals with practical issues and lets the group know briefly what the training will cover. The body of the training will present the main material.

The end part of the training may include an integration exercise and will backtrack on the essential points, give a sense of completeness and allow trainees' feedback. The ending closes the circle. A training that ends because time has run out never gives the same sense of satisfaction as one that comes to a natural, measured conclusion.

There are some principles of appropriate sequencing of ideas and exercises in the body of the training. Teach and ask trainees to practise the less risky skills before moving to the more risky. For example, it might be better to role play managerial skills in a situation involving a small breach of discipline before one of massive confrontation. The more self-disclosure involved, the more risky the skill.

## Concepts versus experience

Now we come to a central choice at the heart of sequencing a training. What makes it so interesting is that it is not just a theoretical issue, we have important beliefs and values of our own about it, often to do with how we were taught. Here is the choice: do you teach concepts first so the trainees can make sense of the subsequent experience? Or do you give them experience first, so they have something to conceptualise about?

Traditional training tends to give the concepts first. There is talk *about* the skills and experience. Then there is the practical exercise to practise the skills. Then there is an integration.

The alternative approach, the one that is favoured in NLP trainings, works in the opposite direction. It gives the sensory-based experience first in the form of exercises. Once the trainees have had the experience, then they have something to talk about. Without the experience, we propose, the concepts will have little meaning.

Secondly, the concepts will inevitably be given with the trainer's own perceptual filters and biases. There's nothing wrong with this, yet why burden the group with your own bias? Education is a passing from generation to generation not only of accumulated knowledge, but also of accumulated biases and limitations. It is much more respectful and fairer to the trainees, we propose, to give them minimum structure so they can get the most out of the experience. That way they will also get more out of your material than you knew was there. They will enrich and enlarge the existing theory and uses of the material and will even teach you something.

This approach is more difficult to bring off, however people like a map of where they are going. Trainees will be more uncomfortable without one and, to hark back to our introductory dolphin metaphor, the reward of fish needs to be bigger and more plentiful.

As with so many questions, the best answer is both-and, not either-or. You can have your cake and eat it too. Some skills can be taught in the traditional way: concept first then experience. Others can be taught the other way round: experience first then the concepts to talk about. Do not be a slave to either approach. We will argue strongly for more of the second approach, because training is highly biased towards the traditional mould.

## Simple versus complex

Traditional training starts from simple ideas and moves on to the more complex. It also builds up by taking small pieces and putting them together to create the larger framework. There are many good arguments for this method and the whole NVQ approach to competencies is built on these terms. Skills build on each other, so teach the smaller components first. One advantage of 'chunking down' complex skills is that you can present them in small enough pieces so trainees experience repeated successes.

There are, however, three drawbacks to presenting complex skills in small chunks. First, trainees can lose track of the final outcome and never actually put the bits together. The second danger is that you can present too many pieces and overload the group's conscious mind which can only manage seven plus or minus two pieces of information at a time (or two plus or minus two on a Sunday morning). The third danger is that the bits never add up to give an integrated whole, just a Frankenstein collection of bits. Frankenstein trainings are all too common.

The alternative to the traditional approach comes from how we acquire really complex skills, such as language. Here, we naturally take in the whole structure, which contains the smaller skills and ideas within it. In other words, we learn many of the structures, ideas and rules unconsciously and implicitly. We know them, but we do not know we know. Language is an amazing skill we all master in a few short years before our formal education process has interfered with our learning circuits. Children start by copying language and then using it to say what they want to say. They also go through a stage when they never seem to stop talking except when they are asleep. They practise like crazy and do not know the meaning of the word 'failure'. When we learn grammar formally we consciously learn about what we were already doing. Children who cannot understand grammar still manage to speak perfectly well. The interesting thing is that they will apply grammatical rules correctly in order to express what they want. For example, by saying 'I thinked' instead of 'I thought', they apply a correct rule to the verb 'I think'. Children will correctly say 'I blinked' rather than 'I blought' or 'I blunk'. They learn the rules and apply them unconsciously, adding to their knowledge of exceptions as they go. If we learned language in the way we learn other subjects at school, we would all stutter.

So a further choice in training is whether to teach large chunks first or build up from small chunks. The first leads to accelerated learning. Its complement, accelerated training, is the ability to transfer skills and knowledge to the trainees' unconscious minds in one step without having to go through the conscious stages. We will talk more of that in Part Three.

---

## DESIGN PRINCIPLES

### *Key Points*

- The trainer delivers content as part of achieving the end goals for the training. The content will consist of:
    knowledge
    skills
    values
- He is also responsible for the process; how the content is put over.
- The trainer will track time frames and use facilitation skills to put over the training content.
- The main principles of a good design are that:
    It keeps the trainees and the trainer in a good learning state.
    It is fun and engaging.
    It provides a set of varied experiences.
- Adequate breaks are important to maintain a good learning state:
    Breaks improve recall of the material.
    Breaks refresh the trainees.
- The design puts the training material into sequence.
- There is an important choice about whether to give the concepts before the experience or to give the trainees the experience first, before introducing the concepts to code it.
- The second important choice is whether you build skills small piece by small piece. This is the traditional learning approach. The alternative is to give the total skill with the small chunks contained in it.
- Accelerated learning is getting the whole skill without building it up bit by bit.
- Accelerated training is the ability to teach to the trainees' unconscious mind, so they do not have to build the skill consciously from its constituent parts.

# DESIGNING FOR LEARNING

## LEARNING STATE

One of the key differences between the NLP approach to training and the traditional approach is that NLP makes the trainees' learning state the priority. Trainees in a good learning state will learn what you offer them and will have good associations with the knowledge that will make it easy to use. Children love learning, yet somehow they often emerge from formal education having learned to hate learning.

NLP studies our experience and our emotional states. Emotional choice is possible. The most important design principle is to create a context where the trainees can enter their best learning state. You are designing a structure for the whole group and yet each person is different and learns in a different way. How can your design utilise these differences as well as the common qualities as resources for learning?

### Common qualities

At a deep level, we all share common qualities. We all have a physical, emotional, intellectual and spiritual part. These parts are aspects of a whole person – touch one and all the other aspects are touched. They form a unity: a human being. The more the training involves the whole person, the more lasting and generative the learning. People learn best when their whole selves are involved in the process.

1. The physical part of a person is their body. A training needs some physical movement in it, either built into exercises or as a break state between exercises. As a musician, I like to use rhythmic movements and games. Other trainers use Kinesiology

exercises or yoga exercises. Use whatever you feel is right. A few minutes of physical exercise can paradoxically give a group more energy.

2. A training will bring out emotions: be responsive to the feelings of the group. However dry the content, trainees will have feelings about themselves as learners. Good training exercises allow trainees to feel good about themselves as learners, whatever else is happening. The content of the training may work directly with emotions, for example counselling or assertiveness training.

3. Traditional training emphasises the intellect and the intellectual, cognitive part of the training does need to be taken care of, for if the ideas are not intellectually satisfying, people will often reject the whole training. It is only one aspect, however. There is often a presupposition, that stems from the school educational model of training, that conscious understanding is a prerequisite to successful learning. Yet think of the significant learning events in your life; they are unlikely to involve conscious understanding of the events at the time. Usually it is the opposite: first the experience, and only later integration and understanding. The 'University of Life' uses accelerated learning techniques. No guru appears to prepare you for what is going to happen.

4. The spiritual is the part that connects us to others in a way that transcends our individual egos. There are many different ways to think about this. Many trainings do not reach this level, while others will touch on a sense of going beyond perceived individual limitations and connecting with something greater.

## Training as equal partnership

Training is a loop where first the trainer is more active and the trainees respond. Then the trainer responds to the trainees' input and the total loop drives the training forward. Both trainer and participant have an equal part to play.

The trainees are not empty vessels to be filled with knowledge and skills by an all-knowing trainer. This model is another school leftover, although many people act as if it were true. To finally dispense with this model is a profound relief. The trainer does not

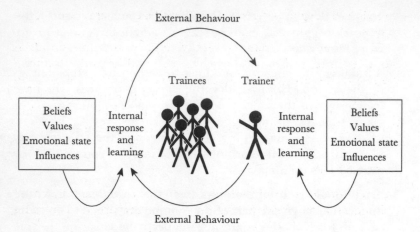

*Figure 2.1 Communication in training*

have the heavy burden and responsibility for the success of the training. He does not have to shoulder all the blame if trainees do not learn. Nor can the trainer blame the trainees if they 'don't get it'. Blame is irrelevant in a working partnership of equal people. Training is a circular, co-operative venture and the trainer has primary charge of creating a context where it is easy for people to learn. Everyone is responsible for their own learning.

The trainer learns too. She may learn new aspects of the material that had never occurred to her or learn more about presenting a topic. She could learn about her own personal strengths and weaknesses. If the trainer is not learning, the trainees are unlikely to be either.

The beliefs we have about learning will help or hinder the training loop. Believing and acting as if everyone has or can create the resources they need to learn is empowering. Beliefs act as self-fulfilling prophecies, creating subtle expectations that feed back to the trainer. In educational research by Rosenthal and Jacobsen ('Teachers Expectancies: Determinants of Pupils' IQ Gains' in *Psychological reports* 19 (1): 115–18) a class of children were divided into two groups of equal ability. The teachers were led to believe that the first group were more intelligent than the second and were therefore expected to excel. The first group did indeed do better than the second. This is known as the Pygmalion Effect and has been borne out by studies in business, politics and medicine. Beliefs and expectations can drive the learning loop in either direction. Believing people are excellent learners empowers them to be so.

Given that most trainings are voluntary and the group is motivated, the trainer still has to engage and keep the trainees' interest. The group will want material that is relevant and meaningful, and will hook onto some existing knowledge for the training to build on. The group will want the training to be fun. Fun is one of the hardest elements to pin down in a training.

## Training for fun

Take a moment yourself to think back to your own experiences of training and learning, perhaps in school, perhaps in a training

|  | Fun experience | Not fun experience |
| --- | --- | --- |
| What did I hear? | | |
| What did I see? | | |
| What did I feel? | | |
| | | |
| What was it about the surroundings? | | |
| About the trainer/teachers? | | |
| About the other learners? | | |
| About the content? | | |

situation, perhaps in a totally different context. Make a list now of what you saw heard and felt that made this experience fun for you. Unpack the word as far as possible. It could be the personality of the trainer. It could be jokes, engaging experiences, material in the training. Think of what was there.

Now think back to a learning experience that was emphatically not fun. What was happening there? What did you see, hear and feel in this situation? Make a second list.

Now you have two lists:

As you look through the lists what are the main differences?

What can you do that will create a context where you can have fun?

What can you do as trainer to create a context where the group can have fun? You will have probably discovered from your lists that if the teacher is not having fun it is very hard for the students to. Walt Disney is quoted as saying: 'I would rather entertain people in the hope that they will learn, than teach people in the hope that they will be entertained.'

## DESIGNING FOR LEARNING

### *Key Points*

- The training design needs to keep trainees in a good learning state, where differences can be a resource.
- Training design can touch people on four levels:
    physical
    emotional
    intellectual
    spiritual
- Training is an equal partnership between trainer and trainees and a loop of mutual influence:
    both trainer and trainees learn
    trainees are not empty vessels
    there is no blame in an equal partnership
    everyone is responsible for their own learning
- Beliefs will strongly influence the learning loop.
    Act as if the trainees have all the resources they need to learn well.
- Find ways of making your training fun.

# DESIGNING THE DESIGN

## Creative designing

Several years ago a major oil company finally realised that what would give them a competitive edge was the creativity of their people rather than the technology they used, which after all could be and was duplicated by their market competitors. The company hired a team of psychologists to find the difference between their creative engineers and the less creative ones. In essence it was a modelling project. They hoped that once they knew what distinguished the creative from the non-creative they could teach all their engineers to be creative.

The psychologists spent three months in the company with a battery of questionnaires observing the engineers at work and asking them questions. The chief difference they found between the two groups surprised everyone. It was very simple. The creative people thought that they were creative and the less creative people did not think they were creative. Creativity is rarely to do with finding a huge difference, but noticing and combining several small ideas. You are creative when you start to let your mind combine many different facts, ideas and processes. The fewer restraints you set on the process the better.

For a training, you may already have designs worked out that work well. You may wish to experiment with them and modify them to avoid becoming stale. Or you may be faced with planning a training from scratch. Whatever the task, you will want a strategy to create the main parts of a design. There is a good strategy modelled from Walt Disney by the American trainer Robert Dilts, known unsurprisingly as 'the Disney strategy'. Disney used it to think about the films he made. You can use it to brainstorm, refine and evaluate your designs.

## THE DISNEY STRATEGY

- Start thinking of the training you want to design. It can be anything from a small exercise to the whole training. You may want to start with a fairly small chunk until you are familiar with the process.

### Dreamer

The first stage is to brainstorm, simply to generate possibilities without regard to how realistic they are. Disney called this part the 'dreamer'.

Choose a place in front of you that you can step into and become the dreamer. Here you are completely free to brainstorm, to create without any restraints. You may want to mark this spot on the floor, perhaps with a coloured piece of paper. Think back to a time when you really generated some creative choices in any area. It need have nothing to do with training. Step into the spot you have chosen and relive the experience as fully and immediately as you can. By doing this, you associate, or anchor, the dreamer, the creative part of your mind, to that spot. Step out when you have finished.

### Realist

Next, choose a different place in front of you and mark it. This is for the 'realist'. Dreams are fine, but then there comes a time when you have to sift them, organise them and act on them. So you need to know how dreams are translated into the real world.

Think of a time when you thought realistically and constructively about an idea and devised an effective action plan. When you have a good instance, step into the marked realist spot and relive that experience. Anchor the realist part of you to that spot and, when you are satisfied, step out again.

### Critic

Next, select a third place in front of you for the 'critic' or 'evaluator'. Then think of a time when you were able to criticise a plan in a constructive way. The word 'criticise' has a bad name; it tends to imply negative and destructive comment. Good criticism is constructive, it identifies what is missing and what else needs to happen. Its positive intention is to improve the plan.

When you have a good instance of this, step into your critic spot and let your mind loose to find the weaknesses. When you have finished, step out.

- You now have three places as anchors for a particular thought process. The first for the dreamer, the second for the realist and the third for the critic or evaluator. Now you are ready to think about your training design.

- Step into the dreamer spot and start to explore freely and creatively. You can brainstorm to your heart's content. You need not think about whether it is realistic or what problems there are – the other positions will take care of that. Let your mind roam and get as many ideas as you can before stepping out. Daydreaming can be a useful and powerful way to pass the time. The best example of this was when a young physicist called Albert Einstein wondered what it would be like to travel on the end of a light beam. His speculations revolutionised modern physics, the 'hardest' and seemingly most objective of the sciences, and started the theory of Relativity.

- Now, take the speculations you have created and step into the realist position. Start to organise your ideas and create a plan. You will probably drop some ideas and elaborate others. How can these ideas be brought together into a realistic series of actions? When you are satisfied, step back out.

- Finally, step into the critic position and evaluate the plan. Ask questions about what is missing and what is needed. Take the participants' point of view. They may be paying good money for this training. Is it worth it from their viewpoint? How could it be improved? Would you pay money to attend it? This stage typically involves talking to yourself.

- You will now have a reasonably refined plan. Step back into the dreamer position and see if you can come up with any more ideas to change the plan creatively, utilising information from the realist and critic. Step out when you have finished.

- You may now want to revisit all three positions until you are satisfied. You can visit any of the positions in any order until the plan is as complete as you can make it.

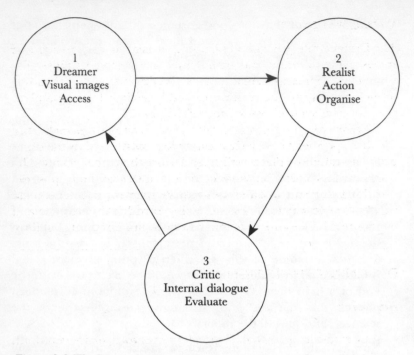

*Figure 2.2 The Disney strategy*

You may find that one of these positions is easier for you to access than the others. This shows the area where your strength lies. To create a really good plan you need all three functions and they need to be separate to work without interference. What often happens is you start to dream and create a plan, whereupon the critic interrupts with a negative comment or the realist in you tells you it is impossible. You never have a chance to really let your mind be free.

The critic is no more realistic than the dreamer, he is just another way of sorting ideas. The critic criticises the plan, not the dreamer.

You may co-design your training with a co-trainer. You can use the Disney strategy together or each represent different parts of it. Aim to use the differences between you to create a synergy, giving a better design than either of you could have done on your own.

## Working with groups

The Disney strategy is a good planning strategy to teach to a group. It has many different and complementary pieces. It utilises the three main representational systems: the dreamer will work mostly in mental imagery, the realist uses bodily feelings for action plans and the critic typically uses internal dialogue.

Whether you run this strategy for yourself or a group, make sure the three positions have a clear physiology unaffected by the other two. The different places will help to sort the three cleanly. The dreamer, realist and critic will have a different body posture, breathing pattern and different gestures. In a group you may need an observer to watch the person going through the exercise and intervene if he sees the same physiology in two different positions.

---

## DESIGNING THE DESIGN

### *Key Points*

- Your creativity is strongly dependent on how creative you think you are.
- The Disney strategy gives a way of designing the design:
  The dreamer brainstorms ideas.
  The realist thinks about how to put them into action.
  The critic notices how they can be improved.
- These functions work best when kept separate from each other.
- Design with a friend or colleague to create synergy.

---

# 9

# ACTIVITY STRUCTURES

Everyone has their preferred methods of learning, and by mixing the ways, you can satisfy everyone and cover the material in a multi-sensory way. There are the auditory ways, such as discussing, lecturing and using cassette tapes. There are the visual ways, such as films, videos and demonstrations. And there are the physical ways, such as role plays, experiential groups and exercises involving physical movement. Some materials lend themselves more to one particular way than others. Good designs have plenty of variation.

## Role playing

This involves simulating a situation that uses the knowledge and skills taught in the training. The trainees act out the parties involved and reach a conclusion. Role play does need to be realistic and to be perceived as relevant by the trainees. Its success involves getting the balance right between a structured situation with a clear issue, while leaving freedom for trainees to improvise. Role playing usually works best towards the middle of a course when group rapport is established and initial inhibitions have been overcome. There needs to be clear instructions that theatrical skills are not important and anyone who does not wish to join in is free to watch without feeling awkward.

Role playing can serve many different purposes. It can be used for people to learn each other's differing strategies for dealing with demanding situations. It can be used to develop awareness of the opposite role to the one where you practise the skill. It can simply develop the skills of a new role until the person becomes comfortable in the role. You may use it to build in a specific new response or to fine tune existing skills to a level of competence or quality. Be clear on your outcomes and design accordingly. Ask yourself, what exactly do I want people to get from this? What would have to happen for them to learn this? How am I going to demonstrate this role play? How may I need to coach people?

Role plays are good for training negotiation skills, often with the added twist that the actors have to change roles in the middle of the exchange on the trainer's signal. Each party has then to argue the opposite case from the one they were just presenting.

Role plays are also particularly useful for rehearsing the skills back in a worse environment after the training. All the old pressures will be there waiting to mould the trainees back into giving the old responses. This rehearsal of new ways of acting and of thinking outside the training is known as *future pacing* and is an essential part of any training. Without it, skills will not transfer outside the training room.

Assertiveness training is another area where role plays are useful. One person may act out a stereotype such as a rude waiter, a shop assistant or a difficult official. Everyone can learn from a role play, not just the person ostensibly on the spot practising the skill. Role playing any part of the action is an opportunity to bring resourcefulness, flexibility and perhaps a secret theatrical talent to bear on the situation.

After a role play it is important to get everyone involved to change their state, get up and move around and do something different for a few minutes to come back to themselves. They need to shake off the role (sometimes literally), before carrying on with the training. In one training I remember the trainer neglected to do this after role playing a difficult negotiation scene that was full of conflict. The training ended and the next day there were many complaints from the group that they found themselves getting into arguments and feeling annoyed and dissatisfied during the course of the evening.

Role play is usually memorable and enjoyable. It involves action and participation. It allows the group to experiment with a new skill in a low-risk situation: a challenge within a supportive environment.

## Lectures

Check your response to the word 'lecture'. In the training context a lecture is simply a verbal presentation to a group, but it is often taken to mean a rather boring one-way passage of complex information from expert to learner. Hand in hand with this goes the mistaken assumption that a person who knows the most about a subject is also best equipped to teach others about it.

Lectures are weakest when they rely on words alone. A lecturer must use examples, metaphors, humour, body language and the space available. Something of a real person must shine through the material, or the group may just as well listen to a tape.

The strength of the lecture format is that the trainer can use all her skills in a live situation to drive the group forward. She can watch the response and change what she says and does as she goes, depending on the live responses she encounters. A good trainer can modify the second half of the sentence depending on the group's response to the first half.

Lectures may be formally or loosely structured, long or short, from five minutes to three quarters of an hour. A short lecture may occur naturally without much preparation simply to bring out a point in the material. A longer lecture will introduce or expand a topic and have a definite structure.

Lectures mimic the training itself on a lower level:

- They have an *Introduction* that connects the material to what has gone before.
- There is a *Middle* where you give the information, in a sequence of key points. This will be a mixture of quotes, facts, anecdotes, real life examples, metaphors and questions, either rhetorical or direct to the group. You can use a flip chart and other visual aids, although these will be secondary to the spoken word. You will be using body language and your voice to emphasise key points. Questions to the trainees are important. They invite the group to think. Have you ever been in a presentation where the lecturer has asked a question that really set you thinking? Questions make the material more interactive, do they not?
- Finally, the *Conclusion:* a review, summary and opportunity for questions from the trainees.

Lectures are good for communicating quickly and effectively with large groups. The trainer knows what to present and in what order and can calculate the time involved very accurately. As lectures tend to put the group in a passive position, the success of the lecture depends to a large extent on the trainer's presentation skills.

## Case study

This method gives a group a set of circumstances based on real or constructed events and lets the trainees use the skills they have been learning by applying them to a 'real' situation.

Case studies work best in small groups of perhaps three to six. The situation must be realistic and relevant enough to engage the groups, and the situation must be interesting and complex enough to have many different possible answers. The 'puzzle' type of case study where there is only one answer and it is up to the trainees to find it is not very useful.

Case studies can be used in many ways and bring out many learning points, for example:

- What questions are needed to get the necessary information?
- What outcomes do the trainees want from this scenario? What are the outcomes of the various parties involved and how might they be reconciled? (This is a negotiation problem.)
- What would the group do in this situation?

Any solutions can be compared with what actually happened in that situation. Business trainings often involve case studies of problems such as staff management, product distribution and manufacturing quotas. It is also possible to analyse possible solutions by using computer software, if figures are available. For example, a case study may involve a business losing money and the problem might involve allocating resources to reverse this trend. Trainees will discuss and work out their own solutions and put their figures into a computer simulation model of the company. The computer runs the model with those figures and trainees see the consequences. The advantage of the computer is that it can run complex systems and output figures without being influenced by hopes, fears or wishful thinking.

Another way to use case studies is to give the group both the problem and the action taken. The group analyse the issue to understand why the action was taken and the possible consequences.

The trainer lays down the rules and limits of the case study exercise, which can be presented through a lecture, report or video. There will be a certain point where no further information will be available. The trainer will also specify how the groups should report back: a presentation, a full written report or a series of main recommendations.

Case studies are useful to get the group to think in particular ways. The danger is that trainees might come away thinking that they have 'the right answer' to the type of situation in the study and attempt to apply that answer regardless of the different circumstances in their workplace.

## Brainstorming

Brainstorming is the 'dreamer' part of the creative cycle and can be done separately or as part of a group Disney strategy. Brainstorming in a group can produce some excellent ideas and the synergy between different people can create quality ideas no one person could have created.

There are some guidelines for getting the most out of group process, very similar to the internal creativity of the dreamer in the Disney strategy:

• Group members do not criticise their own ideas or those of anyone else, either verbally or non-verbally.
• Ideas need not be realistic. No boundaries are drawn on what is possible.
• Everyone can participate equally and everyone's ideas have equal validity. All ideas are recorded.

These rules need to be made explicit to the group and are probably best written down and displayed. The trainer states the outcome to be achieved, for example: 'The goal of this session is to explore what you could do about a work superior who is sexually harassing you.' Set a time limit on the session and stick to it.

Brainstorming, like any exercise, may be dominated by the most vocal individuals. On the other hand, everyone may feel too constrained to say anything. In this case the trainer may have to encourage participation by giving a few totally outrageous ideas in order to show reality is no bar to creative thought.

Brainstorming needs to be followed up, for it is only one third of the creativity process. Once the ideas are generated, they need to be appraised in a 'realist' session and then evaluated. This can be done individually or on a group basis.

## Visualisation and trance

Trance is simply a deepening of a relaxed and receptive state, so trainees will be in and out of such a state constantly throughout the training, and sometimes you can encourage it as a way of giving the group a break or use it more formally as a teaching method. This works particularly well at the end of a day, when trainees are likely to be tired anyway. You can encourage them to get comfortable in whatever way they choose, sitting or lying down, and when they are, using a slow and soft tonality, take them back through the day's material. At the same time, you can encourage them to make their own integration, using very open permissive language:

And as you think about the different things you have learned today, you can begin to wonder how you can apply it in your life, as you may already have some connections, there will be many more that you will find in the days that follow. . .

N.B. This may not be appropriate for some business training.

## Discussion and processing

A discussion is a free exchange of knowledge, experiences, ideas, questions and answers between trainer and group. The term 'processing' is often used to mean any discussion of something for the purpose of learning and typically happens after an activity or exercise.

A discussion can vary from a loose exchange of ideas on a fairly general topic to a tightly structured exchange on a small area. For a useful discussion, trainees need some experience of the subject.

The trainer will want to have some outcome from the discussion and should have some questions of his own that he can ask the group, should the discussion flag. He needs to establish a context where everyone can feel their contribution is heard and valued. This may mean rationing the air time of particularly garrulous individuals.

The danger of a discussion is that it can end up chasing a succession of red herrings or simply turn into a lose-lose argument. Be clear on what the purpose of the discussion is. Decide to what extent you want to control the discussion.

Requesting that all comments are made to you will give you control of the structure. At the other extreme, you may opt for a facilitating role, commenting only on the process of the discussion.

## Tasks

A task is an assignment that is designed to help a person achieve their outcome and lead to new learning. Anyone can decline a task of course. The task can be done outside the training room, perhaps with friends or family, as well as an integral part of the training. There are two main types of task, overt and covert.

An overt task is designed to lead directly to the outcome; the connection is clear. For example, one person was tasked not to smile for a whole afternoon, although she could tell other trainees about her task so that they did not get the wrong impression. This was hard for her because she smiled a lot. She learned two things from the task: how she smiled when she did not really mean it; and that smiling is not the only way to get rapport.

A serious person, on the other hand, may be tasked to make someone laugh or tell a joke. Tasks are designed to expand choice and are difficult only to the extent they counter our predictable habits.

Tasks may also be covert. A covert task switches the person's attention from the real focus of the task to another, overt assignment, which, if accomplished, will automatically achieve the real covert outcome. So the real focus of a covert task is whatever else has to happen for the person to carry out the assignment. The best covert tasks do not depend on successful completion of the overt assignment.

Tasking is used a lot in therapy. One good example is the story of Milton Erickson, the famous hypnotherapist. A man went to him complaining that life seemed drab, uninteresting and boring. Erickson tasked him to go into a nearby field and bring him back two blades of grass that were absolutely identical. Several hours later, the man reported back his inevitable failure at the obvious task. However, the experience of minutely examining so many blades of grass and finding that they were all different focused his mind on difference and how amazing nature is. He was unable to see life as boring after that. Even blades of grass differed. (Or perhaps an afternoon spent examining blades of grass made him appreciate that his life was not so boring after all.)

## Metaphors

Metaphors cover stories, parables, similes and jokes. They are more memorable than just information, for you can make a point much more deeply and effectively with a story than just relating facts.

Metaphors will have several meanings and will affect the group on many different levels. Stories and jokes are engaging, and you can use them to bring the group out of a serious, less resourceful state. You can also use them to organise all or part of your trainings. You can link together themes and topics with metaphors, rather like composers use music in an opera. There will be particular themes or leitmotifs for different characters in a musical drama and when the theme plays, it introduces the character. Stories can act in the same way in a training, bringing you and the trainees back to particular themes that run throughout the training.

You can also use metaphors to organise sections of the training by nesting one inside another. Start with a story which you leave unfinished. . .as you move into the course material. You can start another metaphor at any stage which you also leave unfinished. . . as it leads you to another part of the training material. You can do this a number of times: this sets up what are called *nested loops*. Nested loops require unnesting in reverse order. So the structure is as follows:

Start training
    Story A . . . material A . . .
    Story B . . . material B . . .
    Story C . . . material C . . .
    Story D . . . material D . . .
Now come out by completing the loop by finishing story D...
    Finish story C . . .
    Finish story B . . .
    Finish story A . . .
    End of training

This organises the material for you and the trainees.

Secondly, stories put people into emotional states. Depending on which stories you tell, the trainees will run through a gamut of emotional states. If you choose these states carefully they can be a

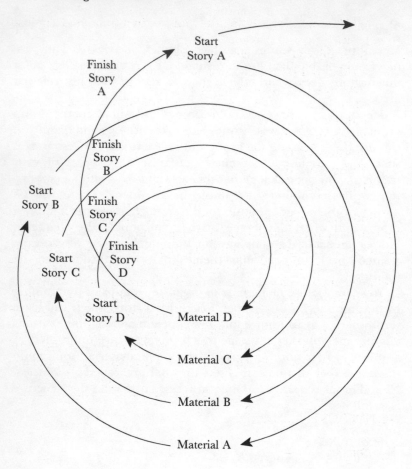

*Figure 2.3 Nested metaphors*

positive help with the material that you are using. For example, suppose you are using these ideas in an assertiveness training session:

> Start story A . . . evokes apprehension.
>     Material A . . . dealing with fear.
> Start story B . . . evokes curiosity.
>     Material B . . . becoming interested in your responses to people.
> Start story C . . . evokes fun, humour.

Material C . . . finding the humour in a situation to defuse it.

Start story D . . . evokes self-esteem.

Material D . . . being able to deal with the situation.

Start story E . . . evokes strength.

Material E . . . ways to deal with a difficult situation.

Finish story E.

Finish story D.

Finish story C.

Finish story B.

Finish story A.

Not only have you put the trainees in a learning state to get the most out of the material, but you have also covertly installed a strategy for dealing with difficult situations: feeling frightened goes to being curious, moves to feeling humorous, moves to feeling your own self-worth, goes to feeling strong and dealing with the situation. This strategy is worth a million theoretical discussions about assertiveness. Trainees will remember it because it evoked real feelings in safe environment.

The success of this strategy, however, depends on the quality of the stories you tell and your skill and congruence as a raconteur.

---

## ACTIVITY STRUCTURES

### *Key Points*

- Good designs are varied and multi-sensory. There are many design structures:

  *Role plays* – simulating a situation that uses the knowledge and skills taught in the training.

  *Lectures* – which depend on the skill of the presenter. They can vary from short lecturettes to hour-long presentations.

  Longer lectures have an introduction and framing part, a middle, giving the material and taking questions, and a conclusion with a summary and final questions.

  *Case studies* – involving the group in a set of circumstances based on real or constructed events and letting them apply the skills they have been learning. Computers can be used in some case simulations.

*Brainstorming* – getting the group to come up with ideas without criticising or worrying if they are possible.

*Trance* – used as relaxation and guided visualisation.

*Discussion* – a free exchange of knowledge, experiences, ideas, questions and answers between trainer and group.

*Processing* – talk about the discussion.

*Tasks* – either overt and covert. Overt tasks are where the outcome is clear. Covert tasks are where the real outcome is different from the given assignment and does not depend on its success.

*Metaphors* – used to organise training. Themes and topics can be linked by metaphor. You can design nested loops of metaphors, each evoking an emotional state and building into a series of steps. This is a covert way of installing strategies.

# 10

# EXERCISE DESIGN

## Levels for exercises

Training exercises can focus on four different levels and most operate on more than one simultaneously. Keep in mind which one you want to focus on predominantly in any exercise.

- *Whole group*
  The group works as a whole, processing, discussing or visualising. An open opportunity for the group to raise any questions or issues is an example of this. Whole group exercises fit well into the beginning and end of trainings, to create or re-establish group rapport.

- *Between groups*
  The groups may be large or small. One example of a between groups exercise is where one group designs and runs an exercise for another group. Other examples are management game models where groups problem solve in competition with each other or run a different part of the management process. Both whole group and between groups designs focus on co-operation and teamwork.

- *Interpersonal within groups*
  This is the most popular structure for practising interpersonal skills and the one we will concentrate on. Typically, there will be an operator or explorer who practises the skill. There will be a client or a subject, who either role plays a problem or issue, or supplies a real problem for the operator to work with. Then there may be the observer, sometimes called 'the meta person', from the Greek word *meta*, meaning 'over' or 'above'. She will keep time, provide support for the operator and give feedback to both at the end. Groups can vary between two and five people.

- *Intrapersonal*
  Here the focus is what happens within the person. The individual increases self-awareness without working with another person. Examples of this would be trance, meditations, guided fantasy or written work.

## Experiential exercise design

Exercise design is at the heart of preparing a training, bringing all the design elements into focus. Exercises are where the group learns by doing in a safe environment. Good exercises give the trainees maximum learning on as many levels as possible.

Exercise design parallels training design. You can use the Disney strategy in exactly the same way: first brainstorm possibilities, organise them in an action sequence and then criticise the design and sort for problems. Creating an exercise creates a context for learning or discovering skill, knowledge and values. It is a microcosm of training. NLP training puts a lot of emphasis on creating a resourceful learning state. However good the exercise, trainees will learn little if they are bored, tired or fed up.

Trainees are unlikely to become proficient after one exercise, but they should leave with a kernel of skill to practise and develop.

There are a series of steps to designing an exercise.

- *Establish outcomes*
  All exercises must have outcomes. If you are not clear about the outcomes of the exercise, then the result will be random at best and you will have no way of judging its success. Be clear about both the overt, stated outcomes and what covert, unstated outcomes you want from the exercise. A good exercise will have both types. Do you want the participants to be consciously aware of the covert outcomes? If you do not, you are teaching to the unconscious mind of the group members. Training communicates to both the conscious and unconscious minds of the trainees. NLP adds to traditional training skills by focusing particularly on covert outcomes and teaching at the unconscious levels. So trainees will come away from a training having learned skills without consciously realising they were at the time.

- *Establish evidence for success*

  How will you know that you have achieved the outcome of the exercise? You will want to be clear what you will see, hear and feel during or after it has run its course. The evidence may come from your observations as you monitor the group during the exercise, and the feedback and group processing at the end.

- *Establish specific steps and activities*

  What are the steps and activities that you will use to achieve the outcome? What time frame will you use? How many people will be in a group? What will be their roles? What will each person be doing?

  You can set up special situations to stretch the participants. For example, in a 'ghost' exercise the group observer will hand the client a 'ghost card' with an instruction on it. The instruction may be something like: 'Start to cry' 'Only ask questions' or 'Lose rapport constantly.' The operator does not know what is on the card, and has to keep working to get the outcome of the exercise in the face of these continuous 'ghost' instructions to the client.

## EXERCISE DESIGN PROCESS

Here is an example of an exercise design:

**Primary outcome:** To increase awareness of the profound impact that simple matching or mismatching body language has on communication, as a preliminary exercise to learning how to use body language to build rapport and improve communication.

**Basic idea:** To have people match and mismatch body language and notice the difference it makes.

Matching body language will involve sitting in a similar posture, giving and receiving the same amount of eye contact and moving their body to the same extent. These add up to what we call 'paying attention'.

Mismatching will involve breaking eye contact, turning away and adopting a different posture from the person talking.

**Rough out the roles:** Three people in the exercise group. Three rounds of three minutes per round plus two minutes discussion time per round: 15 minutes total run time. The client talks about anything he wants. The operator does not talk, but matches the client's body language as naturally as she can until she hears a prearranged signal from the trainer to mismatch. She continues to mismatch for 30 seconds until she hears the signal again, and then returns to matching. The observer notices body language of client and operator. All three are asked to notice the difference in communication of matching versus mismatching. In processing afterwards, you ask what differences they noticed.

## Problem sorting

Now that you have a basic design, you run it mentally in each of the three roles and notice what might go wrong. Let the critic loose on the exercise. Assume the trainees are naïve. When you have identified the places where the exercise is weak, go back and see what instructions you need to give at the beginning to pre-empt the problem. For example, some trainees may be reluctant to mismatch because they feel uncomfortable about being rude. You can deal with this in advance by saying something like, 'You may feel uncomfortable mismatching because it is seen as rude. Remember you are doing it in the bounds of this exercise so both you and the speaker can learn the effect it has.' If this is not enough, what changes can you make to the design to circumvent the difficulty? Recycle through the design process until you are happy with the basic structure. For example, you might think that some people will object that the exercise is unnatural. How can you deal with this objection in advance? Perhaps with a metaphor about how tennis coaches artificially break a serve into the component parts for the purpose of learning. . .?

## Stack the design

Now you have a basic design, how much more can you put into it? How can you improve it? What extra nuances can you introduce so that the participants learn on as many different levels as possible? With a single outcome exercise you will get that outcome . . . maybe. With a stacked design it is impossible for anyone to go through the exercise without learning *something*. Notice the outcomes that are already built into the design. For example, there is a covert outcome of getting familiar with the three different perceptual positions: first, second and meta.

Now go back and look at the stacked design for possible problems. There will come a time when any further changes just make the exercise unwieldy rather than better. There is also a time when the only way to find out if an exercise works in practice is to actually *do* it in practice.

## Identify the evidence of learning

How will you know the exercise has achieved the outcome? In this instance you may go on the differences the trainees report noticing when they return from the exercise. Often you will be noticing changes in skill or behaviour as the exercise runs.

## Evaluate afterwards

This is not strictly part of the design process, but if you want to do the exercise again, you want feedback on how well it worked and whether it needs any changes. Problems that do happen despite your best efforts refine your mental model for problem sorting. There is a principle in theoretical physics: anything that can possibly happen, will happen. In the business of training, assume anything that can go wrong will go wrong (given enough time). Expect feedback. The small comforting thought here is that no one is infallible.

Criteria for a successful exercise:

- That it is possible (appropriately chunked into steps and stages, and given a realistic time frame).
- That the trainees experience some level of success.
- That the trainees learn something.
- That there is at least one overt outcome.
- That there is at least one covert outcome.
- That it stretches participants past their habitual skill levels (their comfort zone).
- That it is easy to generalise to other situations outside the training room.
- That all roles in the exercise are utilised for learning.

## Coaching skills exercise

Here is one final example from a training on coaching skills, designed by the NLP trainer Brian Van der Horst.

This is a three-person exercise.

1. The operator (A) elicits from the client (B) his outcomes for the training. At the same time he coaches B into a resourceful state. This section runs for 15 minutes.
2. The observer (C) gives feedback to A on how he did while at the same time eliciting a resourceful state from A (five minutes).
3. The client (B) gives feedback to the observer (C) on how he coached A, at the same time eliciting a resourceful state from C (five minutes).
4. The observer (C) and operator (A) get together. They give B a task, something for B to do that will help the client achieve his outcomes. This also takes five minutes.
5. The observer then writes a summary of the outcome of the task and the learning he expects the operator to get from performing the task, and gives it to the trainers.

There are three rounds and each person performs each role. At the end each person will have a task to perform from their operator role, and each person will be getting some unexpected help in achieving their outcome for the training from their client role.

This is a good example of a multi-level exercise with many overt and covert outcomes:

- Participants get to practise the skill of eliciting outcomes.
- They practise coaching each other into a resourceful state.
- They give feedback.
- They design tasks.
- They carry out tasks.
- They see and experience different coaching styles and learn from them.
- They experience resourceful states.
- As the first exercise in a training it establishes resourceful states for the training and builds group rapport.
- Everyone becomes clearer about their outcomes for the training.

## EXERCISE DESIGN

### *Key Points*

- Training exercises can focus on four different levels:
  whole group
  between groups
  interpersonal within groups
  intrapersonal
- Experiential exercises are at the heart of training.
- Exercise design parallels training design.
- Establish outcomes, both overt and covert:
  overt outcomes train conscious minds
  covert outcomes train unconscious minds
- Establish evidence for success.
- Establish specific steps and activities.
- Look for possible problems.
- Stack the design to get the most from the exercise.

# 11

# PRESENTATION SKILLS

What you are doing speaks so loud I can't hear what you say.

*Emerson*

## COMMUNICATIONS CHANNELS

When training or presenting, you have four main channels of communication: visual, voice quality, touch and the actual words you say. There is classic research by Professor Albert Mehrabian of UCLA, which makes it clear that the impact and perceived truth of any communication comes mostly from the body language of the presenter, closely followed by the voice quality. The actual words come a poor third. His figures for the impact and perceived sincerity of a communication are 55 per cent body language, 38 per cent voice quality and 7 per cent words.

When these three aspects reinforce each other, the communication is congruent. If there is a discrepancy between the words and the body language, it is the non-verbal part that the listener will pay attention to, often without realising it. Presentation skills are how you give life to your words. They are how you manage the 93 per cent of the presentation. So they are much more important than memorising the words. Presentation skills consist of a number of simple things you need to do and a number of simple things to avoid.

### Appearance

The first impression that a group will have of you will be your appearance. Your appearance is a communication. Is it what you want to communicate? You never get a second chance to make a good first impression. A number of research projects have

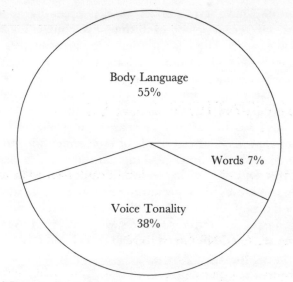

*Figure 2.4 Impact of a presentation*

confirmed that people form their initial judgements about you in under 10 seconds. Generally speaking, you want to feel comfortable, put others at ease and be appropriately dressed for the weather, time of day and occasion. It is generally better to be overdressed than underdressed. Match the colours and styles you like, and if in doubt, err on the side of being conservative, especially in a business setting. Consider how you want to look and dress. Look at yourself from the audience's perspective. Get feedback from those whose opinion you trust. How do they see your hair, clothing, make up and jewellery if you are a woman? For a man, what do they think of your clothes, hair, moustache and beard if you have them, watches and jewellery? Get honest feedback.

## Eye contact

Eye contact with the audience is important and a natural expression of your interest. I like to have made eye contact with everyone in the room before I begin a presentation. If the audience is a very large one, pick up to a dozen of the friendliest people you can see and make eye contact with them in turn. When you speak, mentally divide the room into four or five segments and systematically make eye contact with people in the different segments, a different person each time. Eye contact for about five seconds works best. There is a tendency to dart your eyes away, but resist it. Five seconds is quite a long time. Time it. We make extended eye contact with people when talking with them on a one-to-one basis and groups are a collection of individuals.

In trainer training you can use the following exercise. Have the participants raise their hands. They are to keep their hands raised until they experience five seconds of eye contact with the trainer. The trainer must continue speaking naturally to the group while he does this.

Closing your eyes while presenting in a sort of extended blink is not a good idea. It distracts the audience and you cannot track the audience response to what you are saying with your eyes closed – or, if you can, you do not need to read this chapter. Come and tell us how you do it.

## Posture

You make a fundamental statement about yourself by the way you use your body. An aligned, erect posture communicates ease. Stand your full height. Poor posture is very often based on outdated habits. If you stand, be balanced equally on both feet. Shifting from side to side, going back on one hip, rocking or swaying can be distracting. I remember one presenter who swayed from side to side the whole time he spoke. He put most of the audience in a trance inside two minutes. This was not his intention at all, for his material was linguistics that needed full conscious attention.

To get a good basic posture, stand with your back to a wall. Touch the wall with the back of your head and your backside and as much of the small of your back as you comfortably can. Now step away. Your new posture may feel stiff and perhaps unbalanced to you, but check in a mirror. It is actually erect and balanced. The problem is that we become used to habitual postures so they *feel* right, even though they are not. If you habitually lean slightly to the right, then when you stand upright, it will feel as if you are unbalanced to the left. Use a mirror and ask friends to give you feedback on your posture.

## Gesture

It is a truism that gestures need to look natural and spontaneous. Unfortunately this is the 'Be spontaneous!' paradox. By *trying* to be spontaneous, you make it impossible. To try to gesture spontaneously looks wooden. This being so, the way round the paradox is to eliminate those things that stop you being natural. For example, we all have a 'nervous gesture' – jingling loose change in the pocket perhaps or fiddling with a lock of hair. Five minutes worth of yourself on video and you will see it precisely. When you have identified it, stop doing it. When it has gone, find the next nervous habit to eliminate. These small changes will make a big difference. Also avoid unnecessary gestures. Gestures emphasise a point and if you are always gesturing then they lose their impact, like an orchestra that is always playing fortissimo.

## Space

Use all the available space. Physical space is a metaphor for mental space, so claim what you want from the start. To give the most boring presentation possible, get behind a lectern, put a large bundle of notes on it, look down at them and stay rooted to the spot while you read the notes in a monotone. After five minutes, those members of your audience who are still awake will probably leave.

## Voice

We pick up a rich variety of information from a person's voice, their general state of health, their mood, their social class and what part of the country they come from. In a presentation your voice adds energy and interest. Use it to express the natural emotion of what you feel. Practise with a tape recorder. Whether you train with or without a sound system, you will need to be able to project your voice to the back of the room. Sometimes you will want to catch the group's attention by talking softly, but a soft voice still needs projection.

We do not hear what our voice sounds like to others because it resonates in the bones of our skull. When you listen to yourself on tape the first time it is always a surprise, it sounds like a stranger. Listen to your voice on tape and experiment. Are the emotions, energy and inflection you mean to give out actually coming out? If they are not, then you need to exaggerate and experiment until they do. Remember, it is the audience, not the speaker, who decides what degree of expression there is. If the *audience* does not hear it, then for practical purposes it is not there.

Vocal projection needs good breathing. Our breathing drives our voice. Nervous breathing is quick and shallow, and deprives the voice of range and power. Notice your breathing when you are training. Breathe deeply when you speak to groups. Use the diaphragm, so the abdomen expands when you breathe in.

Take your time when talking. If the group is taking notes of what you say, they will appreciate this. Fast speaking often comes from quick, shallow breathing, so if you speak more slowly, you will automatically breathe more deeply. Visualising while speaking also increases the rate of delivery. Pictures happen quickly and you have to speak fast to keep up with them. Slow down your mental video.

Use your voice congruently with your words. If you want the group to visualise, speak faster. If you want them to hear internally, speak more slowly and rhythmically. If you want them to get into their feelings, speak slower still and deeper. The more choice you have about the range, speed and timbre of your voice, the more you can use it as a musical instrument to communicate with the group. Do not play a flute part on a tuba.

To continue the musical metaphor, it is the spaces between the notes that give the music meaning. The great pianist Artur Schnabel is quoted as saying, 'The notes I handle no better than many pianists. But the pauses between the notes . . . that is where the art resides.' Pauses are the natural punctuation in what we say. The audience appreciates pauses. You can use pauses to think of what you are going to say next and to collect your thoughts. Learn to pause deliberately, so when you do need to pause to think it will not seem unusual. Remember that when you are training, time tends to speed up and a five-second pause can seem interminable to you, while to the audience it is a natural break.

There are also the natural vocal inflections that you can use to create effects. If your voice tonality stays level to the end of a sentence it will imply a statement. If it rises at the end of a sentence it gives the effect of a question. If it drops at the end of a sentence it gives the impression of a command.

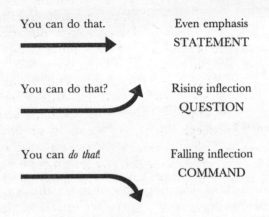

*Figure 2.5 Voice inflections*

## Words

At last, the part we practise, shape and fret over the most. How straightforward are words? Well, unfortunately what the trainees thought you meant to say may not take into account the misunderstanding you tried to circumvent. In other words, words can be tricky. If a picture is worth a thousand words, that is about seven minutes' speaking time at the normal rate of about 150 words a minute.

### Vocabulary
The first obvious point is that we need a rich and varied vocabulary that will give our listeners a taste of the subject. We need to fill in the blanks and give the audience a grasp of the themes. There are some hundreds of thousands of words in the English language and the average person's vocabulary consists of a meagre two or three thousand.

Pick your words carefully, for every word has a different shade of meaning. I have just opened a Thesaurus at random and come across a listing of the words 'authority', 'power', 'permission' and 'right' as meaning the same thing. What do you think?

### Multi-sensory speech
Mix your sensory-specific words, especially at the beginning of the

training. Remember that most people have a favoured way of thinking, either in pictures, sounds, or feelings. If you wanted to communicate effectively with one person you would find out how he thought and tailor your language to that mode. With many people in a group you need to use all three modes to catch everyone. Make sure that the people who visualise well see what you mean, that you come over loud and clear to the people who have keen hearing – and those who think more with their bodies get a good grasp of what you are saying.

## Jargon

Avoid jargon. Unless of course you are in a specialist field and the training consists of learning specialist vocabulary. In many trainings people want and expect technical words and will complain if they do not get them. What is jargon to the uninitiated is technical vocabulary to those who know, or want to know, the field.

If you do use jargon, explain it and be aware that a word that may be very familiar to you may be new to the group. Write key technical words with definitions on the flip chart or have a hand out. The principle here is KISS – **K**eep **I**t **S**hort and **S**imple.

## Reading prepared passages

If you plan to read a passage from a book, mark it in advance and have the book handy. Fumbling around for the right book or right page is not a good prelude for the pearls of wisdom you want to give. Give as much life and energy as you can to the passage you read; it will live or die according to the interest you put in it with your voice.

## Active tense

Use the active tense to involve people in what you say. Use the passive tense to defuse the energy in a room and to detach people from their experience. It is amazing how quickly a room full of lethargic people can be created by you if the passive tense is continually used by you. Was it not?

One can also use 'one'. Read the following three sentences and check out your internal responses to them. Do they have the same effect?

One can make pictures mentally.

You can make pictures mentally.
Pictures can be made mentally.
Make mental pictures . . . *Now.*

## Names

What is the most important word in the English language? Many possible answers here, but I would have thought that your own name would figure high on the list. Use people's names. Thank them by name for any questions and comments. Make sure you know names or, if the group is too large for this to be practicable, make sure everyone has name badges.

## Words to avoid

Now some words to avoid. Do not use cliffhangers. Starting sentences with: 'It is because . . . that . . .' makes them very hard to follow and is liable to generate confusion. Keep subordinate clauses to a minimum. Generally speaking, short sentences with short words evoke direct action. Longer sentences, with more words in them, perhaps with a number of dependent clauses which alter the sense of the sentence as it goes along, not too much mind you, but just enough to make the whole thing an exercise in long-distance sense retention, (if indeed there was any at short distance to start with), can actually get away with leaving out the point of the sentence, because you have forgotten the start by the time you have just reached the end. I hope that makes the point – please do not reread the last sentence! Most adults have difficulty following the sense of a spoken sentence with more than 18 words.

## Instructions

Do not turn instructions into questions, otherwise people will answer them and not follow the instructions.

Do not give a second instruction until the first has been acted on.

## Nervous verbal gesture

Find your own personal nervous 'verbal gesture'. 'Well . . . uhh . . . let me see . . . so . . . um, let's sort of find out . . . ummm . . . what it is . . . [sniff] . . . like . . . alright? OK . . . So . . . ? Mmmmmm . . . what d'ya think?' Hearing yourself on video will soon identify what it is and how often you use it. Once you identify it, it will seem to be everywhere. Catch the verbal fluff in your sentences and start to leave it out, starting with whatever you favour the most. Replace these 'fillers' with something more powerful. A clear sentence – or even a pause – is always more powerful.

### Verbal humour

Verbal humour is a powerful way of getting and maintaining group rapport. I attempt to get the group to laugh within the first five minutes of a training. It is an important landmark. Making people laugh is not a matter of telling jokes. Do not tell jokes unless you are sure you can do it with timing and congruence. A joke that falls flat stays down. Stand up comics will tell you how difficult it is to try to make people laugh with jokes. 'Fun' is not the same as 'funny'. Often all you need do to raise a smile is point out the odd aspects of something quite mundane.

### Practice and feedback

The man with the violin who stopped the passer-by to ask the way to Carnegie Hall got the famous answer: 'Practice.'

There is no achievement without personal discipline and no feedback without practice. Get as much feedback as you can from friends and peers, but watching yourself on video camera is easily the best way. You can review and rehear what you did from an objective position and learn and improve much more quickly. It is also satisfying to track your performance to see how you improve over the course of time.

### Modelling

Watch trainers and presenters you think are good. What are the patterns they have that make them good? Look for patterns in the three areas: body language, voice tone and the words themselves. Try out some of these patterns when you train. Some patterns will suit you, others will not. Take what you want and leave the rest. In NLP 'stealing' behaviour is the greatest compliment you can give somebody. No one has copyright on excellence. What one person can do, others can do.

Watch television for role-models. Watch it with the sound off to concentrate on body language. Listen to voices-only television or radio. Radio presenters have only the auditory channel to work with, consequently they tend to be very expressive with their voices. Mimic a good model from radio and notice how that is different from how you would say the same thing.

When you have found an example of excellence, experiment becoming that model for some short period in training or presenting. Imagine you are in their shoes. How would they present this material? How would they move and speak? You can extend your range tremendously by experimenting with different styles. You will finish with the style that expresses yourself with many of the best of others woven in seamlessly.

Also watch presenters that you think are not good. What are they doing differently? Get a contrast. See what they do and say, and how they say and do it, and you will have some things to avoid. By learning what does not work, you come closer to what does. Do not just learn from you own mistakes; learn from others' mistakes too. It saves time.

### Experiment

You owe it to yourself and your audience to experiment. But be kind to yourself as a learner. The most ferocious criticism is usually self-criticism. We often have the most exacting standards for ourselves that no one else would dream of applying. As you become more proficient at training, there is the danger that you can eat yourself alive with criticism instead of simply using it as feedback to improve. Know that you will never be perfect and then each skill you acquire opens up areas of new skills and refining old skills in what becomes a delightful, endless journey.

Also make sure that your critical circuits do not spoil your enjoyment of any other trainings that you participate in. The intention of criticism is improvement, not punishment. Review, evaluate and then move on.

---

## PRESENTATION SKILLS

### Key Points

- The impact of a presentation is 55 per cent body language, 38 per cent voice tonality and 7 per cent words.
- Presentation skills are how you put across your words – the skill is in what you do and what you leave out.

- Skills mean consistent performance over time, backed by empowering beliefs.
- Skills flow from the good emotional state of the presenter.

BODY LANGUAGE
- Make your appearance appropriate to the presentation.
- Make eye contact with the trainees.
- Have a natural upright posture.
- To keep gestures natural, eliminate the unnecessary and nervous ones.
- Take all the physical space you want.

VOICE
- Project your voice.
- Talk more slowly and use your voice congruently with the material you are presenting.
- Use pauses.
- Use a large, multi-sensory vocabulary and avoid jargon.
- Use names.
- Avoid cliffhangers and long sentences.

FEEDBACK
- Use video to find your nervous verbal gesture and stop it.
- Utilise every opportunity for practice and feedback.
- Learn from models – find what does and does not work.
- Keep self-criticism within bounds.

# BELIEFS AND VALUES

Presentation skills are important, yet they are only a means to an end. What do you want them for and what are you going to do with them? This is a very personal area and your answer will depend on what is important to you about training and why you do it. Your skill as a trainer comes from what you do, your behaviour, backed by your core beliefs and values.

These core beliefs and values underlie your identity: who you perceive yourself to be and what your mission in life is. Is training something you do or do you think of yourself as a trainer? The latter is a statement about your identity.

## BELIEFS

Beliefs are generalisations we make about ourselves, other people and the world around us. They are the principles by which we act. We usually think of beliefs as 'all or nothing' and that what we believe is true consistently. Yet a moment's thought is enough to realise that we have changed many beliefs throughout our lives. It is rather unlikely that you still believe in Father Christmas, for example.

While we do have core beliefs that are fairly fixed and important to us, we can also be flexible about what we choose to believe in certain areas of our lives. If we act as if certain things are true, then it makes many tasks much easier. The old saying applies, 'Whether you believe you can or you can't, *you're right!*' Beliefs act as self-fulfilling prophecies.

It is this proven fact that beliefs have a strong tendency to make themselves come true that gives them their power. If you change just one belief, you will also change a lot of your behaviour. But if you change just one aspect of your behaviour, you are unlikely to change anything else. This is why cleaning up your personal belief systems is a central part of any personal development programme. Useful beliefs act as empowering permissions to use our skills to the full. Others may act as unnecessary limitations. All beliefs have consequences. The question to ask about any belief is, 'Is it useful and does it serve me?' This applies from the big ones – 'Is the universe a friendly place?' – to the small ones – 'Do I believe that reading this chapter will be satisfying and enriching?'

Here are some examples of empowering beliefs that can make a lot of difference to your trainings. Notice which ones you already have on board and which ones you would like. We invite you to act as if they were true in your daily life and notice what difference they make. You can then transfer them into training. All of them will be useful for your trainees.

- **There is no failure, only feedback.**
  The belief that failure is real is one of the most common and limiting beliefs that there is. Believe instead that there are no errors, no mistakes, only results and outcomes. Admittedly, they may be very different from what we had in mind. If what you get is not what you want, try something else and learn what you can from what you did get.

- **Every person has all the resources they need.**
  This goes for both the trainer and the trainees. The trainer need never get completely stuck – and trainees are not empty vessels to be filled with skills and knowledge. Every person has a lifetime of varied experience from which to draw many different resources. How can you tap them?

- **The meaning of your communication is the response you get.**
  When you are training you are a professional communicator. What you say and do will be focused on achieving your training outcomes. When you get a different or unpredictable response from the participants, take that as feedback and do something different. The meaning of what you say or do is determined by the group. This gives you enormous flexibility to change what you do to get your desired outcome, rather than blaming the group for not responding the right way. Remember that whenever you get caught in the blame game, you disempower yourself.

- **The intention of every behaviour is positive. To believe otherwise is to make it so.**
  Every person creates and lives in their own model of reality. Every action they take is the best choice available to them at the time, given their reality. It may be incomprehensible to us, but it is real to them. If you can understand how a person's model of reality works, then you can find the positive intention behind any 'difficult' behaviour. And if you know the positive intention, then you can find the most useful response to make. This does not excuse what they do; it enables you to understand and deal with it.

- **If a training goes badly off course, I can always find ways of getting it back on course and learn a lot in the process.**
  It is much easier to stay on track in the first place, but if things do go awry, this is a powerful belief to have working for you. One way to get things back on course is to utilise whatever happens to learn.

These beliefs cannot be proved true (or false). Treat them as useful principles and add your own favourites to the list

A good way to find the most useful additional beliefs is to take an inventory of your present beliefs about training. Take a few moments to write down your immediate answers to these questions.

1. Why are you a trainer?
2. What are your strengths and potentials as a trainer?
3. What do you believe about the groups you train?
4. What beliefs do you have about yourself as a trainer?
5. How easy is it for people to change?

Now pause for a moment before thinking about:

1. How would you act if you realised your potential?
2. What beliefs would you like to have about yourself as a trainer? (Clue: What feedback from peers gives you the most pleasure?)
2. What beliefs would it be more useful to have about the groups you teach?
3. What stops you acting as if these beliefs are true?

## VALUES

Values are those things that are important to us in our lives. To value something means to place importance on it. Of course, different people will have different values. As a trainer, you are likely to put a high value on relationships, feelings and learning. A line manager may put a high value on results, effectiveness and profitability.

Core values are those values that permeate most of what we do. They are especially important because they are the key to understanding what we do and why we do it. Core values will be things like satisfaction, self-respect, achievement, adventure, independence, learning, growth, integrity, love, joy and peace.

One of the skills that will enhance your training performance is developing your awareness of values, both your own and other peoples'. Here is a simple exercise that you can do in the next five minutes to clarify your own core values.

1. Think of at least three of the most significant experiences in your life. Take each experience in turn and ask yourself what it was you got from it that made it so significant for you. Write a list of key words or phrases.
2. Keep going until you get a cluster of about five words that represent the core values that keep recurring across different significant experiences.
3. Of those five core values, if you had to lose one, which one would you lose? Underline that word and write the number 5 in front of it. Repeat for each in turn until you are left with the single most important value, number 1.

What you have just mapped out is a hierarchy of your core values. Decisions are difficult because they often represent a conflict of values. For example, do you take on that extra work or not? On the one hand, you need the extra income, on the other, you want to spend more time with your family. If you know which is more important, the decision becomes simple.

One of the most powerful applications of this is writing out your life purpose in just one sentence. Keep making up sentences until you have a version that you are happy with. Write it on a card and put it in your pocket. Any time you face a tricky decision, pull out the card and read it. You will find the decision much easier to make. This works so well because it is our core values that give direction and meaning to our life. We are literally drawn to them and by them.

## Training values

Be clear about your own training values and remember that other people may not share them. You can identify them with the following exercise:

1. Choose three good training experiences. These can be from the distant or immediate past. Write down the key words that represent what was important for you about each one. Notice the clusters that emerge from all three.
2. Contrast this with three experiences of bad training. Write down the key words for each and identify the clusters.

The cluster of values you got from step one are your core values about training quality, what you want to achieve, sometimes called your 'moving towards' values, as you are always seeking to fulfil them. Examples might be: fun, learning, enthusiasm. The cluster of values from step two will be your 'moving away from' values – those things you want to avoid in a training. Examples might be: embarrassment, anger, blame, boredom.

## Evidence for values

We use very general words to describe values – 'integrity', 'energy', 'happiness' – and they will mean different things to different people. What specifically do they mean to you? How do you know when they are being fulfilled? What rules do you have to tell you when values are met?

For example, two trainers may both say it is important for them to be well paid, train large groups and get positive feedback from trainees. *But*, for trainer A this means £1,000 a day, a group of 100 and a score of 95 per cent on the happy sheet. His friend trainer B's values are met by £500 a day, a group of 15 and a score of 80 per cent on the happy sheet.

This does not tell you who is the better trainer. The question to ask is whether you are limiting yourself by setting your sights too low or frustrating yourself by setting your sights too high. If you define your values in such a way that they are impossible to meet or are significantly outside your control or are not satisfying, then they are worth reviewing.

### Final questions

Here are a last few valuable questions to ponder:

- Are you satisfied with your core values hierarchy?
- Do you want to make any changes in your core values?
- Can you imagine any training values that could serve you better?
- Are your actions at the moment getting what is of value for you?

---

## BELIEFS AND VALUES

### *Key points*

- Training skills are a means to an end only.
- Beliefs are generalisations and act as self-fulfilling prophecies.
- Changing beliefs is a powerful way of fundamentally changing behaviour.
- Collect empowering training beliefs.
- Values are those things that are important to us in our lives.
- You can discover your hierarchy of values and your hierarchy of training values.
- Values will have rules or evidences attached – these need to be realistic and empowering.

---

# SELF-MANAGEMENT

This chapter is about one of the most important aspects of training, presentation or performance: being in a good emotional state. Self-management is about what 'you' do to manage 'yourself' beforehand to give your best performance. You may have all those wonderful skills in there, but if they cannot emerge in just the right way and at just the right time, you might as well not have them at all. During the actual training 'you' do want to be free to just get on with it and not have to worry about your emotional state. If something happens that sets you back, then you need the self-management skills to regain your state to continue training well. You cannot always control the situation or other people, but you can control how you respond to it.

There are four main issues in self-management:

1. Being in a good state while training to allow the skills to flow.
2. Having recovery strategies in difficult situations to keep or regain your state.
3. Learning from the trainings you do to constantly improve.
4. Dealing with criticism and pressures that could lead to long-term trainer 'burnout'.

## THE TRAINER'S EMOTIONAL STATE

I can clearly remember being at one of John Grinder's trainings when someone asked him what were the most useful things for a trainer to pay attention to. I was on the edge of my chair waiting to hear his response. This was, after all, probably the finest trainer I had ever experienced. His reply was something like this. 'First, pay attention to your own state. Second, pay attention to your own state. And third, pay attention to your audience's state.'

This was not the answer I was expecting, yet it makes perfect sense. When the trainer is in a resourceful state, he will think clearly and quickly and respond to the concerns and outcomes of the participants. It takes attention and energy to rise above an unresourceful state – attention and energy needed for the training.

Emotional state is not an easy subject to deal with in a book. While it is easy to give advice, you have to walk it as well as talk it. 'State' is one of those verbs that masquerade as nouns. Despite the way we talk about it, it is not something you have, it is something you do (or not) and continue to do (or not) while you train. You act.

As you learn to have freedom of choice about your own internal state, that is, your thoughts and feelings, your skills flow and you will be able to be at your best more consistently and with less effort. This is simple to say, but not easy in practice.

However, the payoffs are huge. Training becomes easier and more enjoyable. You increase the flexibility and range of your own behaviour, and you become more effective. And, of course, changing your own emotional state is one of the easiest ways to influence your audience and change their emotional state, and consistently create enjoyable learning contexts.

## Physiology

Our emotional state and thinking are linked with our physiology. Physiology affects thoughts and thoughts affect physiology. It is impossible, for example, to maintain a resourceful state and clear thoughts with a slumped posture, downward-looking eyes and shallow breathing. Alternatively, acting as if you are confident allows you to feel more confident. You can become calmer by relaxing your neck and jaw muscles and exhaling deeply. The myth of the 'good deep breath' is only half right. You need to exhale deeply. This stops the build up of carbon dioxide in the bloodstream that is one of the physiological causes of anxiety. Changing your breathing is probably the most powerful way you can change your state.

Something to bear in mind when starting a training is that there is a difference between unresourceful feelings and the natural feelings of excitement of the body preparing itself. The feelings usually labelled as 'nerves' are your body preparing to act powerfully. The only question is whether the butterflies in your stomach scatter and beat their wings against the glass or whether they fly in formation. There is nothing wrong with these feelings; many experienced performers, actors, musicians and presenters welcome them as a sign of extra energy.

When you are training you are in an altered state. This has two subjective consequences. First, your sense of time is altered. Time seems to speed up. An afternoon can pass in a flash, so clock time needs watching carefully. The reason is when you are training you are fully associated in the moment and not attending to the passing of time. So you need to jump out of this occasionally to track how time is passing in the outside world.

The second consequence is that you will be very sensitive to your own performance, especially where it does not live up to your expectations. Every mistake is magnified and becomes significant. From the position of the audience, however, your 'dreadful gaffe' will be unimportant, if they notice it at all. You will nearly always look better than you feel.

## Resource anchoring

One way to have more choices about your emotional state is to transfer positive resources from past experiences via an association or 'anchor'. We naturally make associations, so it is a simple step to learn to make those that will help us in training. Athletes use lucky mascots in the same way to prepare themselves for competition.

The first stage is to choose the emotional state you want and then associate it with a trigger or anchor so you can bring it to mind whenever you want.

1. Think of a particular resourceful state that you want for training, for example, confidence, humour or patience. You may not have a word for it, it may just be a good state you have when training is going really well.

2. Remember a time when you were in that state. Get back to it strongly, see what you saw then, hear what you heard then and get the feeling as strongly as you can. Then come back into the present moment.

3. Decide what associations or anchors you want to use that will remind you of that state to bring back the resourceful feeling.

Pick one thing you can see in your mind's eye, one sound or word you can say to yourself and one small inconspicuous gesture you can make. Some people clench their fist or touch two fingers together. The picture, sound and gesture should be distinctive and memorable. These are your anchors.

4. Next, go back and fully experience the resourceful state you want to have while training. See what you saw, hear what you heard and feel your full body sense. It can help if you put your body into the same position as you were then, if that is appropriate. When the resourceful feeling is at its height, use your anchors. See the picture, hear the sound and make the gesture. Then come out of the state and think of something else.

5. Test the anchors. See the picture, hear the sound and make the gesture. Notice how this brings back the resourceful feeling. If you are not satisfied, go back to step 4 and associate again. Do this as many times as you need to, so that the anchors do indeed bring back the resourceful feeling.

6. Mentally rehearse using your anchors in a training situation. You can use them to get yourself into a resource state at the start of the training and as a recovery strategy if things go badly during the training.

Anchoring and using your resourceful states are skills and, like all skills, they get easier the more you practise. For some people this technique works dramatically first time. We live in a culture that believes feelings are involuntary, created by other people. Anchoring is one way of gaining emotional choice and so is an excellent tool for self-development generally, as well as for training.

## Confidence

Confidence is one component of a good emotional state. The dictionary defines it as 'assured expectation'. It is firmly based on adequate preparation.

You need to be prepared on two levels. First, you need to know your material. If you do not, you are quite right to feel uncomfortable. Put in the time to learn it.

Secondly, once you have mastered the material, you have to ask yourself, 'Can I deliver what I know I know, in this particular training?' To answer this you need to ask another question: 'What might prevent me?' Now you can go through various scenarios and come up with solutions in advance that you need to rehearse mentally before the training. Most of them are about keeping a good emotional state. With this skill, your confidence is well founded.

The question to ask is, 'Do I deserve to succeed?'

Confidence also comes from experience. If you have done it once, all things being roughly equal, you can do it again. You have a reference experience for success. How many times do you have to train well before you can be confident you can do it again? Once? Twice? Three times? More than that? Never? Different people have different answers. You may want to change the way you think about your skills if you have to prove it to yourself every time you go out.

## Competence

Competence is also about what you do. It is about the ability to act skilfully at every level, to monitor the results and track whether you are getting your training outcomes and participants are getting theirs. A competent trainer has many choices in any situation, something for every eventuality. Competence is probably the most important factor in getting long-term rapport with a group.

## Congruence

Congruence is the third and most important trainer quality. It is sometimes called sincerity. Again, it is not something you have, but something you do, i.e. you act congruently when your body language, tonality and words all give the same message. You act incongruently when they give mixed messages – for example, talking about the importance of valuing group input while actually ignoring their questions or stressing good posture when your own posture is slumped and unbalanced.

There are three levels of congruence. The first level is feeling congruent about doing the training. This is an important question, and before committing to a challenging situation you will want to feel that all your unconscious resources will be there to support you. Be congruent about a training before accepting it. To find out whether you are congruent, you can run through this check.

### Congruence check

You can check congruence in two ways. First, remember a time when you were completely committed to some task or outcome. It need not be a training task. As you think of that, be aware of how your body feels, what pictures you see and what sounds or voices you hear internally. What is it like to be committed? Get to know that congruent feeling. That is a resource to let you know that you are ready to do a training.

The second approach is to remember a time when you were not fully committed to some task or project. What does that feel like? What does your body feel like, what pictures and sounds do you have internally? Many people hear a doubting voice tone in their mind in this situation. This signal is your friend. It is warning you that there is something not yet right about the situation.

If you do not feel congruent, start to think about what the problems are. What would have to be different before you could feel congruent about doing the training? Do you have adequate preparation time? Does it put you under pressure in your life? Is this a time when you need to say no? Do you know the subject well enough? Identify what you have to do, assuming you will be taking the training. Very often it is some preparation or condition that you need to attend to. Then think again and check for congruence.

You cannot fake a congruence check – it gives you an honest answer about your preparedness for a particular training. When you are congruent, you can be confident that you are competent and that your unconscious resources are there to support you.

You can use the congruence check on any area of your life.

### Alignment exercise

Congruence comes from alignment of all your resources, conscious and unconscious. Like an orchestra playing in tune, you want all the different parts of you to work together.

There is a powerful exercise using neurological levels you can do before training to help this alignment process. You can either do this alone or have a friend ask you the questions as you move through these levels.

Start by giving yourself some space to move. You are going to move forward physically as a metaphor for exploring higher levels of yourself.

1. Start by standing where you can take five steps forward. Think of the *environment* you train in. Where are you? Who is around you? What equipment do you use in your training? What times do you train? How long does it last and when is it held? Who else is with you?

2. Take a step forward. This is the next level, where you can explore your *behaviour*. What are you actually doing? Think through what you do in a training situation – your movements, actions and thoughts.

3. When you are ready, take another step forward and consider your *skills and capabilities*. What skills are you using in the training situation? What skills do you have from other parts of your life that you bring to bear when you are training and what general capabilities are expressed by the behaviour you thought about at the previous level?

4. Step forward again and reflect on your *beliefs and values* about training. Why do you train? What do you believe about yourself as a trainer? What do you believe about the participants? What might get in the way of your training? What is good training all about? What do you find worthwhile about training? What would you have to give up if you stopped training? What is important to you about training? Take the time you need to come to some answers that satisfy you.

5. Step forward again and think about your *identity*. What is your mission in life? How does training connect to it? Who are you?

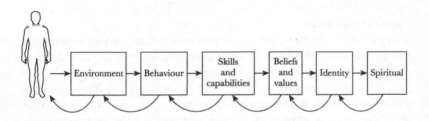

*Figure 2.6 Neurological levels alignment*

Get a sense of yourself and what you want to accomplish in the world. Allow your own answers to come up naturally.

6. Now take a last step forward. Think about how you are connected to all other living beings and whatever is beyond your being. You may think of this as *spiritual* or not. You may have religious beliefs or a personal philosophy. Take the time you need to get a sense of what this means to you.

7. Still feeling this connectedness with others, turn around and face back the way you came. Take this sense of connectedness with you as you step back into your identity level. Notice the difference it makes.

8. Now take this enhanced sense of who you are and who you can be, and step back to your beliefs and values. What is important now? What do you believe now? What do you want to be important? What do you want to believe?

9. Take this new sense and step back to the level of skills and capabilities. How are your skills transformed and deepened by this greater depth of yourself?

10. Step back again to your behaviour level and notice how your skills enrich what you do.

11. Finally, step back into the training environment. Notice how differently you feel about where you are with this greater depth and clarity from your values, purpose and sense of connectedness. Take a moment to allow this to integrate within you and be aware of the changes.

Sometimes we can find ourselves becoming stale, 'going through the motions' of training for no other reason than it's our job. This exercise links us back to what we know is important and opens a channel of energy for us in the present.

You will be congruent if you believe in what you are saying and doing, if you are honest with yourself and your participants. Integrity and authenticity always come through.

### Messenger–message congruence

The second level of congruence in training is known as *messenger – message congruence*. How convincing would a stress-management training be, given by a trainer who bit her nails, twisted her hair and shouted at people? How convinced would you be by a weight-loss course given by someone who tipped the scales at over 20 stone and ate Danish pastries during the breaks? Have you ever been to an assertiveness training where the trainer was dominated by the participants? If the trainer does not embody the main principles she teaches, you have cause to doubt those principles from the start. The trainer acts both as an advertisement and convincer for a course, whether she likes it or not.

Training with NLP means that the trainees learn both consciously and unconsciously. They learn the training material consciously. *How* the trainer teaches and what she does provides the main channel for unconscious learning.

When you use NLP to train, you *do what you talk about*. This is another key difference between NLP training and traditional training, and another reason why congruence is so important.

### Alignment congruence

The third level of congruence means all parts of your communication, words, voice and body language give the same message. A trainer whose words and body express the same message will be a powerful presenter because the same message will be received on both the conscious and unconscious level by participants. A great deal of this book is about specific ways of reaching this alignment.

## RECOVERY STRATEGIES

However good your emotional state, it can be difficult to maintain it in the face of adversity. You cannot prepare for every eventuality in a training. What can you do when something unpleasant happens and you find your state slipping?

### Criticism

Criticism in this culture is usually directed personally and focuses on what the critic thinks you did wrong. Therefore it is easy to find yourself losing your resourceful state if you are criticised by one or more participants, either publicly or privately.

What you need to do is keep your state and, if possible, extract any useful part of the criticism. The positive intention of criticism is to coach you to greater heights. This is not very easy to see sometimes.

There is a useful process you can use to learn from criticism, developed by Steve and Connirae Andreas. You may want to practise it before a training and mentally rehearse it, so that it comes automatically into play if you are criticised during a training. (Or anywhere.)

### Strategy for dealing with criticism

1. Remember a time when you were criticised.

2. Imagine yourself now behind a plexiglass screen or some similar barrier you can see through, but no criticism can penetrate. Safe here, see yourself on the other side of the screen getting some sense of what the criticism means. The important point is that you are safe on this side of the screen and the 'other you' is dealing with the criticism.

   This may seem strange. However, people who deal with criticism well will typically do two things: they detach themselves from the bad feelings and they evaluate the criticism while feeling resourceful. The screen is to protect you. Imagine you see yourself. If it is difficult, pretend or just carry on 'as if' you can.

3. Now, safe behind the screen, you can watch yourself clarify exactly what the critic means, perhaps by asking some questions. The criticism may be simple abuse, in which case you might decide to disregard it. You will want to know what the critic would want you to do differently. This may be useful. It gets you the critic's version of events.

4. When you have enough information, have the 'you' in front of you compare your memory of the event with the critic's version. Do they match? What are the significant points of difference? What were you trying to do? Did you achieve your outcome in doing it?

5. The 'you' in front decides which one or more of the following responses would be the best choice:

   You may agree with them.
   You may want to apologise.
   You may want to give your version of the event if it differs

from the critic's version. You may want to let them know what
your outcome was.

You may disagree completely and let them know that.

You may want to leave the issue for the moment and perhaps
discuss it one to one another time.

You may want to utilise it to make a teaching point.

6. Have the other 'you' rehearse any new response you wish to
   make. See yourself making it.

7. Let the screen dissolve and have the 'you' who dealt with the
   criticism rejoin you. Integrate the new response.

Mentally run through the whole pattern with a number of
different examples of criticism so it is available when it is needed.
The more times you use it, the faster and more automatic it
becomes. The two important patterns in this strategy are
dissociating, so that the inner you remains unaffected, and
responding from a resourceful state. After that you can decide
what you will do next time so you do not attract that sort of
criticism again.

## TRAINING REVIEW

There are three versions of any training: the one you prepare, the
one you give and the one you wished you had given. Constantly
learning from each training you do will narrow the difference
between the second and the third version. Ask the questions,
regardless of how well you have done, 'What could I have done
differently? How will I improve on what I did?'

Do not attempt to process consciously during the training. You
will split your attention and distract yourself from where you need
to pay attention: the participants' needs. Mistakes are irretrievable
in one sense. They can be utilised, apologised for, but not undone.
In training you may open your mouth and put your foot in it. Do
not make matters worse by going back and trying to extract the
offending limb.

At the end of each training, take some time to rerun it mentally
and notice what you can learn. Congratulate yourself on those
things you did well. To learn the most from the training, go
through the following process with anything you are not satisfied

with, anything that did not go as well as you wanted and you want to do differently next time. Again, if it is difficult to visualise mentally, just get a sense of it in any way you can. The process works well whatever the quality of your mental pictures.

## New behaviour generator

1. Imagine seeing yourself in your mind's eye at the beginning of the incident as though you are watching it on a video rerun. Watch and listen to yourself and any others very carefully. Spot the first thing you do that you are unhappy with and pause your mental video. (You can use a real video if you recorded the training.)

2. Ask yourself, 'What would be more effective here in order to get the outcome I intended?' Run this alternative behaviour on your mental video and check whether seems satisfactory to you. Then watch yourself doing it.

3. Now imagine stepping inside the 'you' on video who has just rehearsed the new actions. Get in your mental video and act in the new way that you have decided would be better. Experience it as fully as you are able, seeing, hearing and feeling yourself back in that situation. Enjoy acting what might have been.

   As you act it out, again check that it works well. If you discover something is still wrong, come out, think of another alternative, watch yourself doing it and go through the process again, until you are completely satisfied from both viewpoints: the viewpoint of you watching yourself and the viewpoint of you actually doing it.

4. Finally, ask yourself, 'How will I know when to do what I have just rehearsed?' and identify exactly what you would see, hear or feel, internally or externally, that will act as your automatic cue to use this new behaviour that you have just created. Next time a similar situation comes up, you will be ready for it, the new choice will be mentally rehearsed and available.

When you have finished, store your mental video somewhere safe and forget about it.

You do not have to restrict this process to training. Use it on every unsatisfactory incident in your daily life until it becomes automatic. This is a general process that can be used to learn from what has happened as well as mentally rehearse what is to come.

## TAKING CARE OF YOURSELF

Good trainers care about the trainees and the training. Sometimes it is easy to forget we need to take care of ourselves as well. Taking care of yourself does make a difference to the quality of your training. Read books or listen to tapes on the areas of self-development that interest you. Treat this as an investment in yourself. Set yourself outcomes for your training and for those parts of your life where you want to move forward. Build in new choices with the new behaviour generator where you are not satisfied.

It is not easy to act counter to the cultural belief that other people rather than ourselves are responsible for our feelings, but using anchoring will help you to choose your internal state.

Many of the things that you will do to prepare yourself for training are simply part of a healthy lifestyle. As the Buddhists say, 'Eat well, sleep well and keep warm.' Feel free to add whatever else supports you.

### Avoiding burnout

Burnout can happen in professions like training where it seems as if you are giving all the time and never receiving. That is why it is important to take care of yourself and keep learning from training. Experiment with your training, even if it is one you have given many times before. You owe it to yourself and the trainees to experiment and keep the material fresh.

Relaxing and taking time off is part of taking care of yourself. The Russians have a saying: 'We learn to ski in the summer and swim in the winter.' In other words, a break is an integral part of any learning experience. You need it for refreshment and it actually integrates your learning unconsciously in the time gap, rather like the idea of 'sleeping on a problem' if you want to solve it.

Keep looking for different points of view. Attend other trainers' courses to see how they train and keep the experience of being a learner alive. (But switch off your trainer's critical circuits.) Take a course in a subject you know nothing about. This allows you to appreciate first hand what it is like in the trainees' position. You will understand their outcomes and state better and so train better.

Be aware when your body sends you signals that you are doing too much. The signals will be subtle to start with. It is worth paying attention to them, for if you do not, they will become louder and more persistent, like a child getting an adult's attention. Illness often comes when the body knows of no other way to you slow down. Know your limits. Too much training does not make you a better trainer, it is self-defeating. Just enough training is how to improve.

Stay away from negative people who drain your energy. Their intentions may be golden, but their influence is psychotoxic.

Take any criticism on the level of behaviour. Criticism is about what you did, not who you are.

Work on becoming the trainer and person you really want to be. There is a story of Michelangelo working in his studio one day, when a small boy wanders in. 'Signor,' he says, 'why are you chipping at that block of marble?'

'Because there is an angel inside and I'm helping him to get out,' replies the sculptor.

## SELF-MANAGEMENT

### Key Points

EMOTIONAL STATE
- You need to be in a good emotional state to make the most of your training skills.
- There are four aspects to managing your state:
    1. Being in a good state while training.
    2. Having recovery strategies for difficult situations.
    3. Learning from your training.
    4. Dealing with criticism and pressures that can lead to 'burnout'.
- Keeping a resourceful physiology and breathing pattern is an important part of keeping state.
- Resource anchoring allows you to bring resourceful feelings into any training situation by making a powerful association.
- Confidence is a feeling of assured expectation and is based on adequate preparation and successful repetition.
- Competence is the consistent ability to act skilfully to achieve outcomes.

CONGRUENCE
- Congruence is your full commitment and alignment to what you do. It operates on different levels:

   commitment to doing a training

   alignment of the neurological levels of environment, behaviour, beliefs and values, identity and connection

   messenger–message congruence that you embody the values and skills that you are training

   congruence of verbal and non-verbal messages

LOOKING AFTER YOURSELF
- Dissociate and learn from criticism.
- Review and learn from every training.
- Taking care of yourself is important to avoid burnout:

   experiment with your training

   relax and take time off

   learn something completely different

   listen to your body

   take criticism at a behaviour level and not at the identity level

   work at the difference between who you are and who you want to be

# 14

# THE TRAINING ENVIRONMENT

Training brings together three elements: you, the trainer, with the trainees, in the training environment. A key step is to manage the whole training environment so it supports an excellent training experience for all, yourself included.

The administration and organisation of a training course is a large subject and there are many good books that deal with it in detail. Our focus here is more on what arrangements can be made to ensure that participants achieve a good learning state.

You have some degree of control over the environment. Do not waste time and effort trying to change what is not within your control. Make the best of what you have. No training room is absolutely ideal, except the one you would design for yourself, but be clear about your bottom line of what is acceptable.

## Universal access

Universal access means arranging training as far as possible so that no group of people are automatically barred by nature of their work or disability. For example, training dates and long training days may make it difficult for parents to attend. Certain venues may be inaccessible for people with disabilities. Awareness is growing in this area, but progress is slow.

The problem is most visible with mobility impaired people. The training venue may need to have ramps for wheelchairs, lifts and reserved parking spaces. There are also visually impaired and hearing impaired people. A hearing loop in a training venue is an excellent provision. We have no doubt that universal access will come more and more into public consciousness and everything we can do in training to help that is useful. On a personal note, we are committed to equal opportunities. Everyone is equally valuable as a learner and equally valuable as a person. We seek to run trainings that are easy for everyone to participate in.

## Accommodation

When you have a choice about the room you use, pick one that is comfortable, has good acoustics, as few distractions as possible and sufficient space for the exercise you have planned.

Review the venue from the trainees' perspective. What sort of view do they get?

Check the electrical facilities of the room are adequate. You will need to establish exactly what equipment you need and notify the organisers accordingly.

Natural light is the best. There is evidence that fluorescent lighting hinders concentration and it can be noisy. It is certainly unpopular. You may need to keep the windows closed for part of the time, which will affect the temperature and air circulation. The most enthralling of presentations will induce lethargy in a hot, ill-ventilated room. The room is the culprit, not the training. The best training rooms are between 65° and 68° Fahrenheit (19–20°C) and well ventilated.

The seating is important. The brain can only absorb what the rear end can endure. Comfortable seating is essential and the seating plan gives a message about the training, and the relationship between participants and trainer. Seating arrangements can vary considerably depending on the type of presentation you are giving. A classroom arrangement where the seats are laid out in straight rows facing the trainer gives a message about structure and hierarchy. Many people have a negative association between seats in rows and a school environment that actually hinders them learning. A circular seating arrangement gives a different message, as the trainer has no particular favoured place. Placing the seats in a U-shaped design with the trainer at the mouth of the U is popular, as it encourages interaction and participation. Any unused chairs can be moved to the side for visitors, guests and late-comers.

Providing suitable refreshments in mid-morning and mid-afternoon breaks is part of the practical arrangements that need to be made. Lunch arrangements need to be clear. Dietary choice is important. Feedback from trainees makes it clear that the fact that there is choice of food is more important than whether their own preference is there. If lunch is not available on the premises, then participants will want to know what alternative arrangements there are and the duration of the lunch break needs to be sufficient to allow everyone to eat their meal without rush.

Here is a trainer's check list for the training room equipment and materials:

### Trainer's environmental check list

*Room*
sufficient room space
comfortable seating
special needs resources
seating plan
chairs
layout
sound system for trainer (if any)
sound proofing
sufficient natural or artificial light
good ventilation or air conditioning
enough toilets for both sexes
toilets accessible for the disabled
available telephone
fire escape drill
clear communication channel from outside to trainer and
    participants
tea, coffee, biscuits and soft drinks available
lunch arrangements
security of personal belongings
universal access

### Pre-course check list

*Training materials*
name badges
registration list
handouts
any other learning materials
plain paper
pens and pencils

*Equipment*
overhead projector (OHP) and transparencies
white boards

markers
wiper/duster
flip charts
spare flip chart paper
felt tip pens
blutac
video camera
video monitor
video player
cassette player

*Miscellaneous*
water jug and glass
first aid kit
scissors
'post its'
sticky tape
paper clips

---

## THE TRAINING ENVIRONMENT

### *Key Points*

- The training environment is important to support everyone in the best learning state.
- Take the environment you have, make it the best you can and be clear about what is unacceptable.
- Be aware of problems of universal access.
- Check the rooms for:
    adequate space
    good lighting, acoustics, adequate heating and ventilation
    seating arrangements, comfort and layout
- Have pre-course check list for room and training materials.

---

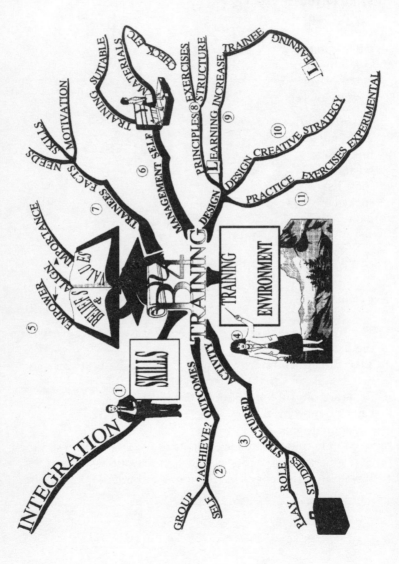

# PART THREE

# DURING TRAINING

## OVERVIEW

The stage is set, you and the trainees are ready. However experienced you are as a trainer, you are likely to have mixed feelings of excitement and anxiety. You have defined your task, set your outcomes in terms of the knowledge, skills and attitudes you want the trainees to learn. You have prepared your materials and presentation. You know the kind of learning environment that you intend to create. You know you will give of your best and look forward to learning from the training. Your audience now awaits you.

What will the trainees be feeling? What will they bring with them? They will have expectations and outcomes, some they will be aware of, some not. They will want to gain useful knowledge and skills in an enjoyable way. They may be there by choice or, in the worst case, under duress. They may be well motivated or they may come influenced by low morale at work. Whatever the situation, no one goes into a training room to have a bad time on purpose.

What would an impartial observer make of training? When you think of it from this viewpoint, it is a very strange phenomenon. People interact in an intricate dance of communication, sometimes one person leading, sometimes another. The person at the front now driving, now responding to the group. Spoken and unspoken messages being exchanged, far too many to consciously keep track of, yet overall there seems to be purpose and pattern to the event.

### Key training skills

To weave the pattern and hold the purpose there are six key training skills that are intricately connected:

- Multiple description: shifting viewpoints.
- Creating and maintaining rapport with the group.
- Personal congruence, the art of giving consistent messages.
- Setting and tracking outcomes continuously.
- Maintaining your own resourceful state.
- Creating resourceful learning states in the participants.

Other skills depend on these key six, so we will touch on each as an overview.

### Multiple description
This is the ability to see different viewpoints. There are your own, the trainees', the organisation's and an impartial viewpoint that watches the dance. Moving between these gives you the ability to make training three dimensional. You can never be pinned down or get stuck, for there is always another way to look at what is happening, another angle on the question.

### Creating and maintaining rapport with the group
Rapport is about building relationship with and between the trainees. Without this, they might as well read the handouts on their own. Rapport at its simplest is the ability to influence, and the openness to be influenced, on many different levels. When you have enough rapport, you will appreciate what is real for the trainees and know what to do next to meet their learning needs and your joint outcomes. Without it, you will give the perfect training that you *yourself* would wish for as a trainee and not the one *they* need.

In any learning situation there is a balance between task and relationship. Rapport builds relationships. The better the relationship, the easier the task.

### Personal congruence
We have already mentioned the three types of congruence. First, your commitment to the training. Second, messenger–message congruence: you are an example of the message you are putting across. For example, if you are giving a financial training, your credibility and capability is not helped if your own financial affairs are in a mess.

Third is your personal alignment. You are in rapport with yourself and comfortable with the participants. All parts of your communication, the words, voice and body language, give the same message. When the different parts of you are working together in harmony, it is like a racing yacht, with the helmsman and crew working in perfect co-operation with the boat and the elements. Good trainers care about training and about the trainees, and this shows. Be yourself and show them how much you care. Your listeners won't care how much you know, unless they know how much you care.

### Setting and tracking outcomes

You will have set outcomes before you start and some part of your mind will need to keep track of them. Outcomes, although flexible, form your basic map of what you are doing. You may need to modify them or even change them completely during the course of the training. For example, I was called in to do some counselling and negotiation skills training for a group of middle managers in a well known organisation. It turned out that there had just been some drastic changes in the company and most of the trainees were demoralised, insecure and resentful. I put my original outcomes on hold because they were not appropriate and set new ones to explore what was happening and how they felt about it. This took most of the first morning and only then were they ready to move on. Once they were ready, we were able to utilise all the material that had come up as the basis for the counselling and negotiation skills.

You will have 'end' outcomes that deal with the largest chunk levels: delivering the training competently and enjoyably, with feedback from the organisation that the training needs were met. Some of your outcomes will deal with the medium chunk levels, for example giving trainees new skills and seeing them demonstrated. There will also be smaller chunk process outcomes: how you are going to move towards these end outcomes; the structure and delivery of the training. There will be still smaller outcomes that serve the larger ones: answering questions satisfactorily, setting up exercises cleanly, keeping on time, doing whatever it takes to keep the larger outcomes on track. Training can be seen as a whole series of process outcomes nested one inside another like a Russian doll, all aligned with, and included in, the main outcome. And at any time you may need to pay attention to such things as re-establishing group rapport or your own resourceful state.

A good trainer will be aware at some level of what outcome she is actively pursuing at every moment. You could stop her at any time, ask: 'What is your outcome in saying or doing that?' and get a sensible answer describing the small outcomes at that moment and how they relate to the larger outcome.

### Maintaining your own resourceful state

The emotional state of the trainer is probably the most important variable that determines the success of a training. All the other skills flow from this. When you are nervous or anxious, you do not think as clearly or act so effectively, as when you are in good emotional shape. Training involves being in front of people, putting yourself forward and giving some sort of performance or presentation, and for many people this is one of life's most frightening experiences.

Nearly everyone experiences some heightened feelings of anticipation before a performance, no matter how many times they have done it in the past. Happily, most successful public performers report that some level of excitement is necessary to give a good performance. There is, however, a threshold level where these feelings pass into disquiet, unease and anxiety, with full blown and paralysing stage fright at the far end of the spectrum. The task here is to make use of the excitement and keep it at a level where it is helpful.

Creating resourceful states is an important part of preparing to train and maintaining these states whilst training is essential. This is easy when all is going well. The test comes when the unexpected happens, when someone asks a particularly difficult question or behaves in a way you find hard to cope with or brings up a topic that you are unsure of or sensitive about.

### Creating resourceful learning states in the participants

You need to elicit states of learning and curiosity in the trainees or your fascinating material will fall on stony ground. Once you have their attention and interest, the material will be easy to present and, more importantly, be easy to learn.

This is much easier to do when you are intimate with the material you are training. You can then enter the training room with an 'empty mind', ready to respond to whatever happens in the moment. Your conscious mind will have quite enough to attend to with all these process levels, without having to think consciously about the material. Paradoxically, when you are less concerned with the content, it becomes easier to deliver. Trust your unconscious competence – always provided you have done your homework. You do not want unhelpful internal dialogue about remembering the content to take up any of your precious attention.

There are two more facets of training that penetrate all the above. First, you have to pay attention to the outside world. This seems obvious – how will you get rapport, track outcomes and attend to all the myriad other matters unless you notice what is going on in the group? Paying attention to the world outside is sometimes called being in *uptime*, yet often trainers get so caught up in their own thoughts about the material they fail to respond to the group. The other place is *downtime*, inside your own head. Although you may dip into that place occasionally, to answer a difficult question for example, when you are training you should be a tourist there and not a resident.

The second is a commitment to learning. If you can learn to learn and teach at that level, your trainings will always be full. Give a hungry person a fish and you feed them for a day. Teach them how to fish and they can feed themselves and others. Teach them how to teach whatever is needed and you create growing abundance. One of our prime motivations for writing this book is to make the wealth of 'learning to learn' strategies that NLP has recently evolved more widely available.

## Unconscious learning

As you read through this section, do bear in mind that people learn in two very different ways: consciously and unconsciously. Your trainees' conscious attention will be engaged mostly in understanding the material, while they will be processing many more things at an unconscious level. One of the skills of training is to make sure that the important parts are processed unconsciously.

Some trainers go so far as to say that training is about entertaining the conscious mind and teaching the unconscious. When training imparts skills, for example, too much thinking and analysing can interfere with the learning by doing. Far better to have a training where the learners leave able to perform the skills, even if they are not completely clear about the reasons, than a training where they leave unable to actually perform the skills, even though they understand them well. This is the danger in teaching too much to the conscious mind. Trainees will leave knowing *about* the material, but not very competent to *do* anything with it. The trainees will be learning unconsciously throughout the training anyway. The only questions are, 'What are they learning?' and 'Is it part of the shared outcomes of the course?'

## Adding choices

There is no 'right' way to run a training and you will find many different ideas in this section. Our aim is to give you more choices about what you do. Use them if they are useful, improve them if they do not work for you and generate more of your own. Training, like reading a book, takes place over time and so has to follow some sequence. The pieces of the training will fit together as a whole, which is more than the sum of its parts, just as the pieces of a jigsaw make a picture you cannot predict from any one piece.

In this section we are laying out and separating the patterns in a sequence, to make them easy to understand. Of course, the ideas all interrelate as parts of the jigsaw. Our intention is to bring out the important elements in successful training and isolate them momentarily for your conscious attention. We offer examples to bring these skills alive and invite you at every turn to question:

'How else can I think about this?'
'How can I adapt this pattern?'
'What is the best way to make use of this idea?'

---

## PART THREE OVERVIEW

### *Key Points*

- There are six fundamental training skills that empower all the others:

  **Key training skills**
  Multiple description, by shifting viewpoints.
  Creating and maintaining rapport with the group.
  Personal congruence, the art of giving consistent messages.
  Setting and tracking outcomes continuously.
  Maintaining resourceful states in yourself.
  Creating resourceful learning states in the trainees.

- To make these skills work, you need to have your attention outwards.
- Train and think at two levels: learning; and learning how to learn.
- What people learn unconsciously is at least as important as what they learn consciously.
- Identify the patterns in this section that you can use and adapt them to your purposes. If they work, use them. If they do not, ignore them.

# STARTING THE TRAINING

## Begin on time

The seminar has a beginning, a middle and an end. Start on time, unless there are very good reasons to delay. It is part of your time frame management and courtesy to your group. Many people have a threshold of about 10 minutes after start time, after that you are late. If you are going to start late for any reason, announce this to the group and give a revised start time.

## PRACTICALITIES

First on the agenda, after your opening comments, will be dealing with practicalities: how long the seminar will run, when and how long the breaks will be, where smoking is allowed and so on. You may want to draw attention to any practical difficulties. For example, I remember a training at a venue with many modern art pictures hung round the walls. The room was an unusual shape with several entrances and exits. We drew attention to these things right at the start and framed them as distractions 'only if allowed to be'. When we forgot to do this, we found either people complained afterwards or would be distracted during the seminar. A shared recognition of practical difficulties renders them much less of a problem and helps build rapport.

If the training is being videotaped, explain what is happening and why. If video is going to be used with the trainees as part of the training, explain how it will be of benefit to them. Decide in advance if people can tape record the seminar.

Complete any other practical points and close this by asking for questions about any practical concerns you may have missed.

For you, the training will have started. Do you want it to have started for the trainees? You can separate these practical issues from the main body of the seminar by saying something like, 'Before we begin, there are some practical issues that need attending to.' Spatially separate this by standing in a different place from your 'training spot' and using different body language. After this, shift body language, move into your 'training spot' and begin. People will usually get the message unconsciously, but you can observe the interesting shifts in their posture, breathing and focus of attention when you move back and start 'for real'.

### Create rapport with the group

Build group rapport from the time you enter the room. The easiest way to start this is by sharing a positive experience, an amusing story or a humorous comment. Get everyone laughing together. You can anchor this positive state with a word or gesture and return to it later if you want to. It is good to make eye contact with everyone in the group in the first five minutes, even if you have already met them before the start.

You also need to pace group expectations, beliefs and values. The type of group you have will determine much that you do. A group of business executives will be very different from therapists or teachers. For some groups you may need to establish credibility with a reference to your published material or a carefully chosen previous experience.

#### The expert audience

Sometimes you will be training an expert audience, sometimes an audience who merely think they are expert. Here you may need to tread with care to bypass the danger of a response like: 'Oh yeah, let's see if you can teach *me* anything!'

Start pacing by saying, 'I would like to remind you that you all know far more about your jobs than I do. My role is to offer you additional approaches and skills that may help you to produce even better results, if you are willing to try them out.'

#### The reluctant audience

Possibly the most challenging people to work with are those who are there under sufferance, who have been told to be there. You could start by saying something like: 'Some of you are here because you want to be and some of you are here because you have been told to be. I know when that's happened to me it's not pleasant and it made it hard for me to get anything of value from the experience. I would like to make our time together as useful to you as possible and would appreciate your help in thinking about the best use that you can make of this training.'

### Culture

There is also the question of different cultures. Clearly, training in different countries needs different approaches. America, England and France, for example, are very different culturally. Generally speaking, groups will give you the benefit of the doubt, if you come from a different country, and the more you can fit in right from the start the more rapport you will get.

In the same way, corporate cultures are very different. When you do in-house training for a business, make sure you know their technical language. Do not assume a word means the same thing in different business cultures. For example, the corporate culture in Apple computers is very different from that in IBM. Different firms will have different ways of doing things and different values. Similarly, within a company you will often get surprisingly different cultures in different parts of the organisation. Join the culture you are in as far as you can.

## INTRODUCTION

There are many ways of beginning a training course and a great deal depends on personal style, numbers of trainees and the desired outcomes. A group of a dozen people are a very different proposition from a group of a hundred. You will tend to become more of a performer and less of a facilitator as group size increases.

One useful move as you introduce yourself is to disclose some particular interests as well as recounting a few experiences that build credibility. The trainees get to know something about you and so can start to relate to you as a person rather than just a trainer. This also gives them points of contact by way of shared interests.

Whichever kind of introduction you choose will have several functions. It will gain the attention of the trainees. It will start the process of trainees and trainers getting to know each other. It will establish your credibility and set useful frames for the whole training.

## The 'yes set'

You can incorporate a technique known as the 'yes set' in your opening comments. Build participation in a sequence, for example by starting with obvious statements about the training venue, the weather or the training material. Everybody will nod imperceptibly. Then progress to asking questions like, 'How many of you have had training on this material before?' or 'How many of you are managers/teachers/salespeople?' Ask for a show of hands. You can gather information while increasing participation and group involvement.

A different choice is to start with controversial statements as a way of getting them to sit up and take notice. The worst choice here would be to present something unimportant in such a way as to invite argument.

## SETTING FRAMES

Setting a frame means establishing a context for a purpose. A frame is a way of looking at a situation. For example, the frame (of mind) you would bring to reading this book for pleasure would be quite different from that of proofreading for errors. The frames you set give people ways of making sense of the content of the training. They are crucial because they establish the filters through which you want the material interpreted.

In some of the trainings we give, we will state explicitly at the beginning: 'Some of this material may challenge your beliefs. When this happens, notice the challenge, notice how you feel about it and put it to one side for future evaluation. This will let you get the most from the material and you can keep all of your existing beliefs intact if you still want to.' Suspending disbelief in this way can effectively avoid what could have been significant difficulties. This kind of framing beforehand to avoid a problem that you think may arise is known as *outframing*. Once you do have a problem, changing the way the trainees perceive it is known as *reframing*. This can be difficult. An ounce of outframing is worth a ton of reframing.

Another useful frame comes from the learning model where the most uncomfortable stage, that of conscious incompetence, is also the stage when you are learning the most.

There are general frames that you may want to put in place at the beginning. For example, requesting all comments and questions are addressed to you ensures effective use of group time and avoids unproductive arguments between trainees. Asking the group to let you know when they are having difficulties is a way of getting useful feedback. Request their help in starting and being back from breaks on time. If *you* stick to these time frames, they will too.

### Tell them three times

One of the many 'Golden Rules' of giving presentations is: 'Tell them what you are going to tell them, then tell them and finally tell them what you have told them.'

Repetition of key points is important for learning. What was that? Repetition of key points . . . Yes, but they *do* need to be artfully dispersed. If you were to read this book for structure, you would find key points reiterated in different ways at different places. So a good choice is to give your trainees a map of the training by telling them what you are going to tell them. On the other hand, you can use the magical mystery tour model and just dive straight in. If you go for the mystery tour choice, tell the trainees at the start, otherwise they might get lost and blame you.

## TRAINEE OUTCOMES

Trainees will have outcomes and there are a number of advantages to bringing these into the open right from the start. It gives the message that you do care. You may also want to check that your outcomes as trainer for the group do not diverge greatly from those of the group. Good training relates your outcomes and their outcomes in a win-win situation.

The downside of explicitly eliciting trainees' outcomes is that they can act as hostages to fortune. Once out in the open, you have no excuse for not making an effort to meet them!

Trainees may not be sure of their outcomes and it is one of your tasks as trainer is to help them clarify these. If people come to a training not knowing what they want, it makes it rather hard for you to satisfy them, and you, the trainer, will have to deal with the feedback – which may be very clear indeed.

## Eliciting trainees' outcomes

There are several ways to elicit outcomes without interrogating people. You can tag them onto the end of a round of introductions. Invite everyone in turn to introduce themselves to the group, to say their name, a little bit about their work, their prior experience and knowledge in the field of the training course and what they want to go away with at the end of the training. Set a time frame for this, say about one minute for each person.

If you have a large group and such introductions would be too time-consuming, then invite them to form small groups and introduce themselves, for five minutes, while generating some outcomes for the group. One person from each group then gives some key words to cover each group's outcomes for the training. These key words can be put up on a flip chart or white board at the start and serve as a reminder to all (including yourself!) throughout the training.

Another variant is 'hopes and fears'. Have each person say a few sentences about the best and the worst that could happen. You can pair off the trainees to explore their hopes and fears before reporting back. This self-disclosure tells you what to avoid as well as what to do and builds group rapport at the same time.

## OPENING EXERCISES

Eliciting outcomes can also act as a warm-up exercise or icebreaker. These initial exercises have as the main outcome of putting people at ease and establishing rapport.

There are many different warm-up exercises and books devoted to them. You can practise and develop your own favourites. Sometimes you may make them up on the spur of the moment to fit a particular need. Here is an opening exercise to start you off.

### Exercise for contrasting states

We were starting a trainers' training on the twin themes of maintaining your own resourceful emotional state and eliciting resourceful states from trainees. We invited half of the group to remember a poor training they had experienced, while the other half looked for changes in their physiology. After a moment, the trainer broke that line of thought and immediately asked the first group to remember some good training they had experienced. When they came out of this memory, they were asked for some key words to describe the experience of good training and in contrast some key words to describe their experience of poor training. When they had done this (the whole exercise took less than five minutes), the other group who had been watching were taken through the same process while the first group watched. There was then a brief discussion with everyone about the differences they noticed. We finished by putting the keywords for good and poor training on separate flip charts on the wall and explained that it was our intention to create these good qualities, but if they experienced any of those other ones, would they please let us know immediately.

The exercise focused the group on their criteria for good and poor training and on calibrating to the subtle physiological changes in posture, breathing and muscle tone in the other group as they went through the two experiences. It was also a demonstration of eliciting emotional states in trainees. We were careful to finish with the experience of good training. The exercise was also useful for us, as we could see what the group looked like when bored and dissatisfied, and when energised and interested.

## Learning names

During the first part of a seminar you will want to learn people's names, if they are not wearing name badges. It is important for group rapport that the trainer knows everyone's name.

One memory strategy is to visualise the trainees' names printed on their forehead as they introduce themselves. A more auditory one would be to repeat a key feature with their name, for example, 'Fred has curly hair' or 'Sarah has a Scottish accent', etc. Avoid clothes as features, because people change them.

Use the names at every opportunity at the beginning until you have mastered them.

You can make your own game of name learning by going for personal bests in terms of how quickly you can learn how many names. As a measure of what is possible, we would like you to know of one trainer who can learn 80 names in an hour, whilst speaking continuously to a group. . .

## STARTING THE TRAINING

### *Key Points*

- Begin on time.
- Deal with all the practicalities.

CREATE RAPPORT WITH THE GROUP
- Establish your credibility.
- Outframe the expert audience.
- Reframe the reluctant audience.
- Look for cultural differences and pace them.
- Use the 'yes set.'

SETTING FRAMES
- Use frame setting to establish filters.
- An ounce of outframing is worth a ton of reframing.
- Use a control frame to channel all communication through you.
- Frame discomfort as evidence of learning.
- Tell them three times.

TRAINEE OUTCOMES
- Elicit trainees' outcomes and dovetail them with yours.

OPENING EXERCISES
- Warm-ups.
- An exercise for contrasting states.
- Learn names.

# 16

# TRAINEES' EMOTIONAL STATES

One of your main tasks as a trainer is to bring out the curiosity of the participants and help them to learn and enjoy learning. The skill and knowledge you gain depend on the state you are in when you are learning. This is obvious, yet so often forgotten or only paid lip service to. NLP puts this firmly centre stage.

For example, if you learned mathematics at school, found it hard, did not understand it and felt bad about it, then every time you do maths after that will bring back those bad feelings associated with it. School is not a special case. Instil skill and knowledge in a good emotional state.

## Traditional models

There is a model of training which comes originally from the world of education, where one knowledgeable person pours their precious, scarce knowledge into empty vessels, who are duly appreciative. However, learners are not empty vessels. To try to understand education or training as a one-way passage of information from trainer to participant is like to trying to understand the rules of tennis by restricting your observations to one half of the court. You might make complex statistical analyses of how often the player hits a backhand, but the essence of the game will elude you.

Some unfortunate consequences come from this one-sided 'empty vessel' model. First, if the participants do not understand, then everyone assumes it must be their fault. They must be stupid. This gets you into the nefarious 'blame frame', where fault and blame are rolling about like a loose cannon. It must be *someone's* fault—and if it is not their fault, it must be yours! Enter self-recrimination, bad feeling and eventual burnout.

Once you see communication as a loop, blame is irrelevant:

there are only results. These results give you the feedback that you need to improve. If you do not get the response you want, then do something else, until you do. Your awareness of the trainees and your flexibility of behaviour will get you your outcome in time. This is also 'response-ability', the ability to respond. Whatever happens, you learn from it.

## Eliciting learning states

There is a sense in which you cannot teach anyone anything. You can, however, create a context to draw out their desire to learn. One of the most effective ways of doing this is by eliciting emotional states. How do you elicit states? Before we answer that, there is another question: what state do you want to elicit?

Suppose you wanted to elicit a state of intense curiosity. This would be an extremely useful state for trainees, and make your training very easy and enjoyable, wouldn't it? There are quite a few ways of doing this and we have found one really excellent way, which works like a charm every time we use it. As far as we know it has not appeared in print yet because trainers guard it jealously, as a sorcerer would a magic spell. Before we tell you about it, a question: How curious are you? How disappointed would you be if there were no foolproof method? Do you think the outcome of this paragraph was to make you feel curiosity, anticipation and then disappointment? How far did it succeed?

Another way you can change people's emotional states is to tell a story. It need not be complex – common, shared experiences work best. This morning, for example, I was running late for an important meeting. I made good time on the main roads and arrived at the building with two minutes to spare just as someone pulled into the last parking spot for two miles. Have you ever toured back streets looking for a parking spot and watching the minutes tick away? Just thinking about it makes you impatient, doesn't it?

Think of some simple examples like that to use to elicit the sort of states you want: curiosity, relaxation, learning, enthusiasm, joy.

In our trainers' training we run an exercise to give the trainees an opportunity to elicit states.

### State elicitation exercise
This exercise is for groups of four.

1. Each person thinks of three states they would like to be able to elicit in the groups they train. Each state is written down on a separate piece of paper and folded, so the writing is not visible.

2. Each person puts their three target states into the middle to form a pool of 12 target states.

3. The first person takes the role of trainer for the group. She takes a random piece of paper from the middle and attempts to elicit that state from the other three people in the group. The group does not know what the state is. The trainer stops when she thinks she has succeeded or after about one minute, no more, and asks what sequence of states each person experienced.

4. Each person briefly indicates the states they went through and the state they finished in. Their task is not to guess the target state, but simply to respond to what the trainer does.

5. If the trainer is successful in eliciting the target state, then it is another person's turn. If the trainer is not successful, then she tells the group what the target state was. The group then demonstrates to the trainer how they would look and sound if they were indeed in that state. The trainer makes note of this and can try again for up to a minute.

6. Each person takes turns at the trainer role.

This exercise is fascinating and the processing afterwards usually brings up some very useful points. For example, states have very general names and people may call similar states by different names. Someone may be slumped in a chair eyes half closed, face relaxed and report their state as either trance, boredom or relaxation.

Also, the trainees use many different strategies in the exercise. Some go into the target state first themselves to demonstrate it. They change their physiology, posture and breathing pattern, and this affects their group.

Another strategy to elicit states is to evoke the state directly through your behaviour. If you want to elicit curiosity, then act in a strange and mysterious way. Exactly what you do is irrelevant, but your manner is important.

Alternatively – and this one depends on the particular state – you get the group to move. It is harder to get excited when you are glued to a chair. Dance, charades and exercises are all possible. You can ask the group to access a time when they felt the state either directly or indirectly. Asking for it directly would be: 'Think of a time when you were curious . . .' Asking indirectly would be: 'Think of a time when you knew something was going to happen and you did not know what it was . . .' You can also ask them to imagine a context where that state would be natural: 'Imagine you are an explorer and you have found this strange object in the great pyramid. As you turn it over it looks as if . . .'

The possibilities are endless: you can give the group a task to do; you can tell a story, real or imagined . . . The only limitations are our own self-imposed rules. Every trainer has their self-inflicted rules, picked up from direct instruction, modelling another trainer or transposed into training from another context. Ask yourself: 'What are my rules for trainer behaviour?' As you read this book, we hope that you are challenged by some of the ideas. Every time you think: 'I could never do that' or 'I should never do that', ask yourself: 'What would happen if I did?' or 'How do I stop myself?' You might find yourself pushing the boundaries – only as much as you want to, of course – and finding the constraining walls are actually elastic. Some rules are necessary, but how many? As Einstein said, 'Let things be as simple as possible, but no simpler.'

## Sensory acuity

There is always more to the world than we see hear and feel. Reality, as they say, leaves a lot to the imagination.

As a trainer, you need to put attention out onto the trainees, if you are to help them stay in a good learning state. Once your attention is out, you can develop the filters to know what to look and listen for.

Here is an entertaining exercise that will help develop these filters. It gives practice in tracking attention levels in a group. We use it in our trainers' trainings and find it works best with small groups of between five and ten people.

### Attention tracking exercise

1. The exercise begins with one person acting the role of the trainer in front of a small group. He can choose what he is going to talk about for three minutes.

2. A second person stands behind the trainer. Her job is to point to certain people in the group who will then gradually cease to pay attention to the trainer. The trainer cannot see these signals, so does not know who is being influenced.

3. The task for the trainer is to notice who is losing attention and catch their attention again as smoothly as possible while continuing the presentation. If the trainer is overloaded, he simply stops and says so.

4. The group task is to notice the different strategies each trainer uses to bring individuals' attention back.

There are many choices for the trainer. He can gesture, do something unexpected, tell a brief anecdote, ask a person a question, mention their name or engage the group in some physical activity. These are useful strategies to bear in mind.

---

## TRAINEES' STATES

### *Key Points*

- Learners are not empty vessels and training is a two-way game.
- Avoid the 'blame frame' and take personal responsibility.
- If what you are doing is not working, keep changing it until it does.
- Develop your skills for eliciting positive learning states:
    give examples of them
    tell a story
    go into the desired state yourself
    use your voice tone
    do something that will evoke the state naturally
    get the group to move
    ask directly
    ask indirectly
    create an imaginary context
    give them a task
    describe a personal example
- Identify and reduce any self-imposed rules that limit your flexibility.

- Sensory acuity:
    keep your attention out on the trainees
    develop your filters for the states you want
    learn how to keep high quality attention from everyone on you

---

# LEARNING STYLES

Learning is the goal of training for the trainees and the trainer. It is a natural talent. In fact we cannot *not* learn. Trying and effort are evidence, however, that sometimes learning does not happen easily. They act as signals to make changes in the learning process.

This goes against some of our cultural beliefs that learning is hard and trying is good. We would not want to belabour the point that the formal education system tends to reinforce this belief.

While we are all natural learners, we also have preferences for what and how we learn. As a trainer, you also have your particular strengths and weaknesses in how you think and how you put over material. Being aware of your own learning style and the different styles within a group means you can get past your own preferences and put over the material in different ways, making it easy for everyone.

## METAPROGRAMS

*Metaprograms* is a technical term used in NLP to describe unconscious and habitual filters we have learned to put on our experience. They determine what information gets through and how. There is so much information we could attend to and our conscious minds are limited, so some selection is necessary. Think of a glass of water. Now imagine drinking half of it. Is the glass half full or half empty? Both, of course. Some people notice what is positive about a situation, what is actually there, others notice what is missing.

While many patterns could qualify as metaprograms, here is a short summary of the more useful ones in the training context. None are of these patterns are 'better' or 'right' in themselves. As you read through, you may find yourself sympathising with one particular view in each category. This is a clue to your own pattern. Metaprograms were developed originally by Richard Bandler and Leslie Cameron Bandler and further developed especially for use in business by Rodger Bailey as The Language and Behaviour (LAB) Profile.

Understanding metaprograms will help you to understand the attitude behind certain questions and reactions, and give you some clues about how best to deal with them.

## Towards and away

One important difference in learning styles is between the person who goes towards the positive outcome and the person who reacts away from problems and difficulties. Many people are motivated towards what they want. They will often ask direct questions about how they can achieve results with the training material. Others will bring up the possible problems. They are motivated to avoid difficulties. They have a fine eye for what can go wrong and will pick out possible problems in your material with unerring precision.

To deal with this, you need to pace the problems. Acknowledge that, yes, there is a possible problem here and then say how it can be avoided. Other times you may have to say that there are literally an infinite number of things that *could* go wrong. The only way to find out for sure what happens is to *do it*.

## Internal and external

It is important for many people to decide for themselves and define their own standards. Such people are internally referenced. In contrast, externally referenced people take their standards more from the outside and seek direction and instruction from others.

The internally referenced person needs time to assimilate the material. Once they take it in, they will be very clear about its value and be willing to put it into practice. The externally referenced person will be more likely to take the material in and use it immediately. They are often more co-operative as demonstration subjects.

## Options and procedures

A third pattern is about following procedures. Some people are good at following set courses of action. They are motivated by, and good at following, a fixed series of steps. They like sequences. Others want choices and find it more difficult to follow set procedures. They like to have alternatives. It is good to build in some degree of flexibility into any fixed procedure for these people. Alternatively, if it is important they follow the procedure to the letter, you can explain how doing this will enable them to have many more choices in future.

### General and specific

Probably the most useful distinction in learning styles in the training context is between general and specific. General people are most comfortable dealing with large chunks of information. They pay little attention to detail. Specific people pay attention to detail and need small chunks in order to make sense of the bigger picture.

When you are presenting information, be prepared to 'chunk down' by going into detail, as well as 'chunking up' to give the larger picture. As a presenter, be aware of your own style, so as to maintain a nice balance of general and specific material.

### Similarity and difference

Some people mostly notice what is the same about things. They also tend to like stability and continuity in their lives. Others notice what is different and often seek out different experiences and work. These will point out the differences and are prone to get involved in arguments.

In any comparison, there are always both similarity and difference, just as this page is both black and white. So when you make comparisons, highlight both. A person that chunks down and sorts for difference will go over information with a fine tooth comb, looking for discrepancies. This is very useful in many classes of work, but alarming in a training context.

## SENSORY CHANNELS

People prefer to take in information in different sensory channels. Some like to see the material. You can satisfy them with demonstrations, handouts, flip charts and overhead projections, videos, film, etc. These students remember what they see.

Others are more auditory. They like to hear the material. For them a lecture-based format is ideal, with lots of questions and answers. They will remember what was discussed and their memory of the training may be in the form of an audio tape, either a mental one or an actual audiotape of the presentation.

The kinesthetic thinkers need to do exercises and enjoy role play. They learn by doing and may want to move around a lot. This does not mean they are not paying attention. It is a left-over idea from schooldays that learners need to sit still to pay attention.

What are you to do? You cannot please all of the people all of the time. What you can do is please some of the people some of the time and make sure that the 'some of the people' keeps changing, so that all styles are catered for. Modelling excellent teachers shows consistently that they teach in all three ways: in pictures, in sounds and in feelings.

Have training materials that appeal to all three main senses and choose your words to stimulate thought in all three channels. This is the verbal equivalent of using training materials that engage all the senses. People can see the point, get on the right wavelength and come to grips with the material.

Listen to a recording of your own language patterns when training and notice which system you favour and which is weakest. A trainer who mixes her language to include all the senses will engage everyone. This is one aspect of verbal rapport.

Make your non-verbals congruent with your words. So, if you are asking the group to see an idea, speak a little quicker and gesture upwards to suggest the eye pattern for visualisation. When dealing with auditory material, speak a little slower, use your voice expressively and move and speak more rhythmically. Models for this type of presentation are musicians' workshops, as you might expect. Finally, if you want the group to access emotions, speak slower and lower, and gesture downwards to their right. It is likely that you are doing some of these things anyway. You will be asking the group to see a picture you can already see, hear a sound you are hearing and feel an emotion you are in touch with. This is a part of presenting material congruently.

There are very few studies on this, mainly because the feedback is difficult to evaluate precisely. One study was done at the University of Moncton in New Brunswick, Canada. The study was testing spelling, a skill that needs the ability to visualise the words to check the spelling with a remembered image. Groups who were told to visualise correct spellings got 35 per cent better results than those that did not, with almost 100 per cent retention of the words.

## CONCEPT, STRUCTURE AND USE

This is a broadly useful model of how we learn, currently being developed by Florence Kesai, Deanna Sagar and Michael Miller in California. The model is that people fall into three broad categories. When learning new material, some people prefer to hear the concepts first. Concepts are the philosophy, theory and thinking behind the material. Others like to understand the structure first. Structure is to do with the organisation of the material, how the pieces fit together, maps, diagrams and how it all works. A third group likes to know what it is good for first, the uses and the practical applications.

People differ in their preferred sequence. One person might like to get the theory behind the ideas first, then work out how the information fits together and finally look round for ways to apply it in practice. Another person may just want to start doing and using the material without knowing or caring very much about the rationale behind it. She may then find and develop the inherent models in it, and finally develop the theories behind the models. You may like to deduce my preferred sequence from the way I lay out this section on Concept, Structure and Use.

There are three important ideas for trainers in this model. One is that everyone has a preferred starting-point. You can use a warming up exercise to bring this out, known as the 'Three Door Game'.

Tell the group that you want to share some new information with them. There are three doors. Behind Door One are the concepts, theory and philosophy. Behind Door Two are the structure and connections, how it works. Door Three hides the applications, uses and benefits.

Which door would the trainees like to go through first? This will divide the group into three and will give you a broad idea on how you might best sequence the material.

A second aspect of concept, structure, use is to utilise all three in your presentation. When giving material or information, give some elements of the concepts and philosophy behind the ideas.

This will satisfy the conceptualists. Give some structure, how the pieces are organised and fit together, with diagrams if appropriate. Thirdly, make sure you give the uses, the practical applications, otherwise your idea will remain nice and structured, yet impractical.

A third element in this model, possibly the one with the greatest potential, is that we tend to leave out the last one in our sequence. For example, when I present information, I have a sequence that goes concept, structure, use. You probably knew that already. Once, when I used to train, I would give people the concepts, show how it all fitted together and skip over the applications. Now I know my sequence, I make sure I mix up the order in which I present, sometimes concept, sometimes structure, sometimes use first. I make sure I cover all three. This one change made a big difference to the trainings I give. Finding your weak link can do the same for you.

---

## LEARNING STYLES

### *Key Points*

- Learning happens naturally.
- Good training makes learning easier.
- *Metaprograms* are systematic and unconscious habitual ways of thinking. Awareness of them can help you to tailor material to different styles:
    Towards – Away
    Internal – External
    Options – Procedures
    General – Specific
    Similarity – Difference
- Sensory channels:
    Alternate between all three main sensory channels in the language you use.
    Align your gestures with the sensory channel you want the group to use.
- Concept, structure and use:
    Learners will have a preferred starting-point and sequence.
    You may have a tendency to leave out the last step in your sequence.
    Use all three in your training.

---

# EXERCISES

## Purpose

Exercises are structured activities where trainees practise skills in a supportive setting. As such, they are at the heart of experiential training. Their form and purpose will vary – for example, a warm-up exercise for introducing trainees to each other and a long negotiation role play are both exercises. The best exercises not only take people through a sequence that leads them to discover for themselves the skills or knowledge embedded in the exercise, but install them as well. A really good exercise will allow learners to make discoveries you had not even realised were in the material.

We will focus on the process of exercises in training, taking as an example a classic exercise design for interpersonal skills training. You may have a specific exercise of your own in mind as you read.

We will track training exercises through the following stages:

- preparation
- setting up and framing the exercise
- demonstrating
- clarifying the demonstration
- running the exercise and coaching
- processing the exercise

Not all exercises will go through all these stages, so adapt and apply them to suit your own material.

## Preparation

Review your actual or mental notes before the exercise and mentally rehearse so that you know you can do it the way you want to. Check that necessary props or visual aids are ready. You may need to prepare an overhead transparency or write the exercise instructions on a flip chart beforehand. Review your outcomes for the exercise, both covert and overt, and think through your links, so the new exercise fits into the flow of the training.

### Roles

Part of your preparation will be clarifying the different roles involved in the exercise. Exercises can involve any number of people, from one person to a whole group, depending on the nature of the material. The classic experiential exercise designed to install a behavioural skill will involve three different roles:

The first is the person who is practising the new skill, known as the 'operator' or 'explorer' role.

The second is the person the operator is practising with – the 'subject' or 'client' role. The client role plays himself or another character so the operator can practise the technique. He needs to genuinely enter into this role.

Finally, there is the 'observer' or 'meta person'. The observer has several responsibilities. She is the trainer's representative in the group and keeps the client and operator on track making sure that neither is overloaded. The observer usually has responsibility for keeping to the time frame given to complete the exercise, and is in the perfect position to give feedback to both explorer and client – involved but uncommitted. (The difference between being involved and being committed is nicely demonstrated in a breakfast of bacon and eggs, where the hen is involved but the pig was committed.)

Experiential exercises are usually quite short – 5–20 minutes a round. There will be 3 rounds, so an exercise will run between 15 minutes and an hour.

### *Setting up and framing the exercise*

You need to introduce the exercise, link it to what has gone before and what will follow. Set frames for the exercise; how do you want the trainees to perceive it? Of all the possible things they *could* pay attention to, where will you direct their attention? Be explicit about the outcome frame (what the exercise is designed to achieve). Cover the why, what and how – why they are doing the exercise, what the concepts behind it are and what uses it has. What the exercise is. How it runs, the steps and the practical details. Make sure the participants are clear on all these points.

If the exercise is designed to deal with a particular kind of problem, seed this early, so people have plenty of time to think of a specific example for role play.

## Demonstrating

You now have a choice to make about how you set up the steps and practical details of the exercise. The most effective way is usually a demonstration first. A good demonstration shows the exercise procedure, so that trainees are not struggling to understand instructions. However, demonstrations are double-edged. Trainees will copy what they see, which puts an onus on you to demonstrate cleanly.

How you demonstrate depends on the complexity of the exercise. In an intricate exercise involving negotiation skills, you may want to do a complete round. Alternatively, if the exercise is a repetitive one, like turning a closed question into an open one by asking a question in return, you may want to show just enough repetitions to get them going.

If for any reason you depart significantly from the technique you are demonstrating, announce this to the group at the time.

You may want to make ongoing comments about the course of the demonstration to make teaching points. When making such metacomments, mark them out cleanly by shifting your attention, voice tone, posture and position. When you have finished, shift back to the demonstration. This keeps the two aspects of the demonstration apart.

### Identify ideal demonstration subjects

If you need a demonstration subject, ask yourself what kind of person is likely to give the best demonstration for the exercise and who in the group is closest to the ideal. Choose a person who you know will be co-operative.

There are two types of people who can make difficult demonstration subjects. The first is the person who is habitually in meta position, tending to be dissociated from their experience.

This is not very useful if you want expressiveness and emotional impact. For that you need a subject who associates fully into the experience. The second type of difficult subject is the very internally referenced person. He will be deciding and judging for himself throughout, rather than automatically following you. People with these patterns will tend to sit at the back of the room, often with their arms folded and leaning back in the chair.

You can find out who are the externally referenced, co-operative people right at the beginning of the seminar by asking everyone to engage in some small task, like moving some chairs. Make a mental note of the first people to respond. They will usually make the best demonstration subjects.

### Enlisting your demonstration subject

Having identified your potential helpers beforehand, the simplest way to enlist them is to ask directly for their help: 'Carole, would you be willing to help me to show the steps of this next exercise?'

Or you may prefer to be a little more subtle and say: 'In order to show you how this goes, I will need some assistance and I'm wondering who would be willing to help me?' As you say this you move your eye contact over likely helpers, ending the question on the person you would most like. You can also extend a non-verbal invitation with a gesture.

After the demonstration, thank the subject and let them return to their seat, unless it is important that they stay up front to answer questions about their experience in the exercise. If you want them to stay, check they are comfortable to do so.

Your job as trainer in a demonstration is primarily to demonstrate the exercise to the group and only secondly to benefit the demonstration subject. If these two outcomes conflict, the group comes first. You may want to set a frame about this before you start so that if you find the demonstration taking too much time, you can step aside and say so. Check with the person that it is OK to stop there for the moment. Make arrangements to continue to work with them later if appropriate. Then thank the person, dismiss them and either enlist another volunteer or describe what you would have done if the demonstration had continued to the end.

### If you do not demonstrate. . .

If you want trainees to find their own style of using the skill, then give clear instructions for each role, but do not demonstrate. Give instructions for each role from a different spot, so the roles are spatially marked out and the instructions are clear.

## Clarifying the demonstration

After the demonstration and before the exercise, you can elicit the steps of the exercise from the group. Keep asking, 'What did I do next?' Write up the main steps of the exercise on the OHP or flip chart. Alternatively, you can tell them the steps directly or give them a handout. Now the group have a behavioural demonstration, a visual reminder and auditory instructions. You have covered the three main ways of learning.

You need to clean up by taking any questions. Frame this by asking for questions about the process only. Say, 'Do you have any questions about how to *do this now*? Please save any other questions for after the exercise.' Answering questions on, 'What if such and such had happened instead?' is not useful. The purpose of the exercise is for people to discover for themselves.

When questions dry up, ask if everyone is ready to start the exercise and scan round for congruent agreement. Give the time frames clearly: 'This is an exercise for three people at 10 minutes a round, so 30 minutes in all.' Let them know they can call you with any questions during the exercise.

## Running the exercise and coaching

You will probably spend most of your time supervising the exercise, with the question in mind: 'What can I do that will make the most difference to the quality of learning?' Coaching is a skill in itself and there are books written on this alone. Here are a few key ideas.

First, as experiential learning happens through discovery, resist intervening to the last minute. Intervene only if the exercise is significantly off track, if the learner is stuck or if you are specifically asked for help. If the observer looks uncomfortable, that is often a cue for intervening. If you are not sure what is happening, ask the observer in a whisper. Often it is best to wait until the end of the exercise before offering comments.

When you do intervene, avoid the trap of being the expert who can 'do it right', coming in to show the poor incompetent operator. A learning given is forgotten, whilst a learning elicited is theirs for life.

Second position the learner and from their point of view decide what approach is likely to work best: gentle or more challenging; overt or covert. A good habit to get into is the 'feedback sandwich'. Start by acknowledging what they are doing well, ask a question to probe any difficulties and finish with another acknowledgement. Few of us suffer from too much appreciation in this culture.

Here are some useful questions to ask:

'What points were you not clear about?'
'What else could you have done there?'
'What do you think person "X" would have done?'

You may want to ask questions to shift the operator to a more resourceful state:

'How would you have to feel differently to be able to do this?'
'. . . and when is a time that you have felt like that?'

You may want to ask him to step outside the group of three and imagine rerunning the last few minutes of the exercise from the observer position to get a new perspective.

If you draw a blank from the operator you may respectfully offer them choices:

'What do you think would have happened if you had done "X"?'
"Would you like some other possibilities to consider?'

Above all, resist the temptation to come in and run the exercise for them. If you do, neither you nor your trainees will learn very much and they will lose a significant learning opportunity.

Finally, future pace the operator:

'So next time, you can . . .'

As you are responsible for tracking the time, having a bell or tuning fork to mark out the stages or rounds of the exercise can work very well. You may want to announce the last few minutes of each round as time for the groups to process the exercise.

Finally, develop an effective set of ways of bringing people back to the main group. What you say is important. Contrast 'Can you wind up now?' with 'I would like you to *finish off now*, and as soon as *you're ready to* you can *return now* and as you *do this*, notice the comments and questions *you are* bringing *back now.'*

### Processing the exercise

You will need to process the exercise to complete the learning cycle. The group will learn from each other's experience and your job is to create the context for this and facilitate the process. So after the exercise invite comments, observations and questions, setting whatever frames are appropriate. Use the opportunity to make key teaching points and weave the material together. Clear up any misunderstandings and start to generalise the material into other situations, either with examples or by asking the question, 'What else can you do with this material?'

### Future pacing

The final part of an exercise is future pacing or mental rehearsal. Skills work well in the co-operative atmosphere of the training room. The outside world is not so supportive. This is doubly so when trainees have to go back to a work environment with all the old associations and people who try to return everything to the status quo that existed before the training.

Traditional training pays little attention to future pacing; NLP makes it an integral part of every exercise. Ten per cent is the minimum training time that should be spent future pacing, otherwise the skills will not transfer.

You can set up a whole future pacing exercise where trainees will role play difficult customers, unsympathetic managers or cynical spouses for trainees to rehearse the new skills.

---

## EXERCISES

### *Key Points*

- Preparation for the exercise:
    focus clearly on the purpose of the exercise and your outcomes for the learners

decide if you are going to demonstrate the exercise and if so, identify good subjects
- Set up and frame the exercise:
  cover the why, what and how
  give clear instructions, spatially marked out for the different roles
- Demonstrate the exercise if necessary.
  take only questions that clarify the procedure
- Run the exercise:
  supervise and coach
  intervene as little as possible and only to draw out their learnings
  coach by acknowledgement of what went well, as well as what should be done differently
  manage the time of each stage and reconvene the group at the end
- Process the exercise:
  take comments, observations and questions
  generalise the material, give examples and future pace to transfer the skills out

# DEALING WITH
# DIFFICULT PEOPLE

> There is no such thing as a resistant trainee, merely inflexible
> trainers.

Difficult people, like difficult questions, come in two main
varieties: those who deliberately set out to be difficult and those
the trainer just happens to find difficult. From the trainer's point
of view, both can be a challenge and an opportunity. Think how
boring training would be if everyone agreed with you all the
time – although sometimes this certainly seems an attractive
proposition.

We plan to avoid giving stereotypes which talk about 'The Know-
it-all', 'The Distracter', etc. Although this is only a shorthand, it is
more useful to focus on the behaviour rather than the person.
Treating someone as if they *were* their behaviour is likely to make it
more entrenched. Separate the behaviour from the person in your
mind and always keep yourself in a resourceful state.

The converse is also important: people are responding to your
behaviour, not to you. Your identity is not under threat.

Resistance is not something someone has, like red hair or a grey
suit. Resistance is a response to someone else pushing. It is
impossible to resist nothing. So the first question for the trainer to
ask themselves is: 'How am I contributing to this person's
resistance?' or ' What am I doing that is maintaining this person's
problem?'

Preventing resistance is always easier than dealing with it, so the
frames you set are important. When you review a training
difficulty, always ask yourself what frame you could have set that
would have defused the problem before it started. Listen for any
negative commands embedded in the language you use. If you say
things like 'You won't *find this difficult*' or 'Don't *let this worry you*',
guess what will happen? The trainees are likely to notice

difficulties and start to worry, even if the idea had not entered their minds. You will tend to get what you ask for. 'Any objections?' will elicit objections.

Respect trainees' points of view and do not get drawn into trying to win an argument. If you do win the argument, your adversary, and probably the group, will feel bad. If you do not, you will lose credibility. Change the frame to create a situation where you both win, like, 'That is one way of looking at it, here is another . . . What are their respective advantages?'

Gather information about the group's concerns and interests. Acknowledge their reality. When you elicit resistance, play what they say back to them to check you have got it right. Say something like: 'So the way you see it is . . .' and use their words. This will build rapport and reassure them that you do care about their concerns. You may need to apologise: 'You are right. I made a mistake. Now, how else could I have responded?'

One difficult behaviour to deal with is when someone constantly questions your credibility or the credibility of the material. It is fine to be sceptical, but to get the most from any training you have to be prepared to suspend disbelief. Anyone who is not prepared to do this is wasting his time at your training. He could be doing something more useful elsewhere – and you can remind him of this. Turn the tables and ask him to be sceptical *enough* to test the material to see whether it works.

Have a downside plan prepared for the worst case. What would you do, for example, if someone persistently and aggressively interrupted? You cannot know in advance. Over the course of time you will have gone through a number of moves: deferring to the break, identifying positive intention and reframing, asking to be allowed to continue, etc. If these have not worked, step aside to a new position you do not usually use and say something like this: 'I'm sorry I cannot continue to train in this situation. My job is to present this material. Your interruptions are preventing both myself and the group from achieving what we are here for.' At this point you can ask the person what he is achieving by staying and what he proposes to do. There may be a little more negotiation before he volunteers to leave. Alternately, you may simply ask him to leave. If he does, you step back to your normal position and carry on as if nothing had happened. Another option is to keep sweetly and reasonably answering him, until the group cracks and challenges him for you. A more likely scenario is a dissatisfied trainee leaving during a break.

Be curious about any unusual behaviour. Suspect a hidden agenda if someone persistently questions or disrupts the seminar, or brings up irrelevancies. He may feel you have not dealt adequately with his concerns or that his beliefs are bruised. These covert outcomes or hidden agendas will occur more in in-house trainings if there are relationship and power struggles within the group.

If you suspect there is a particular hidden agenda at work in a group, there are at least three ways you can deal with it.

First, you can tackle it openly. Step to one side, away from your training spot, to mark out what follows as different. Say something like, 'I am getting a strong impression – and I could be wrong – that there is some concern in the group about [suspected covert outcome]' and address it.

Secondly, you can be oblique. 'With the last group I taught this material to, the group were concerned about . . . and I said . . .' Or you can bring the conversation around by saying, 'Some people in this sort of situation have concerns about . . . How would you answer them so *they* have more choices about dealing with it?' This dissociates the problem from the group and makes it easier to talk about.

Thirdly, you can tell a story that suggests and deals with the concern without mentioning it directly at all.

Not all difficulties are so high profile and often the group will take care of itself, perhaps with a little skilful facilitation on your part. Facilitation, rather like coaching, is a whole subject in itself.

Sometimes one group member will consistently speak for another person's experience. Remind her to speak from her own experience. Her mind reading can arise because she is not confident enough to give her own experience in the group. She may be speaking up for a quiet group member. Of course, she may just be a habitual mind reader.

The opposite pattern is when a person projects their own feelings onto the group. So she will say things like: 'People are angry that you are not going to do this . . .' People who project, disown their statements. Even if the projection is true, you must challenge the projection. Unless people speak for themselves you will not know how they feel. You may need to say something like: 'Let's check out whether other people are really experiencing what you say they are' or 'I understand that is the way you feel. Other people will need to speak for themselves.'

A difficult behaviour to deal with is when someone is persistently disruptive in mild ways, yet denies any foul intent. He may act naive, make mistakes or just be unfortunate. He seems to be hostile, yet expresses it indirectly. He may initiate side conversations with others, or maintain a uninterested or slightly superior expression. Keep in a resourceful state and make a general evaluation. Your best approach is probably during a break. Ask how he is getting on with the course or, if this draws a blank, express your concern about a specific behaviour and allow him to respond. This usually surfaces some issue. A direct expression of hostility is a step forward. If you were inaccurate, you can apologise for your misunderstanding.

If someone is taking more than their share of the air time during questions and answers, explain that you want to be fair to everyone by allowing each person only one question or comment per session. You can then interrupt the excessive talker legitimately: 'Excuse me, David, you may have forgotten that you have already used your comment for this session and so you'll understand as I ask the rest of the group for any other comments, please.'

Another awkward situation is when someone keeps adding to what you say or correcting you. He knows a lot about the material and obviously wants you and everyone else to know that. Sometimes he will nod, interrupt and agree with you at every opportunity while the group gets more and more fed up. His intention is to support you; in fact he is doing just the opposite. A metaphor will often help here. Tell it ostensibly to the whole group but gesture non-verbally to the person as you tell it. Avoid an argument at all costs. If his information contradicts yours, then thank him, point to the mismatch, restate your position, if you are sure of it, or give your references and say you will check the information. If he is right, thank him. You have learned something. It's OK to be wrong. The only way you will be discredited in the group's eyes is if you cling onto being right regardless.

Distracting questions or comments can be dealt with by asking how they relate to the topic under discussion (with the presupposition that they do not), as long as you have set limits to the discussion. Some people may intellectualise and overcomplicate questions or comments. You may want to ask them to be more specific, to ask their question simply or you may need to restate their question for them in a simple way and check with them that you have it correctly.

Some people are very good at spotting possible problems. They will say some variation of, 'I think that this bit is wrong', 'I do not agree here' or 'Don't you think there is a danger of . . . ?' They say, 'Yes, but . . .' in many different forms. To deal with this you can say that yes, there are an infinite number of ways something cannot work, so how could they adapt it so it would? Or you might turn the pattern on itself by asking them to think about the worst problem that looking for problems creates. You can also utilise and schedule their behaviour. Ask them to be the Devil's advocate in the group and to wait until you have had a fair exposition before they chip in. Now they are doing it to order.

I also like to tell a metaphor. When I was young I was a rather fussy eater. I liked hamburger and chips and not a lot else. My parents started to tempt me onto more exotic foods. I was a match for them though. When confronted with something new I would ask: 'Supposing I don't like it?' I managed to avoid discovering many enjoyable foods and experiences for some time with this question, for my parents could not answer it.

We each have our internal rules of training. One rule many trainers have is: 'I have to satisfy this person and I have to do it now.' This is a limiting rule in the context of a group training. You can break rapport with one person within the larger frame of group rapport and shared outcomes.

Being heckled is a good challenge. Remember that stand up comedians, far from avoiding hecklers, love to interact with them. They utilise what the heckler says and turn it back. You can turn this into a simple exercise for two (or more) people:

1. The person acting a trainer sets a training context, e.g. 'I'm just in the middle of explaining reflective listening . . .'
2. The partner heckles.
3. The trainer utilises and responds to the heckler.

You can ask hecklers to comment by saying, 'If you were me how would you have dealt with that?' You can invite the heckler up to the front onto your territory. It is much easier to heckle from the safety of the audience. Get him to say whatever he wants to say. This usually shuts him up. Then thank him and propel him firmly back into the audience.

Whatever type of training you do, there will be particular kinds of 'difficult' behaviour you encounter. Treat these as invaluable sources of learning by designing and using a range of interventions until you find the most effective. You can do this on your own with the new behaviour generator or the learning from criticism strategy. It can be more fun with a partner and you can test out different responses. Finally, remember that people with difficult behaviour often 'resist' the most just before they do a 'U' turn and become your biggest fan. There is a wonderful psychological term for this. It is called the extinction burst. Would it be useful if you looked on every piece of difficult behaviour as an extinction burst?

## DEALING WITH DIFFICULT PEOPLE

### Key Points

- You learn the most from difficult situations.
- Ask yourself, 'How am I maintaining this difficult behaviour?'
- Focus on the behaviour, not the person, and maintain a resourceful state.
- Preventing resistance is easier than dealing with it.
- Respect all points of view and avoid arguments.
- Have a plan prepared for the worst case.
- Stay alert for and address hidden agendas, either overt or covert.
- Challenge comments for relevance to the topic being discussed.
- Simplify over-complex questions or statements.
- The group's outcomes are more important than any individual. You do not have to respond.
- Either enjoy playing with hecklers or be so patient that the group controls them.

# QUESTIONS

> The important thing is not to stop questioning. Curiosity has its own reason for existing. Never lose a holy curiosity.
>
> *Albert Einstein*

What is a question? Do questions represent the intersection of language and learning? Can you elicit questions, frame questions, outframe questions, utilise questions and answer them by asking other questions? How much do you think the quality of the questions you ask yourself determines the quality of your thinking and the results you create? Is it possible that questions are the ultimate mental bootstrap programme by which we evolve? Are questions the answers?

Questions drive communication. They are clearly critically important, yet in a room full of highly educated people, if you ask how much training they have had in asking questions, the typical answer is one or two days, and the most usual distinction learned is between open and closed questions. Isn't that odd?

We have intentionally made this chapter one of the longer ones in order to redress this balance. Even so, it barely touches the surface. If you want to explore the patterns of questions and language more, read the chapters on Meta Model and Milton Model in our previous book, *Introducing Neuro-Linguistic Programming*.

### Question about questions

The quality of the answer depends on the quality of the question or, in computerspeak: GIGO. Garbage in, garbage out. How can we improve the quality of our questions? By asking questions about questions, or *metaquestions*, of course! Here are some useful ones:

What is the most useful question I can ask right now?
What is the most useful way to think about this?
What am I missing that is important?

The following metaquestions in particular help to communicate with others:

What question can I ask that will best serve the other person?
What needs to happen here and which question is the key to it?
Are these people unconsciously indicating in body language what their concerns are?
Is there an unspoken question in what they are saying?

## ASKING QUESTIONS

You will often want to ask questions, either to the whole group or to individuals. Be clear what your outcome is in asking a question. Ask yourself, 'How does this question further my training outcomes?'

You can then ask a series of questions, notice the response and use that response to ask another question until you are satisfied that you have the outcome you want or are close enough to it. When you get an answer, always thank the person and acknowledge the response in a positive way. Trainees equate 'making people wrong' with bad training.

### Purpose of questions

Within the overall frame of the training outcomes, you can ask questions for a number of different purposes. You can ask them to arouse interest and encourage thinking. You can use them to focus trainees' attention on particular areas. You can use them to empower people to access their own resources and learning states. Questions can shift trainees' existing viewpoints or offer new ways of thinking. When used well, questions make people curious, and curiosity and its magical cousin fascination are the two most powerful learning states.

Questions can also be used to evaluate understanding, but remember that it is possible to have an intellectual understanding, but be unable to use the material. Knowledge is useless unless it makes a difference to what you can do and gives you more choices. The most valuable evidence that trainees have learned the material is that they can use it, even though they may not understand it consciously yet.

Finally, questions can be very useful for giving you information about the group's reality, their concerns and interests. When in doubt, ask.

### Socratic, loaded and other questions

You can ask questions in different ways, for example, to teach with the Socratic method. Here you lead the group to a particular conclusion by a series of open questions. (A less kind commentator would say 'loaded' open questions.) The advantage of the Socratic method, if skilfully used, is to get people thinking round an issue in a particular way, so they seem to discover the answers for themselves, as opposed to the trainer simply telling them (although the same unkind commentator would say this is simply telling them indirectly while pretending they are finding out for themselves). The dangers are that unless this is carefully and respectfully done, the trainer can find herself asking a series of more and more loaded questions if the group does not come up with the 'right' answers in a scene reminiscent of a classroom nightmare. If you have something you want to tell the group, just tell them. There is merit in simplicity. If you don't want to tell them directly, design an exercise so they explore it for themselves.

Beware too of the 'creeping poison' question technique, which is to ask each person in turn a question. This leads to tension in those whose time has come (try second positioning the next person in turn if you doubt this) and relief, often accompanied by switching off, afterwards.

Then there is the 'heart failure' method when the trainer pounces on a participant without warning. Good if you want to gain attention. Usually bad for rapport and learning. Anxiety and an open learning state cannot co-exist.

## ELICITING QUESTIONS

Trainees' questions are feedback. You want their questions in order to find out their concerns and what they are clear about.

They can guide you towards mutual outcomes.

Also people's questions are one of the best ways of making you think about the material in a new way and so learn more about it. There is a saying, 'If you want to learn something, teach it.'

The words you use in eliciting questions are important. Compare the effect of these three requests:

- 'Are there any questions?'
- 'What questions do you have on the material so far?'
- 'Take a moment to become aware of any questions you may have about the material covered so far, notice whichever ones could be the most useful to you and ask only when you are ready to.'

The first example is a closed question. It may elicit silence. It does not presuppose that there are any questions, nor are you requesting the group to ask them even if there are.

The second example does assume there are questions, but does not explicitly ask for them.

The third example not only assumes there are questions, but also guides the trainees through a short process (*'Take a moment . . . become aware of any questions . . . notice. . . the most useful . . . ask . . . you are ready . . .'*) and does request the resulting questions be asked. If you want more questions, or higher quality ones, phrase your request in this kind of way.

Another option is to form small 'buzz groups' to clarify their questions for a few minutes.

Another way of eliciting questions is to make a series of provocative statements deliberately. There are risks here, so if you want to sail close to the wind, do it with care and have some recovery strategies in place if it goes wrong. Utilise challenges to bring out teaching points and admit to being provocative if necessary.

Finally, you do not need to elicit a question in order to answer it. You can yourself ask questions on behalf of the group and then answer them. For example, you might say; 'I am sometimes asked what happens in a seminar if no one wants to ask any questions . . . What I say to them is . . .'

## Choreography

You can use question and answer sessions as they form natural breaks in the presentation of the material, giving space for thought and integration. You can also set aside definite times for questions. When you do, have a place that you use consistently when you want questions. We have already referred to this as spatial marking or *choreography*. It forms an unconscious association between where you stand and the kind of activity you want. You can consistently use other spots for input, demonstrations, summaries, stories, etc.

## Framing questions

When you ask for questions or comments from the group, how you frame your question will determine the responses that you get. The frame can be as tight or as loose as you wish. An example of a tight frame would be: 'Are there any questions about the purpose of this next exercise?' A more relaxed frame would be, 'What questions do you have about the material we covered in this last session?' Your questions control the scope of the questions you get, so that any questions outside of this scope can be elegantly deferred.

You will also want to control the duration of the questions by setting time frames at the start. You can say: 'Now I'd like to take no more than five minutes for your questions on . . .' People will keep track of this and be ready to move on five minutes later.

### Open frame

If you say something like 'I'd like to respond to any comments or questions that you have', then you have set an open frame, wide open. You will get a wide range of responses and can hardly complain if the open frame takes off into outer space!

Be careful with open frames, but they can be useful, particularly to catch the questions that you have excluded from the tighter frames. They are also good for filling the short periods of time when trainees are late arriving back or on the (rare) occasions when you have met your training outcomes ahead of time.

## Closing questions

When you want to finish any question session, you can ask for a closing question by saying, 'I'll take one final question on this topic before we move on to the next piece.' After the one question, say you will be available in the break if there is anything else they would like to ask, but *now* you are moving on. At the same time your tonality needs to be congruent. Speed up your rate of speech and put a little urgency into your voice. You can also use humour to get your message over by saying something like, 'Were there any more questions we don't have time for?' or 'What other questions didn't you have?'

## RESPONDING TO QUESTIONS

Answering questions visibly deals with the group's concerns. Some people in the group never ask questions and rely on the more high profile members to ask for them. Sometimes one dominant person takes on the role of questioner for the group. Satisfy him or her and the group is satisfied.

The general principle in responding to questions is to deal with them in a way that directly or indirectly advances your training outcomes. Trainees need to understand something to proceed and questions show their level of understanding.

Although you need to maintain group rapport, do not feel you have to answer every question directly. Some trainers do and are led off track too easily.

### Dealing with irrelevant questions

When a question comes up that is outside the frame you set, you can simply defer it and mark it out with a specific gesture like opening your hands so that the questioner and the whole group can see. Do this consistently and it becomes an anchor for relevancy, a very useful training tool. Whenever a participant asks a question that is not relevant to the topic or to your training outcomes, you gracefully defer it and use the anchor at the same time. This ensures the message is received by the group at both the conscious and unconscious levels.

You can also defer the question if it is better dealt with at a later stage in the training. Explain this and ask the trainees to ask it then.

When a question arises that is only of interest to a minority of the group, you might say something like, 'That's an interesting question. I don't think I can go into it at the moment, we don't have time. Ask me at break.'

I remember an example when I was training and someone mentioned Psychosynthesis. Five minutes later someone asked

'What is Psychosynthesis?' He addressed the question more to the person who had mentioned it than to me. I said something like, 'A very interesting system of psychology that is an ideal topic to *talk about during break.*' Random cross group discussion is rarely useful.

## Motormouth syndrome

Some people speak before they think and seem to make the question up as they go along. Eventually they may have rambled on and actually asked two or three questions. You can interrupt their pattern by asking them to pick their key question or to be clear about their question before they ask it.

Some trainees hog question time and monopolise the group's attention. They always seem to have a question or an observation to make. Groups can get annoyed at this and they will get annoyed at you if you do not attend to it. Here you may need to say something like, 'Thank you for your question. You are unusually good at asking questions and have asked a number already. I'm sure you'll understand as I ask what questions are there from the rest of the group?' You have a responsibility to the whole group, but also to the questioner, to ensure he or she does not become unpopular.

## ANSWERING QUESTIONS

There is a saying, 'Behind every question there is a statement.' And behind every statement there is a world view. Statements can be thinly disguised as questions. For example there is the question in the form so beloved by Members of Parliament: 'Is it not a fact that . . . ?' This is hardly a question, it is using the opportunity to ask a question to make a statement. You are unlikely to get anything so blatant. If you do, you can ask for the purpose of the question.

### Open and closed questions

A *closed question* is one that closes down possibilities, one that is framed in such a way as to get a 'yes' or 'no' answer. The parliamentary question above is an example. Closed questions usually begin with 'is' or 'isn't', 'does' or 'doesn't', 'will' or 'won't'.

They have assumptions behind them. Often the best way to answer is to examine the question, rather than answer directly, don't you think?

*Open questions* are designed to open up and explore new pathways. They usually start with 'how', 'what', 'where', 'when' or 'who' and they cannot be answered by a simple 'yes' or 'no'. How could you make use of this difference to explore different types of question?

## Information-gathering questions

Many questions are simple requests for information and these are usually the easiest to deal with. Give the information if you have it. If you do not know, say so and ask if anyone in the group knows. If no one knows, then you can offer to find out the answer or refer the questioner to a source.

## 'Why' questions

'Why' questions come in various forms. 'Why are we doing this?' is a type of question that needs a conceptual answer. You need to chunk up and relate what you are doing to the bigger picture. The unspoken part of this question may be, 'What use is it?' Address this by showing how you can use the material in the real world outside the training room.

Another type of 'why' question refers to cause and effect in the past, e.g. 'Why did this happen?' invites a reason as the reply. Any reasons you give have to make sense in the questioner's model of the world, not yours. You could ask them, 'Why do you think it happened?'

## 'How' questions

'How' questions are usually about process and procedures, the structure of the exercise or course material you have presented. You usually need to chunk down to answer them, showing how the pieces relate together.

## 'What' questions

'What' questions usually ask for information, e.g. 'What is the next step?' Although, because the English language is so rich, they can also ask for concepts and reasons – 'What's the meaning of this?' – or for uses – 'What can I do with this skill?'

'Why', 'what' and 'how' questions need to be addressed at every stage of a training. Why are we doing this? How is it useful? How do we do this? What processes do we go through? What are the steps? What information do we need?

When answering a question, you want to have a question of your own in mind first: 'What is the intention behind this question?' or 'What does this person need?'

Always thank the person for their question, especially if it is an interesting one, and if someone asks a good question, say so. If you do not understand the question, also say so and ask the questioner to clarify it.

If someone asks a question to help them understand the material, then an answer that includes examples drawn from the questioner's own interests or profession works very well.

When a group member asks a question, notice how the group responds to the question. Do they lean forward slightly, interested in the response? Is there a lot of shuffling? Or is there a deathly silence? In the same way you need to notice whether the questioner is satisfied with the answer. If you are not sure, ask them. Pay more attention to their body language than their verbal answer, which may just be polite. If the group has shown interest in the question, is the group satisfied with the answer? There is a skill to knowing when to stop answering a question. Watch the questioner as you answer, so that you know when to stop. Avoid over-complicated answers that can bring up further issues and lead to unwelcome questions.

## UTILISING QUESTIONS

A good trainer is able to utilise anything that happens to achieve the desired outcome and questions are no exception. You can utilise questions to introduce new material in your answer or to weave together disparate intellectual strands. You can also reframe questions or use them as a starting-point to explore an area or to change the subject. Sometimes you can use the material in the question to answer the question. That way the group gets two answers to the question – one consciously on the intellectual level and one less consciously on the behavioural level. A question can become whatever you want.

We were in the middle of one seminar on meeting and negotiation skills and were explaining that once you have all agreed on a shared outcome for the meeting, you can use it to challenge anyone who takes the meeting off at a tangent. Someone asked me to clarify this relevancy challenge. He was unclear what it meant and how to do it. I started by saying, 'The relevancy challenge is a very useful idea. For example, I was in a meeting last week, no, the week before, I think it was Thursday. I had had a difficult drive into town and had to eat a quick snack at the motorway service station. Those service stations are *awful*. They are always packed and I had to wait even to get a seat. I was quite hungry, so I thought I would try the shepherd's pie. "Not much you can do wrong with a shepherd's pie," I thought . . .'

At this point the questioner shifted in his seat and said, 'How exactly does all this answer my question?' My rambling forced him to make a relevancy challenge – so he could learn by doing.

Here is an example of answering the question with the pattern the question is asking about: we were asked to explain reverse mind reading and of course replied, 'You should have known we wouldn't be able to answer that!'

This is part of a more general pattern that links your answer to the questioner's real sensory experience, as well as to his intellectual understanding. You can use the opportunity a question presents to tell a story or give a personal example.

You can also answer questions behaviourally. I remember one amusing example when I was training some material on hypnosis and someone asked me what a negative hallucination was. I looked round the group, saying 'Who said that?' When she repeated the question, I did the same thing again. She got the point, amid general laughter, that negative hallucination means not seeing something that is there. (Have you ever lost your car keys and then found them in the most obvious place, just when you gave up looking for them?)

Think of questions as pointers to where your presentation is unclear or incomplete. Are there two or three questions or objections you tend to get repeatedly in a training? You can probably easily answer them. How could you change your presentation so that these questions would never need to be asked explicitly?

A very effective way of using questions is either to ask a question in return or give the questioner a task that allows her to discover her own answer. For example, in one of our seminars a question was raised about outcomes: 'Is there a danger that you can get so caught up in the process of making outcomes you don't notice it isn't making any difference?' This is a closed question, inviting a 'yes' or 'no' answer. The answer we gave was something like: 'Yes, evidence is an important part of getting outcomes. Unless you keep track, you will not notice whether you are getting them either. Only you can answer this for yourself – and here's how.' We suggested he keep an outcome diary, keeping track of the outcomes he set week by week, putting clear time-scales on each and recording progress on every one. Thus the first half of the question provided the answer to the second half.

We also told a metaphor: 'A very fine trainer we knew used to be a pilot. He told us on any flight from San Francisco to Hawaii the plane was off course 95 per cent of the time. He only knew he was off course because the cockpit instruments were so sensitive. Every time he noticed he would correct the plane and sure enough in a short time it would be off course in the other direction. Still, he always made Hawaii.'

## Dealing with difficult questions

How do you deal with a 'heart failure' question from a trainee? Direct challenges and criticism often come disguised as questions, making them more acceptable and harder to evade. Use the criticism strategy (see page 112) on the spot if you need it.

A new slant on the material that never occurred to you is also tricky. First, any question is a difficult one when you are in an unresourceful state. So keep or recover your resourceful state before you respond to a question. Secondly, mentally separate the questioner's intention from the question itself. Ask yourself, 'What does this questioner want?' or, sometimes, 'What does this questioner want that he does not know that he wants?'

There are also assumptions built into every question. Ask yourself: 'What has to be true for this person to ask this question?' This is especially important when you cannot understand how what they are asking could possibly be a problem.

Remember Murphy's Law? 'If something can go wrong, it will.'

The training equivalent is: 'Everything that can go wrong will go wrong, if you train for long enough.' Be as prepared as possible. Think of a couple of questions you might possibly get that would stretch you. It does not matter if you have never had them (yet). Think of a context where they might occur. What material would you be covering? Now, how could you answer in a way that not only used the material you were training, but also furthered your overall training outcomes?

Do not try to bluff an answer if you really do not know it. Trainers do not have to be all-knowing. You will lose credibility irretrievably if you bluff and are seen to bluff. Better to keep quiet and be thought a fool than open your mouth and prove it.

Make sure that a question is only difficult *once*. Whether you think you answered it well or badly, debrief afterwards by asking, 'How else could I have dealt with that question?' Generate at least three options. That way, the question and others like it will not be a problem again.

Some questions come with built in warnings. Beware the question that starts, 'I don't want to be negative here, but . . .' This is fair warning there is something negative coming up. Any question that starts, 'I don't want to be . . . but . . .' guarantees that it will be so. Fill in the blank.

One way to deal with a negative pattern is to use the same pattern back. So respond, 'I don't want to dismiss your question but...' and then dismiss it (elegantly of course). The group will get the unconscious message here. Some may even get it consciously and laugh. Another option is to say, 'Then how would you rephrase that question so that it is stated more positively?'

On the other hand, 'Sorry to ask a boring question . . .' usually guarantees a lively and challenging one. The questioner may be out to nail you to the wall. In the same way, 'I want to be constructive here . . .' can mean 'I am going to rip your argument to shreds.'

Then there is that wonderful word 'but'. 'But' qualifies or negates what precedes it in the sentence. For example: 'I think you are absolutely right, but . . .' Avoid 'but' in your answers for this reason. Use 'and' instead. But it could be difficult. But it's well worth it. And you always have the choice.

If someone is asking questions that seem to indicate that they want an argument, tell them they are right. It is not possible to have an argument with someone who agrees with you. Is it? . . .

Well, you're absolutely right!

If you are not clear about the purpose of the question, ask, 'What would answering that question get for you?' This goes to a higher level and makes the questioner clarify exactly what she wants. The question may be very general, so you may want to ask the person to be more specific or give a specific example. Give a specific example in your reply as well, if you can.

A question may still catch you unawares and you need time to think. Automatic responses like these will gain you a little more thinking time:

'Let me think about the best way to answer that.'
'That's an important point. Thank you for raising it now.'
'There are several ways to answer that question.'

If you need more time, use these:

'Good question. I'd like to open that up to everyone and I'll comment afterwards, if appropriate.' (This is known as the 'ricochet' technique.)
'That's what they call a "good question", and I would like some more time to think about it, before giving you an answer. Let me come back to you on that in the next session.'

Here are two different ways of reframing and transforming any question.

1. You can chunk up from the original question. This essentially says, 'That question is an example of questions about this problem.' You then address this larger problem – which means you need not necessarily answer the specific question in detail.
2. You can also chunk down from the question. You say, essentially, 'There is an important part of this question that needs to be talked about before we can answer the whole question.' You then take a smaller part of the question and go into that.

   For example, I remember a question: 'How do you maintain your own integrity and fit into the organisation you are working for?' The answer we gave went: 'The first question here is to make sure you explore the organisational culture first before accepting the contract. Only if you feel congruent about working there, do you accept the contract.'

Humour can work superbly in responding to tricky questions – or it can embroil you deeper. You may experience what stand up comedians call 'dying' on stage. So tread with care. One of your main standbys will be a stockpile of carefully chosen analogies and metaphors. These go straight to the right brain and are hard to argue with. Identify some of your regular questions and then go off on a hunt for suitable analogies and metaphors to address them.

As an example, one question that comes up regularly about NLP is the issue of manipulation. NLP has very effective skills and techniques. As people begin to realise just how effective they are, they can become uncomfortable about how these skills may be used to influence people, especially in a business or sales context, against their best interests.

One response we make is by analogy. This is both brief and effective: 'Most people have access to a powerful car, which is extremely useful for getting from place to place. It can also be deadly if driven without due care and attention, and horrendous if driven irresponsibly. However, few of us feel that this is a reason for cars to be abolished.'

Another response is the straightforward one: the ethics of the user are a separate issue to the usefulness and power of the skills or techniques. You could also argue that to avoid possible exploitation, *everyone* needs to know about these powerful communication tools. You cannot not influence people. You can, however, be aware of the influence you have. NLP communication skills give more precision and more opportunities to create a win-win situation.

Or you might say, 'Of course you're right. NLP skills are very powerful and should not be abused. If there is anyone in the room who plans to use them unethically, would they please leave now!'

---

## QUESTIONS

### Key Points

- The quality of our thinking is reflected in the quality of our questions.
- Questions drive communication.
- *Metaquestions* are questions about questions. One important one

to ask yourself is, 'What is the most useful question to ask?'

- Asking questions:

    Questions are one of your most powerful tools for furthering training outcomes.

    Always be clear on your outcomes when asking questions.

    Be cautious if using 'Socratic method', 'creeping poison' or 'heart failure'.

- Eliciting questions:

    Use presuppositions intentionally when asking for questions.

    Use spatial marking to indicate when you want questions and when you do not.

    Frame your question sessions to set any limits you want – frames can be open, or very tight, as appropriate.

- Responding to questions:

    Use the questions you get to move towards your training outcomes.

    When questions are outside the frame you have set, use the relevancy challenge to defer them.

    Ensure all questions and answers flow through you, rather than across the group (unless you want this).

    Use pattern interrupting and ask for a summary of rambling questions.

    Ensure that question times are not hogged by a few verbose trainees.

- Answering questions:

    Listen for the statements or questions behind the question.

    Do not answer closed questions, address the assumptions behind the question.

    Open questions are information-gathering questions. Give the information if you have it. If you don't know, say so. You can then ask the group or offer to find out.

    Be clear on the outcome of the questioner. If the question is not clear, ask for clarification.

    Calibrate to physiology to know when the questioner or group have got a satisfactory answer. Keep your answers as simple as possible and shut up as soon as you get these signals.

- Utilising questions:

    Use the questions you get in any way that advances the outcomes of the training.

    Whenever you can, answer on two levels: a behavioural demonstration as well as a verbal answer.

Use the kinds of question you get as feedback to let you know how to change your material or presentations.

Where possible, have the questioner discover their own answer to the question by asking them a question or giving them a task.

You can use questions to go in any direction that is useful.

- Dealing with difficult questions:

    It is easier to avoid difficult questions than to deal with them.

    Difficult questions are invaluable for learning.

    Plan how you will deal with expected difficult questions in advance.

    Ensure a question is only difficult *once* by generating three different answers.

    Have automatic responses to buy thinking time.

    If you don't know, say so and either pass the question to the group or defer it till later.

    Reframe the question by chunking up or down and answer that question.

    Use humour, analogy or metaphor.

    Use the 'learning from criticism' strategy if necessary.

    Use the 'learning to learn' question: *'What would I do differently next time?'*

# 21

# METAPHORS

There is a story told by Gregory Bateson, the anthropologist and systems thinker, who wrote extensively on cybernetics, biology and psychology. In his book *Steps to an Ecology of Mind*, he tells of the man who wanted to know about the mind, what it really was and whether computers would ever be as intelligent as humans. The man typed the following question into the most powerful contemporary computer (which took a whole floor of a university department): 'Do you compute that you will ever think like a human being?'

The machine rumbled and muttered as it started to analyse its own computational habits. Eventually the machine printed its reply on a piece of paper. The man rushed over in excitement and found these words, neatly typed: 'That reminds me of a story . . .'

We will use the word *metaphor* to mean any story, joke, parable, experience or example that refers directly or indirectly to the material you are presenting. A straightforward example would be an analogy. This chapter is rather like an adventure game. The purpose is to enjoy it and anticipation of the unexpected is an important part of what makes it a pleasure. The Bateson computer story is more complex and your mind may still be turning it over as you continue to read.

We might have chosen to tell you of the work of Arbib, a leading neuroscience researcher. He makes the strong case in his book *The Metaphorical Brain* that the human mind is literally a creature of metaphor in that there is nothing but metaphor in sight. Everything is metaphorical in that it represents something that it is not. As you read this sentence, these funny black squiggles are turned into neural impulses, which are transformed into word-shapes and next into sounds. Then, by complex unconscious association processes, you make sequences of images, feelings and more word-sounds. Finally, if you are still with it, your conscious mind becomes aware of some meaning. Now here's an interesting question: which did you prefer, the Bateson story or the literal description?

Most people love being told a story. Recounting a story, or giving an example, is a way of making the material more meaningful. When you present ideas, give some specific examples to make it real. There are many ways to do this and the easiest way is to remember a personal example. Metaphors do not have to be clever stories and often recounting a simple personal experience will make the point very well. Each person will make up a meaning that is relevant to them. The power of a metaphor is not measured by the storyteller, but by the recipient and what their unconscious mind does with the story. Trying to pass conscious, precise understanding is hard. As everyone has different experiences and models of the world, the more precise you become in your model, paradoxically, the more people you will miss in the group. Metaphors, on the other hand, cannot be right or wrong, they are just . . . stories. A good metaphor will have many different levels of meaning, enabling you to speak to each person individually and simultaneously.

I remember when I was young, my father would tell me stories before I went to sleep. I looked forward to these stories. You can probably remember your favourite stories when you were young. The stories I remember the best are those my father and I created together. I would give an idea or a character and he would weave it into an existing story and before long the whole story was transformed. I was never aware of it at the time, but the characters in the stories often faced situations that bore some relationship to the trials and tribulations of my own young life.

Because we made them up as we went along, I had no idea what would happen next and I doubt whether my father did either. We had a beginning and the story seemed to move unpredictably towards a happy ending, which was what I wanted. I suppose he wove together personal experiences, archetypal themes and stories he had read or seen as plays or films to make a tale that was alive from moment to moment. He would not always complete the story in one evening. He knew where to set up a cliffhanger to leave me with a sense of anticipation, so that I was always left with something to look forward to . . .

Because it is important never to explain a metaphor, I really shouldn't tell you that when I was doing my Practitioner training in NLP with John Grinder, I first discovered that you can design a metaphor for any situation. All you need to know is a little bit about the situation and the person's outcome. You then transfer this over to a different situation with a similar structure and build in a resolution of the problem.

I went to the newsagent's the other day and found a very traumatised elderly lady telling the shopkeeper how she had just been mugged. The story went on and got worse. Awaiting my moment, I interrupted and recounted the tale of my friend who was beaten up in her home and could not seem to get the incident out of her head. Then, a few weeks later, when she realised what she was doing, she said, 'Being beaten up is bad enough, but I'll be damned if I'll give them the satisfaction of ruining my life' and she decided to push the whole incident so far away that it was as though she had forgotten all about it . . .'Can I have a *Guardian* please?'

The old lady paused, her eyes focused off into the distance, and then her state changed and she calmly walked out of the shop. The unexpected thing was that as I left with my paper, the person behind me smiled and said two words: 'Nice work.'

What do you think would have happened if I had tried to explain the metaphor to the old lady? Explaining a metaphor is like explaining a joke. If you do, it doesn't work.

## Humour

Be careful about deciding in advance which stories or jokes you are going to use. The essence of a humour and intuition is spontaneity. It takes all the skills of a stand up comedian to make prepared jokes work. It is much easier to be spontaneous. The best jokes seem to be the ones that arise naturally from the flow of the material and just come to mind at the right moment.

This will happen effortlessly if you build a personal collection of stories, jokes, and analogies. You do not have to remember them all consciously. Whenever you read or hear one that you like, make a note of it. You will be surprised how they surface at the right time. Once you set up a 'filter' for these you will discover them in books, films and everywhere. The Sufi religious tradition is particularly rich in good stories. If you write them down when you catch them, they are yours for life.

## Analogy

Casual metaphors may be as simple as an analogy. The right analogy works like the right key in a lock to open understanding. You can almost hear the clicking! Here is a three-person drill for creating useful analogies:

### Analogies exercise

1. The first person makes a statement about the content of the training, some fact, theory or basic assumption, for example: 'There is no failure, only feedback.'

2. The second person specifies a random context, for example: 'In the context of high street shopping.'

3. The third person generates an analogy that illustrates the statement as quickly as possible. 'If you go out to buy something and the shop is out of stock, you don't think, "I've failed." You go and get it somewhere else.'

Keep changing roles. You can also use this format to brainstorm examples on your own. Write down the ones you like.

## Quotes

A simple pattern that comes under the metaphor heading is called 'quotes'. Quotes is when you say something you want to say directly, but attribute it to someone else. So when we discussed our plan for this book with our publisher, she said, 'A book about training focusing on these sorts of skills will be quite unique and really valuable.'

Using quotes, no one can argue with you directly, because *you* didn't say it, someone else did. It still has impact, however. We are, of course, much too modest to say, 'We believe this is a really useful book.' Or to tell you of the colleague who said, 'This book will open the eyes of trainers to the vast potential NLP offers for enhancing human learning.' But quotes is a pattern you may find a use for.

## Metaphors for training

You can design and run a seminar based on one encompassing metaphor. One training on modelling superb acting skills started with the line from Shakespeare: 'All the world's a stage, and men and women merely players.' This provided a rich context for thinking about acting skills and exploring the notion of choosing a role in any situation to get the most from it.

Think for a moment of seminars that you give. Is there a metaphor that comes to mind, short enough to be memorable, yet rich enough with meaning that you could use as a foundation for a training?

This leads to the question of the metaphor that would describe how you think about training generally. What metaphor comes to your mind for training? A dance? A long-distance endurance test? Three-dimensional chess? A brain massage? A colouring book? You do not have to restrict yourself to one description. Take a minute to write down whichever metaphors spring first to your attention.

## TRAINING IS LIKE . . .

What answers did you get? Take a moment to explore one or two of those answers. If training is like that, what else follows logically? Expand the metaphor. For example, we started this section of the book, 'During Training', with some metaphorical descriptions of training. If you did not consciously notice them, go back for a minute to the beginning of the section and find them:

- 'The stage is set, you and the trainees are ready . . . Your audience now awaits you.'
- 'People interact in an intricate dance of communication, sometimes one person leading, sometimes another.'

Training is like a play. Training is like a dance. For us, these are useful metaphors that make training a pleasure. Occasionally, I find myself thinking in the last hour of a training weekend, 'OK, now we are on the last lap.' I never say this out loud. If I did, I would risk the group's physiology going downhill (another metaphor) as they realise (unconsciously) the last two days have been a marathon run. Never underestimate the power of a toxic metaphor.

Practise listening to the metaphors that other people use and this will sharpen your metaphorical filters for the day-to-day metaphors we all use in everyday life. I have a friend, a wise and respected consultant, who uses operating metaphors as a primary tool for diagnosing organisational cultures. Operating metaphors are unseen, unheard, basic assumptions that make such a difference, especially when we train.

Metaphors can be nested one within another. You can start one metaphor and, without finishing it, move into another and then another. Opening loops like this builds anticipation and the group will be waiting for the close of the stories. You will have their attention. Some trainers will use metaphors as anchors so that key words bring back the idea of the story at particular points during the training.

## Using metaphors to resolve difficulties

Difficult situations in training can be elegantly addressed by metaphor. It's hard to argue with a story. I remember one trainers' training, when the trainees were in a freeform negotiation to determine how they wanted to structure the last afternoon of training. The trainers had given some frames and guidelines, reserving the option to comment on process, if necessary. After an hour, the process was bogged down. The group was still at the stage of finding out what everybody wanted, nowhere near attempting to negotiate an overall structure that everyone could go with. Two hours were left.

I told them about a conference that took place a few years ago. This conference was rather unusual, it was a conference for people who were expert at running conferences. The overall goal of this conference was to produce a paper and some definitive guidelines about running conferences. As the conference got underway, these experts were very familiar with the typical course any conference would take. They knew that the first half would be wasted in a battle of egos, jostling for position and setting outcomes for how the overall goals were to be achieved. They knew too, that at some point about halfway through the allotted time, the participants would realise they were not actually producing anything and get down to some work. Consequently, the experts at this conference were not worried when nothing had been achieved by the halfway point. They were still jostling for position and setting outcomes. They saw this as inevitable. However, because they were not worried, there was no incentive to *do something different*, so they continued to argue and the conference produced nothing.

Sometimes trainees may think they already know it all. There is the story of an American professor who had made a lifetime's study of the Japanese tea ceremony. He was the Western expert. He heard there was an old man who was a master of the tea ceremony living in Japan. He had never talked to this master, so he made a special trip to Japan to see him. He found the master living in a small house on the outskirts of Tokyo and they sat down to have tea together. The professor immediately started talking about the tea ceremony, the study he had made of it, all the things he knew about it and how he was looking forward to sharing his learning with the old man. The old man said nothing, but continued to pour tea into the professor's cup. While the professor talked, the old man poured, the cup filled and the old man kept pouring. The professor continued to talk and the old man continued to pour. The tea spilt down the sides of the cup onto the floor, yet the old man did not stop. 'Stop!' said the professor. 'You're crazy. You can't fit any more tea in that cup. It's full.'

'I was just practising,' replied the old man, 'for the task of attempting to pass learning to a mind that is already full.'

## Structure of metaphors

Metaphors also give information by how they are structured. When you looked at this book for the first time, the whole layout and structure gave you a message about what sort of book it is, even before you read the contents.

It reminds me of an incident in my daughter's primary school class. The whole class was asked to write an adventure story. The next week the teacher asked some of the class to read out their stories, and a small boy, whose name was James, was first to read. He stood up and read: 'The pirates went to the island and got the treasure.' The teacher wisely did not question him further at the time, although all the other stories from his classmates were much richer in detail and storyline.

When she asked him later why his story was so short, she found out he had an incredibly rich, full version of the story in his mind. When asked why he didn't write it all down, he said something like: 'Doesn't everyone know the story? They can make it up like I do, so there's no point in writing it all out.' When the teacher explained that not everyone could make such vividly detailed pictures in their head as he could, the boy was amazed. He went home and wrote the story in full.

Learning to use metaphor is a bit like learning to swim. The more you practise, the more streamlined and competent you get. And everyone has their different learning styles and rates of learning. Some people have a 'toe in the water and one small step at a time' approach. My daughter Lara gained confidence a bit differently. She had been going swimming from a very early age once or twice a week. She always wore armbands, and would cling to her mother as if her life depended on it. She never struck out into the water on her own and the constant clinging was disappointing. We began to wonder if she would ever gain any confidence in the water.

One day when she was two-and-a-half years old, we were at a swimming pool in California. It was getting on for evening, the heat had gone from the day. It was a perfect time to swim and wash the dust of the day's journey away. Lara imperiously ordered both my wife and I out of the pool and proceeded to swim five widths without stopping. She never does anything until she is ready. Then she just does it.

You never know where metaphors may go or the effect that they have. Well placed metaphors can be one of the most powerful influences for change. They breed and have a life of their own. Some of the stories my father told me many years ago were eventually told on television many years later and published in a book.

And that reminds me of another story . . .

---

## METAPHORS

### *Key Points*

- In a sense all explanations are metaphor: they are about the thing they describe.
- Metaphors, meaning stories, analogies, parables, personal examples and jokes, bring a training alive.
- Develop the skill of designing stories for any situation.
- Metaphors can be direct for the conscious mind or indirect for the unconscious.
- Build up a collection of stories and jokes that you can draw on spontaneously.

- Notice your own metaphors for training and choose the ones that work best for you.

# 22

# ENDINGS

How do you end a training? Endings are an important and very neglected area of training. First, the musical metaphor: when you perform in public, make sure you play the last few notes right, because these are the ones the audience remembers. Wrong notes in the middle will be forgotten. Second, there is the so-called 'halo effect': our recall is good for beginnings and endings and hazy for what goes on in the middle. One function of breaks is to provide a series of mini beginnings and mini endings for the trainees to help recall.

Simply in terms of the satisfaction for the conscious minds of the trainees, a good ending can make a big difference. If you are using written feedback sheets, you can hand them out at the end and ask trainees to complete them before leaving. This works fairly well, except that it allows the energy to dissipate and makes a weak ending. It generally works better to distribute the sheets before the last break, so that the group can fill them in at their leisure during that time.

Again, like a piece of music, the ending will tend to flow naturally from the rest of the training. A downbeat ending to an upbeat training can seem incongruous and vice versa.

There are five things a good ending needs:

- information backtrack
- emotional impact
- integration
- future pacing
- and a sense of closure

## Information backtrack

A good ending will backtrack the material, to help the trainees sort out the most important information. There are several ways to do this. Simplest is to give a lecturette at the end that summarises the important points. You can also go back over the OHP or flip chart notes that you have made during the training or have a summary handout of the key points, perhaps in the form of a flow chart.

You will have set up key words and phrases in the training, perhaps in a particular tonality or with a gesture. Use these as you backtrack. They will provide immediate links to the rest of the material that was associated with them.

### Emotional impact

This can come in several ways. Sadness that the training is over, gratitude at what has been achieved or excitement at going out to use the skills. There does not have to be an upbeat, noisy community ending to have emotional impact.

### Integration

You can design your own exercise that will integrate all the skills in the training. One excellent integration exercise is to use the neurological levels, taking people through wider and wider levels of experience.

#### Neurological levels integration exercise

Start with the group standing at one end of the room, with sufficient space to take half a dozen unimpeded steps forward. Talk the group through the process roughly as follows, adding your own touches and tailoring your talk to the content of the training.

- Environment
  'Think about the environment that you want to take your learning back to . . . Imagine you are in that environment and notice what it looks like as you see this mental picture . . . and listen to the sounds you hear from it . . . Build this image of where you want these skills as vividly as you can . . . When you are ready, take a step forward and begin to think about what you will be doing in this environment . . .'
  *Wait until everyone has stepped forward.*

- Behaviour
  'What are you doing in this environment . . . ? What do you want to do . . . ? Take a moment to review your behaviour here . . . and when you are ready . . . step forward to begin to think about your skills . . .'
  *Wait until everyone has stepped forward.*

- Capabilities
  'Now think about your skills . . . What skills do you already have in this situation . . . ? What skills do you want . . . ? What skills do you want to use . . . and what skills have you learned in this training that you can use . . . ? Take a moment to review your skills here . . . and step forward when you are ready . . .'
  *Wait until everyone has stepped forward.*

- Beliefs and values
  'What do you believe here . . . ? What beliefs do you have about yourself and others in this situation . . . ? Notice how your beliefs may have changed during this training . . . What would you like to believe is possible . . . ? What is important to you . . . ? What are your values in this context . . . ? Take the time you need to explore some of your key beliefs and values . . . and when you are ready, step forward to start thinking about yourself as a whole person . . .'
  *Wait until everyone has stepped forward.*

- Identity
  'Now think about who you are, this unique person that is you . . . What is your mission in life . . . ? What do you really want to do . . . ? What is it that makes you unique . . . and how do you express your uniqueness . . ? Take the time you need to think about this...and when you are ready . . . step forward to consider your connection with others.'
  *Wait until everyone has stepped forward.*

- Connection to others/spiritual
  'Now, think about how you connect with other people, not just your family, but everyone . . . You may have a religious or spiritual way of thinking about this. You may have a different way . . . Whatever way you have . . . think about what it means for you to be connected to others . . . Take the time you need to do this now . . .'

*After some small amount of time, ask everyone to turn around and start to move back through the levels, integrating each level as they go:*

- Moving back and integrating
'When you are ready . . . step back into your identity space, bringing with you your sense of connectedness . . . Let this sense of connectedness enrich you . . .

When you are ready . . . take this sense of yourself and step back into your beliefs and values space . . . Notice how your beliefs and values are enriched by your sense of self . . . Become aware of any changes . . .

When you are ready . . . take these beliefs and values back and notice how these beliefs and values release and allow you to do those things that satisfy you and others . . . Take a moment to appreciate how these higher levels of yourself enrich and widen your skills . . . how much more effective you are in what you do with these other levels backing you up . . . as you are acting as a whole person . . . completing this process in your own time and way . . . whether consciously or unconsciously . . .

Now take these skills back and notice how they transform what you do . . . making it more effective and satisfying for yourself and others . . .

And step back into the environment you are going to . . . Know how much more you can bring to it now . . . Take a moment to appreciate this . . . as you return your attention to the here and now.

And when you have finished, you can go back to where you were sitting.'

## Future pacing

The neurological levels integration exercise is powerful, for it not only integrates, but also acts as a future pace for what the participants have learned.

The most straightforward future pace of all is an exercise in twos or threes. Each person in turn elicits from another where and how she is going to use the new skills and information. The third person will listen or help elicit. Alternatively, you can do this in larger groups in a free for all, so that everybody can exchange ideas.

## A sense of closure

Another option is to ask the group members for a one word summing up of the training. Put the words up on a flip chart. They need no comment. If the training has focused on a particular skill, say, assertiveness, then ask for words to complete the sentence: 'Being assertive is like . . .' The results can be revealing and funny. I remember I was doing a training on modelling: how to take another person's skill, learn how they do it so you can do it and teach others to do it too. One answer to a final round of 'Modelling is like . . .' was, 'Modelling is like juggling with someone else's balls!'

A satisfying closing ritual that works well is to have everyone fasten a piece of paper to their back. They then mill round and write on each other's back one thing (at least) that they enjoyed and appreciated about that person. Everyone finishes with a piece of paper full of positive strokes from the other people in the training.

A final way to end the training (and none of these endings exclude any of the others) is to have a short relaxation or trance session:

As you begin this final piece, slowing and lowering your voice, you can invite your audience to get comfortable, really comfortable . . . to feel the weight of your body on the chair . . . as your attention focuses in . . . and you become more aware . . . of how pleasant the feelings of deep comfort are . . . becoming more relaxed with every breath you take . . . as your unconscious mind . . . explores the possibilities of what you have learned . . . and you can begin to wonder . . . what changes . . . you will notice first . . . as you apply your learning . . . in satisfying ways . . . becoming more . . . curious . . . about the possibilities . . . and you do not even have to be aware of them yet . . . because you know they will always come . . . in their own good time . . . with a wisdom and a balance . . . that enables you to . . . really enjoy the feeling of not knowing when . . . you will get a pleasant surprise . . . as you find yourself using your learning and skills . . . and remembering that . . . there will be many more learning opportunities for you to look forward to.

*Bring your voice back up to normal speed and tone.*

And while your attention is returning to what we like to call a 'normal' state of consciousness, notice when you want to move or stretch.

Acknowledge and thank your people. Make any practical announcements, such as where to leave the feedback sheets, and close. Whether you get spontaneous applause or not, you have earned it. Appreciate yourself.

For now, the curtain closes, the play is done, the dance is over, this part of training ends and the next begins.

---

## ENDINGS

### *Key Points*

- Trainees remember endings.
- Aim to provide an information backtrack, emotional impact, integration, future pacing and closure.
- Backtrack systematically using visual aids and associations you have set.
- Use finishing exercises that incorporate future pacing as well as some combination of emotional impact, integration and closure, like:
  neurological levels
  mental rehearsal
  guided relaxation
- Future pace the training.
- Appreciate and thank your audience, make any practical announcements and close.

---

# PART FOUR

# EVALUATION

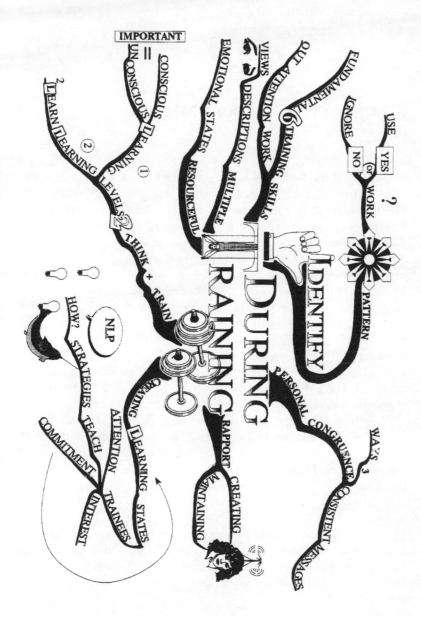

# 23

# EVALUATING TRAINING

Evaluation is the final part of the training cycle and the fourth key role in the National Standards of Training and Development. What difference has the training made? Think for a moment of how you evaluate the results of your training courses.

Here is our definition of evaluation: 'Evaluating systematically looks at the results of the training, notices the difference it has made and determines its value according to preset measures. These results are used as feedback to refine the training.'

These are a dense couple of sentences and need a bit more explanation.

### Systematic

First, collecting information is *systematic*. This means it is not only thorough and careful, but also systemic, that is, you are looking at the whole interconnected system.

Whether you are looking at change in individuals or organisations, cause and effect are not always obviously connected. There is nearly always a time lag and often unexpected consequences. Think carefully about how you look at the results of training.

### Results

The results are what the training actually achieves, not what it is intended to achieve, although hopefully the two match up. Evaluation involves collecting information and evidence of these results in many ways: observation, interview and testing performance.

### Difference

Now we have that small but significant word 'difference'. Difference implies two states and a comparison. You need information about the situation before, as well as after, the training to make a valid comparison.

Unless there is a purpose to the training, an identified need which the trainee perceives, training will mean no more than a 'tick in the box' on the training record. To avoid this the manager needs good enough interpersonal skills and a good enough relationship with the trainee to ensure that the trainee is clear about the benefits and is well motivated. Usually this means the trainee being involved in the Training Needs Analysis process. The Training Needs Analysis (TNA) and/or S/NVQs set the initial outcomes and standards, and learning and training are evaluated in terms of these preset outcomes. Training without outcomes is throwing money down the drain.

## Level

Outcomes can be at the organisational, occupational or individual level. Public seminar training is likely to be at an individual level only. In-house training encompasses all three. It is clear that without a change at the individual level there will be no change in the other two levels, but you cannot assume that individual learning will necessarily lead to a difference in the other two.

The most complete evaluation will be at all three levels, and the information you gather and the way you gather it will be different for each level. This is an aspect of systematic evaluation which looks at the results at each level in terms of preset outcomes and achieved outcomes.

## Values

The very word 'evaluation' implies values: a judgment about what is important. Your values set filters for the information you gather. So evaluation is intimately linked to values at the organisational level as well as the individual level. None of the assessment information has any *meaning* unless some values are associated with it.

An individual may decide the training was valuable if it was fun and made him more effective at his work or gave him new thinking skills. It does not necessarily have to make him more money – his values about work may focus on improved performance and greater job satisfaction.

Organisational values, however, are usually linked to profit. Somewhere, the organisation will want to see a return on its investment in money terms:

- Efficiency
  The money may come from improved organisational efficiency, which is getting the same results at a lower cost. The efficiency of the training itself will be evaluated on the principle of whether the programme achieved its objectives in a reasonably economic way.

- Effectiveness
  Training may lead to greater organisational effectiveness, which is getting better results without increase in cost. It is about improving performance. An effective training achieves major changes without extra resources or effort.

- Productivity
  This is about getting better results with less effort. A training programme that can do this is very valuable. It is both efficient *and* effective, and this is where quality programmes aim to make a difference to the organisation.

These three principles can be applied to the individual as well as the job and the organisation. You are more efficient if you can get the same results with less effort, time or resources. You are more effective if your results improve, given the same effort, time and resources. You can be more productive by getting more with less. All of these are evidence of learning.

## TYPES OF EVALUATION

Evaluation needs to be done at different stages and we will devote a section to each.

First, there is *live evaluation*, where you are tracking what is happening minute by minute. Remember the aeroplane flight. It is only by constantly adjusting and looking at your instruments that you stay on course. A navigator who looks at the compass at 9.30 a.m. and then not again until lunchtime may find himself disastrously off course.

Second, there is the *end of training* evaluation, where the trainees evaluate the training and the trainer. The trainer also evaluates the training and her performance.

Third, there is *transfer evaluation*: however well the trainees performed in the training, it is no use if they leave their skills in the training room when they leave. Have the skills transferred to where they are wanted?

Lastly there is *organisational evaluation*: how has the training contributed to organisational goals?

The final purpose of evaluation is to provide feedback to improve the training cycle. It may give some research data that adds to our knowledge of training principles. Evaluation has the role of quality control. Have trainer and trainees achieved their outcomes, and have the original needs been met at every level? If the training has not achieved the outcomes, this is not failure, but feedback – very useful information that enables you to improve and refine the next training.

## Public assessment

Evaluation may be linked to a public certification which may be S/NVQ based. The S/NVQ standards are put into coherent groups that are valuable for employment purposes.

There are five levels of qualification broadly defined:

Level 1 – Competence at a routine level of activity.
Level 2 – Competence in a more varied range of activities.
Level 3 – Competence in complex tasks with more autonomy and responsibility.
Level 4 – Competence in a broad range of complex tasks, often with responsibility for others.
Level 5 – Applying principles and techniques across a wide range of tasks with responsibility for every part and often for the work of others.

*All extracts from S/NVQs are Crown copyright, reproduced with the permission of the Controller of Her Majesty's Stationery Office.*

The Training and Development Lead Body currently (1993) sets three levels of qualifications for trainers:

Level 3 is to deliver training designed and specified by others and assess the outcomes. Also to design training.

Level 4 is to design, deliver and evaluate training to meet individual and organisational objectives.

Level 5 is on the level of strategic design and identification of future requirements.

At the level of public certification the rules are fixed. The trainer needs to be competent beyond the level she is assessing and play the game according to the rules.

So evaluation is a simple idea, yet it changes like a chameleon depending on which point of view you take. The more points of view the more complete your map. The more complete your map, the more choice you have in where you go and the easier it is to get there.

---

## EVALUATING TRAINING

### *Key Points*

- Evaluation is the last stage in the training cycle.
- Evaluating systematically looks at the results of the training, notices the difference it has made and determines its value according to preset measures. These results are used as feedback to refine the training.
- Evaluation deals with the setting and achieving of objectives that are important to the individual or the organisation.
- Training may improve efficiency (same results and lower cost), effectiveness (better results at same cost) or productivity (better results at lower cost).
- There are four stages of evaluation:
    1. Live evaluation during the training.
    2. Evaluation after the training.
    3. Evaluation of the transfer of knowledge and skill into the individual's life and work.
    4. Organisational evaluation: how training furthers organisational goals.
- Evaluation provides feedback to improve the cycle.
- Evaluation may also be part of public assessment and certification.

---

# 24

# LIVE EVALUATION

## MONITORING THE TRAINING

Live course monitoring is like looking at the compass to check
you are on course – assuming you have charted a course in the
first place. Even your smallest bit of behaviour will have an
evaluation stage built into it, if it is purposeful. For example, think
about a time when you are making an important training point.
You evaluate in order to know when you have said enough to
continue.

During a seminar, evaluation is the process that lets you
know you have got your outcome and it is time to move on,
or you have not and need to do something else to get it.
Without this evaluation process, you might either leave a lot of
the group behind or bore them to tears. You need your attention
fully out, because the better you pay attention to the group, the
more accurate your evaluation will be. Good trainers will keep
track by continuous evaluation without thinking about it
consciously.

### Personal evaluation

You will want to evaluate your own performance to improve your
training skills. Are *you* satisfied, regardless of anyone else? Are you
getting your outcomes?

### Trainees' experience

You also need to second position the trainees to get their
description. As they see it, are they getting the outcomes you have
set for them? In your imagination, put yourself in their shoes and
read off your intuitions about what is going on in their experience.

This is a very powerful strategy for knowing what to do next and good trainers can do this uncannily accurately. However, it is another skill that works mainly at the level of unconscious competence, so they are unlikely to know consciously how they do it. To develop it for yourself, do it consciously whenever you remember. Set yourself an outcome for the training to do it at least every 20 minutes and always if you feel stuck. Make 'feeling stuck' a signal to do it immediately.

Even without this mental jump, the non-verbal behaviour of the group or individual can tell you a lot about what is going on.

If all else fails, ask straight out. A general question to the group like, 'How are you doing?' will get you some feedback. Ask the question and *look*. The verbal feedback may be useful, the non-verbal certainly will. In particular, watch the unconscious leader of the group. This is the person who most accurately reflects the state of the group. If he or she is satisfied then all is usually well. You can tell who the leader is in advance by watching for the person whose movements set other people moving. This is not easy to see as it happens, but if the group is on video you can pick it up afterwards by watching the video at double speed with no sound and noticing the patterns and ripples of movement. Look for their 'epicentre'. Larger groups (over about 18 people) will have more than one such leader.

Another way you can evaluate and get feedback is to ask the group where they would put themselves on a scale of one to ten, where one is semi-comatose and ten is a wonderful learning state. Ask them to notice where they are and if anyone is not satisfied with their own rating, invite them to explore how to change it in whatever way they can. If you build in this frame right from the beginning, you have set up a means not only for the group to track their learning state, but also for them to take more responsibility for it, instead of relying on you for stimulation.

You can ask for feedback in specific situations. For example, having just set up an exercise, you can use the straw poll technique with the whole group and ask for hands up on either 'Who is clear enough that you are ready to do the exercise?' or 'Who would prefer a final summary?' This evaluates readiness for a particular task. How well the exercise goes reflects how cleanly you set it up and so gives you more feedback. Seeing the difference between what you intended and what you actually got tells you how to change the set up next time. You can use the break times to review what you did, what happened and what you would do differently in future.

More informally, if you have noticed that particular people seem to be having some difficulty, you can ask them in break time, 'How is it going?' and find out their individual concerns.

### Evaluation from peers

Another live evaluation strategy – often the most useful – is from observers and peers. They may be apprentice trainers, co-trainers, training managers or training assessors.

Decide what kind of evaluation you want and ask for it. Take all opportunities. Feedback, as they say, is the breakfast of champions. Make sure you have the criticism strategy available to deal with any inept feedback and avoid indigestion. Remember, if it does not help you to do something differently, then it is not feedback.

### Combining evaluations

Taken together, these strategies enable you to collect evaluative descriptions from your own point of view, from the trainees' point of view and from that of any skilled observers. It is particularly important to have good feedback if the main focus of your training is the 'soft' areas of people skills rather than the 'hard' areas of technical skills. Soft training areas, which include interpersonal skills, personal development or attitude change, are notoriously difficult to evaluate.

One trainer's tip here: it is well worth keeping your trainer's learning log at the trainings with you, so that you can write down what you need to do before, or during, the next training.

The main weakness of live evaluation is the GIGO factor: garbage in, garbage out. In an organisation, if the Training Needs Analysis (TNA) is significantly off course in either trainee selection or training content, then your training is heading for the wrong destination anyway. To labour the metaphor, you may be an ace pilot, steer brilliantly, land at Heathrow and then find the passengers needed to go to the Bahamas. Live evaluation keeps you on the track that has been set. The TNA and your design based on it set the destination which is evaluated at a higher level.

## LIVE EVALUATION OF SKILLS

If you are training skills, there will be times when you want to evaluate the learner's skills during the training. If you are dealing with hard skills, technical or sensory-motor, there are usually fairly straightforward ways of doing this. For instance, with a sensory-motor skill like touch typing, you measure rate and accuracy, words per minute and error rate. If you are teaching more sophisticated computer skills, say desktop publishing, you can set a range of tasks and assess competency on the basis of these.

Evaluating interpersonal skills is much more subjective. When dealing with interpersonal skill such as coaching, you can start by breaking it into a few major component parts. For instance, one part is the skill of being able to elicit an achievable outcome. Next, you will need to design an exercise with the main purpose of assessing this part. This can be a role play in a simulated context as much like the real life situation as possible.

### Multiple description

Unreliability of assessment is going to be your biggest problem here and there are two main ways of tackling this. First, use a very skilled assessor. It may be a problem, however, for one person to get around to see a fair sample of all the trainees. Even when you have a very skilled assessor, get as many descriptions as possible by having more people doing the assessing. This can be some combination of trainers, line managers, assistants or trainees (peer and self-assessment). The descriptions do not have to agree. The more descriptions you get, the higher quality the information, and the better chance of coming to a fair and accurate evaluation. More people will also be able to cover all the trainees in the limited time available.

In practice, you can get good quality learning and assessment by combining skilled assessors with the multiple description of peer and self assessment.

Here is the outline of an example for assessing the skill of drawing out an achievable outcome. As you read through this example you might find it useful to substitute a skill that you are interested in assessing and think of the changes you would have to make to enable the process to work for your example.

### Identify key subskills

Dissect the skill into the minimum of necessary and sufficient subskills using Occam's razor (no more things should be assumed to exist than are absolutely necessary). In this case, the trainee will first need the rapport skills necessary to be able to build and maintain the relationship with her client so she can ask the necessary range of outcome questions.

## Rapport skills

* Body language rapport skills:
  the matching, pacing and leading of body language

* Voice quality rapport skills:
  the matching, pacing and leading of voice quality

* Verbal rapport skills:
  the matching and pacing of key words, beliefs and values

## Outcome elicitation skills

* Knowing the five basic criteria of achievability.
* Eliciting an achievable outcome with appropriate questions as necessary:
  1. Identify negative outcome statements and elicit positive alternatives.
  2. Identify statements with no ownership and elicit alternatives that are within the person's control.
  3. Identify statements that are too vague to be of use and elicit more specific alternatives.
  4. Identify any outcome that does not have sensory-based evidence and elicit what the missing evidence would be.
  5. Identify the wider-ranging consequences of achieving the outcome. Elicit alternative outcomes or actions that are needed to resolve possible problems.

### Identify the evidence for each

Specify your criteria of competence for each of the skills in question. Criteria need to be sensory-based evidence, i.e. what the observer would see, hear and feel that would let them know that a basic performance standard of competence had been met. For instance, the evidence for meeting the first of the criteria above would be, when you hear the client describe any outcome in the negative, the next question you hear from the operator must be designed to have the client turn the negative into a positive. For example, the response to 'I don't want "X"' is 'What would you rather have than "X"?'

### Design the exercise
Design an exercise structure that allows sufficient opportunities for the multiple assessments to take place. For example:

- 3 roles: operator, client, and observer
- 3 rounds of 15 minutes for each person in each role

- Operator's tasks:
    establish and maintain rapport with client
    identify an appropriate real problem chosen by the client
    use questions to enable the client to turn the problem into an outcome
    evaluate own performance

- Client's task:
    identify an appropriate real problem that you would like to explore
    be yourself
    notice what the operator does that helps or hinders you

- Observer's task:
    pay close attention to the interaction and look for behavioural evidence from the operator for each of the skills
    evaluate their skill levels

- Trainer's task:
    set up exercise
    manage time frames
    manage the team of assessors
    see each operator in action

Each person will have an assessment sheet with criteria for each of the skill parts.

| Strengths | Potentials | Rating |
|---|---|---|

Exercise . . . . . . . . . . . . .    Operator. . . . . . . . . . . .
Assessor . . . . . . . . . . . . .

**Outcome elicitation skills:**

| Strengths | Potentials | Rating |
|---|---|---|
| | areas for developing | |
| Key words | Key words | Score |
| to reflect | to reflect | out of 10 |
| verbal | verbal | |
| feedback | feedback | |

*Figure 4.1 Assessment sheet*

At the end of each round, there are 10 minutes for feedback and assessment:

2 minutes for the operator to give verbal self-assessment
2 minutes for the observer to give a verbal assessment to the operator
2 minutes for the client to give a verbal assessment to the operator
4 minutes for each person to fill in numerical scores and keywords on the assessment sheet for the operator

At the end of the round, the operator will have three assessment forms, one filled in by the client, one by the observer and one by himself.

Collect in all the assessment sheets, judge the skill of the assessors and weight them accordingly, say 3:1 assessors:trainees.

Calculate the weighted averages for each trainee for each of the main skills, starting with the first set, in this case outcome elicitation skills.

For example:

21 trainees
3 assessors
Trainee A scores 7 from the observer, 8 from client, 7 from self: Total 22
He gets 7 from each of three more skilled assessors. Total 21.

Multiply this by three to weight it: Total 63. Add this to the trainees' score: 63 + 22 = 85

Total number of scores (2 + self + 3 x 3 assessors) = 12 at a maximum of ten each

Weighted average = 85 out of a possible 120 = 70.83 per cent for outcome elicitation skills

The meaning of this figure will depend on the circumstances. For example, if it is substantially higher or lower than the overall average, then it is significant. Also if it is very much higher or lower than her scores for other skills on the sheet, that is also significant. Low scorers are candidates for extra coaching. High scorers are candidates for modelling how they achieve them, which is what you need to coach the low scorers.

Multiple description based assessment approaches are probably the best way of evaluating very subjective skills during a training. You can design a version to suit your needs.

---

## LIVE EVALUATION

### *Key Points*

- Live evaluation is done moment by moment during the seminar to check it is on track.
- Everything you do in the training that has purpose will have evaluation built in.
- The trainer will do live evaluation from three viewpoints:
    her own view (first position)
    the trainees' view – by intuition, asking and noticing non-verbal behaviour (second position)
    observers' and co-workers' view (third position)
- Live evaluation tracks your preset course. For full training evaluation in an organisation, you need to also look at the Training Needs Analysis.
- 'Hard' skills are relatively simple to measure quantitatively as rate, accuracy, quality.
- 'Soft' skills can be evaluated by multiple description assessment exercises.
- You can evaluate by combining multiple description and splitting the skill into smaller chunks by:

having a number of assessors
dividing the skill into subskills
deciding on criteria for competent performance
designing an exercise to test the subskills
pooling the different reports by the assessors

# SEMINAR EVALUATION

## Immediate evaluation

Immediate evaluation at the end of the seminar is the most commonly used evaluation process. The purpose of immediate seminar evaluation is:

- To look back objectively on the seminar. Notice what went well and what you would do to improve the seminar the next time you do it.
- To find out what the trainees thought of the seminar. Their feedback gives an important description of the training.
- To assess the seminar and your training skills from your personal point of view and to gather feedback from any peers.

Then you can evaluate your course outcomes from all three points of view.

## Self-evaluation

There are a number of actions you can take to make the training complete for yourself and learn the most from it:

- Try to predict the trainees' reactions before reading their feedback. This is useful for checking your second position skills. If you think they had a wonderful time and their written feedback is the opposite, you know you have some learning to do.

- Ask yourself what went well and what did not. You may change what you do next time for two reasons: one, what you did worked so well, it is no longer interesting, you want a fresh challenge by doing it differently; or two, what you did failed to achieve the outcome.

- Evaluate your process outcomes. Did you carry out the training tasks you set for your own self-development?

- Was the content of the seminar good? Are there any holes that need filling?

- Was the venue adequate? Is there any feedback you need to give here?

- Ask any peers at the training – co-trainers, assistants, training managers, assessors – for their feedback on the seminar and your performance.

- Give feedback to any colleagues on what they did.

- Make notes in your log of the key points and action to be taken.

## Evaluation by trainees

The classic form of seminar evaluation is a reaction questionnaire (also known as a 'happy sheet') completed by the trainees in the last 10 minutes or so of the seminar. The obvious weakness is that the trainees have not had enough time to assess what they have got from the training and may be pressed for time, so their response will not be carefully considered. Also, the responses you get will only be as useful as the questions you ask.

### Qualitative questions

The questionnaire will usually have two different kinds of questions. One kind is closed questions asking for numerical or quantitative evaluations of one or more 'soft' quality functions. This can be done either as a percentage or a mark out of ten or by ticking one of a series of options ranging from 'poor' to 'excellent'.

Be careful interpreting these figures. For example, you may get an 85 per cent average excellent rating from the group. Is that good? It depends on whether your usual average is 75 per cent or 95 per cent. An individual may rate you as poor because last week he had two amazing, transforming days with the world's top trainer.

These questions will pick up very dissatisfied individuals and very contented individuals. The group average will give you some benchmark over time of your training skill from the group point of view.

There will also be open-ended qualitative questions for the trainees to write brief answers to. For example:

What did you like most about the seminar?
What would you have most liked to have been different about the seminar?
What was the most useful learning that you made from the seminar?

One question might be as simple and open as, 'Please indicate your evaluation of the seminar.'

The strength of open-ended questions is that you can design them to gather information from people on whatever aspect of the training you want to know about. Trying to get any meaningful statistics from them, however, is a nightmare. Even compiling a useful summary is difficult. Stick with some simple rules. If roughly the same number of people say you went too fast as say you went too slow, then you know you got the pace about right. Conversely, if you only attracted comments about going too fast and none about going too slow, then you know that you needed to slow down.

In practice, most reaction feedback sheets will have a mixture of closed quantitative questions and open qualitative questions. Keep it brief and stay with as small a number of questions as you can. The questions above work well and only take five minutes to answer. Trainees will not appreciate a long and complex inquisition at the end of the day and if you insist on one, your feedback will be of much lower quality.

You do not have to try to cover every eventuality on the form, simply leave a space at the end marked 'Any other comments' to catch any issues not covered that people think are important. If a person asks to take the form home and complete it at their leisure, remember that if they do, you have a less than 10 per cent chance of getting it back.

Using a simple instrument like this can tell you a great deal (as long as you hold it constant through a period of time and do not keep tampering with it). For example, over the last six months the average rating of our NLP seminars was about 87 per cent, with a normal distribution ranging between the extremes of 79 per cent and 97 per cent. Individual trainee ratings showed a skewed distribution between 70 per cent and 100 per cent as shown in Figure 4.2.

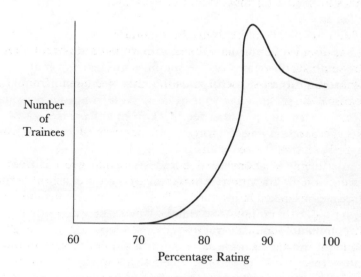

*Figure 4.2 Skewed distribution of individual trainees' ratings*

These kinds of very simple figures can be perfectly adequate as a baseline quality indication. Remember the saying, 'There are lies, damn lies and statistics.' Statistics can give any impression you like, depending on the context you put them in. Make sure they are comparing the same thing and then decide if any deviation is significant or not. If it is, then action is needed.

### Quality measure
The average numerical rating for each seminar correlated well with different trainers' evaluations of that seminar. Experienced trainers can predict the numerical rating of a seminar they have just given to within one or two percent. This gives us a numerical fix on the quality of each seminar and an important quality control measure of trainees' satisfaction. However gratifying it may be to us as trainers to get good scores on reaction sheets and however clear we are that enjoyment is a necessary precondition to learning, it tells us little about the learning that actually took place. For that we need a learning evaluation.

## SEMINAR EVALUATION

### Key Points

- The purpose of immediate seminar evaluation is:
  to look back objectively on the seminar and learn from it
  to find out what the participants thought of the seminar
  to assess the seminar and your training skills from your personal
  point of view and to gather feedback from any peers
- A self-evaluation is useful for:
  reviewing the whole training
  identifying what worked well and what you would change
- Evaluation by trainees is usually taken with a reaction form.
  Trainees are asked to give:
  a numerical rating to the training
  comments about the training
- You can use the numerical rating as a general quality control
  measure.
- You can use the written comments as feedback about their
  perceptions of the training.

# 26

# EVALUATING LEARNING

*Individual learning*

In the evaluation stage we are no longer concerned with the process of learning, only the results. How do you know that you have learned something? There has to be some change in the way you think or act. Trainees will take these changes back into their lives and work. The purpose of in-house training is that these changes lead to improved work performance and, perhaps, to a consequent improvement in organisational effectiveness. But it all starts with individual learning.

There are many different ways to think about what we learn and therefore what we evaluate. We will use knowledge, attitude and skills as a broad framework. These do not exist in isolation – any training will contain all three – but one will usually be predominant.

There have been several surveys of managers that ask the question: 'Why do subordinates fail?' The three answers that invariably come top of the list are:

1. They do not know *what* they are supposed to do. This is a lack of knowledge and also a sad comment on the prevalence of the 'mushroom system of management' (keep employees in the dark and cover them in manure).
2. They do not know *why* they should do it. This is the domain of values and attitude training.
3. They do not know *how* to do it. This is the arena of skills training.

Research also indicates that some two thirds of the causes of these problems are within the manager's control, not the subordinate's. Deming puts it at 90 per cent.

## KNOWLEDGE EVALUATION

Knowledge (remembered facts) is easy to evaluate with a multiple choice questionnaire, consisting of a number of questions, each with four or five possible answers. The trainee ticks their choice of answer. For example:

What does NLP stand for?

a) Natural Language Processing
b) Neuro-Linguistic Programming
c) Neighbourhood Living Project
d) Neuronal Lipopigment
e) Nano Longevity Processor

The correct answer is a), b), c) and d) (all these exist but we made up e)) – which shows the pitfalls of constructing such tests. The original question needs to be more specific, i.e. what does NLP stand for in this book?

Multiple choice questionnaires should be clear. Only include positive statements and do not give clues by repeating keywords in the correct answer. The incorrect answers should be plausible and in random order. To cancel out the effect of random guesses being correct, the scores should be re-scaled, so the number of correct answers you would get by randomly guessing becomes the baseline.

Using a multiple choice questionnaire at the end of a training will give you a measure of *knowledge*, but will not give you a measure of *learning* if you do not know how much the trainees already knew when they started the training course. To measure learning, that is, *change* in knowledge, you need a 'pre-test'. This is a similar questionnaire given at the start of training or in the workplace beforehand to measure the existing level of knowledge. Do not use the same questionnaire that you will use at the end, but make up a pre-test of similar kinds of questions. The difference in trainee scores between the pre-test and the post-test gives you a direct measure of on-the-course knowledge learning.

### Learning and difference

Here is an interesting proposal: the person who shows the greatest improvement in score, regardless of her absolute score, has learned the most. So a person that scored 10 per cent on pre-test and 60 per cent on post-test has learned more than her friend who scored 80 per cent and then 90 per cent.

If our target standard is 75 per cent, then 90 per cent passes and 60 per cent does not. However, if we are interested in learning, the 60 per cent scorer has learned more.

## Gain percentage

You can be more sophisticated and take a 'gain percentage' to allow for different pre-test scores. Calculate the gain percentage like this:

$$\text{Gain percentage} = \frac{\text{Post-test score} - \text{pre-test score} \times 100}{\text{Maximum possible score} - \text{pre-test score}}$$

Our first trainee would have a gain percentage of 55 per cent, the second 50 per cent.

This is a measure of how effective the programme was in teaching what an individual needed to learn. The average gain ratio over all the trainees gives a useful measure of course effectiveness. Research has shown that a good trainer mixing input and practice will average around 50 per cent. One-to-one tuition will show higher gains and individual computer-based training can exceed 70 per cent, whilst a talk with questions will be around 20 per cent.

In an organisation, knowledge will be taught in the belief that it is useful in the job that the person is returning to. It is worth checking this later with a questionnaire asking how useful the knowledge is in the job and, what, if any, difficulties the trainees have had in applying it.

## ATTITUDE EVALUATION

Evaluating attitude change is harder than evaluating either skills or knowledge. Attitudes are beliefs, values and opinions. They are on a higher level than skill and not easily influenced. Examples of attitude training would be training to engender a stronger drive towards customer service in a company's front-line staff or awareness training about racism, sexism and anti-discriminatory practice generally.

Effective skills training will influence attitudes, because to use a skill, you have to see some value in it. For instance, unless the training convinces you that certain communication skills are valuable, you may be able to use them perfectly, but still not bother. For the skill to actually make a difference in your life, you have to be motivated to use it and believe you can use it. This may involve an attitude change if you came to the training thinking these skills were not very useful. It may also involve a change in belief, if you didn't believe you could do it. So any skills training must install the beliefs and values that the skill is possible and valuable (if these did not exist already).

Beliefs and values do not increase skill level as such, but they are necessary if the person is to use the skill to the best of their ability. Attitude change will lead to changes in behaviour, but not necessarily to changes in skill. This is the reason why some 'interpersonal skill' training is disappointing. It is labelled skills training but it is really only attitude training.

## Attitude questionnaires

How do you measure a change in attitude, value or belief? What behavioural changes will there be as a result?

Attitude changes can be picked up in an informal way at the end of a course by asking such questions as, 'What have been the important things about this training?' and 'What will you do differently when you return to work?' To measure the change, there has to be some pre-test, usually by self-analysis or personality inventory. The same inventory after the training will pick up any changes, providing the person does not answer what he thinks the assessor wants to hear.

The simplest measure of change in attitude is a kind of self-analysis questionnaire called a 'semantic differential'.

## Semantic differentials

A semantic differential starts with a concept that is a belief or value and a scale to mark an opinion between two extremes. For example:

*'The meaning of the communication is the response it elicits.'*

> *Circle 1 if you strongly believe this is a useful concept.*
> *Circle 5 if you strongly believe it is a useless concept.*
> *Scores between indicate varying degrees of belief.*
> *Continue for each set of poles.*

| useful | 1 | 2 | 3 | 4 | 5 | useless |
|--------|---|---|---|---|---|---------|
| true | 1 | 2 | 3 | 4 | 5 | false |
| practical | 1 | 2 | 3 | 4 | 5 | academic |
| strong | 1 | 2 | 3 | 4 | 5 | weak |
| warm | 1 | 2 | 3 | 4 | 5 | cold |

*Figure 4.3 Semantic differential*

There are some interesting variations of this. First, the right-hand column can be left blank for the trainees to put their word for the opposite of the left-hand word. More radically, trainees can be invited to fill in both sides and supply seven pairs of opposite or complementary statements.

This can be expanded to a group exercise. Take the value, belief or attitude and ask the group to come up with possible descriptions of it. This way you can build up individual or group definitions of key attitudes. You can do it throughout the training and the descriptions the group generates are likely to become more sophisticated as they become clearer about what the value means in practice. This is where a skilled facilitator to manage the process is essential.

## Change in behaviour

Is an attitude change of any value if there is no change in behaviour? Can it be said to exist at all? What people do is a better indication of how they think than what they say. So when looking at changes in attitude, look for changes in behaviour.

There are a range of evaluation techniques called 'behaviour scales' that are designed specifically for evaluating changes in behaviour. Some of the pioneering work was carried out by Rackham and Morgan and is described in *Behavioural Analysis in Training* (1977). The following scales are adapted from their work:

**Supporting** involves a conscious and direct declaration of support or agreement with another person or concepts.

**Disagreeing** is a direct declaration of difference of opinion, or criticism of another person's concept, with reasons.

**Defending** defensively strengthens an individual's own position.

**Attacking** attacks another person and usually involves emotional displays and value judgments.

**Open** behaviour is the opposite of defending. It exposes the person who makes it to loss of status. For example, the admission of mistakes without excuses.

**Testing understanding** seeks to understand if an earlier contribution has been understood.

**Summarising** restates previous discussions.

**Proposing** puts forward a new concept or course of action.

**Building** extends or develops another person's proposal.

**Blocking** places a difficulty or block in the path of a proposal without offering either a reason or an alternative. For example: 'It won't work' or 'I can't do that.'

**Seeking information** seeks facts, opinions or clarification from others.

**Giving information** offers facts, opinions or clarification to others.

**Shutting out** tries to exclude another group member, for example by interrupting.

**Bringing in** is the opposite of shutting out and tries to directly involve another group member.

*Adapted from 'Categories of behaviour' in*
Evaluating Trainer Effectiveness *(McGraw-Hill, 1991) by Peter Bramley;*
*source:* Behavioural Analysis in Training
*(McGraw-Hill, 1977) by N. Rackham and T. Morgan;*
*used with permission.*

This list can be useful. It is quite specific and describes behaviour that we can see and hear happening frequently during an interaction. The behaviour is also described in plain English without jargon. You can tailor the list to suit different specific situations and count instances of particular behaviour before and after attitude training to evaluate changes.

For example, where a manager is coaching an employee you would expect a high rate of:

- bringing in
- seeking information
- testing understanding
- proposing
- supporting
- building

and a low rate of:

- shutting out
- blocking
- attacking
- defending

### Language

The other indication of change in attitude is what people say. Talking is behaviour and a very revealing one, although we do not usually think about it that way. It is easy to see how behaviour scales must be reflected in the language people use. Language and behaviour are integrated.

At present there is a great deal of awareness training in anti-discriminatory practice to counter racist, sexist and other forms of discrimination. Political correctness is the extreme result of making a simple link between language, attitude, thought and action. This is a vast subject, but there are two important issues for the trainer:

- A change in attitude will usually result in a change in language, but not vice versa. A person can easily use the right words without thinking or acting any differently.
- Language has many resonances at the personal, cultural and political level. It is so complex that it cannot be taken in isolation. Actions speak louder than words.

## SKILL EVALUATION

Actions, knowledge and values bring us to the area of skills. Skill is the ability to carry out some task consistently to a specified standard. There is a mental and a physical component to any skill. Mathematical skill is mostly mental, changing a car wheel is mostly physical. When modelling skills with NLP, you look at the physical actions, the beliefs and the thinking strategies as one integrated unit.

Skill evaluation can be based on tasks. There are two different ways of approaching this:

- A task is set and the result is inspected. It may be possible to measure the result quantitatively. If the skill is precision engineering, you can measure the results to see how they compare to industry standards. The skill may be complex, but the result can be easily measured numerically. There is also an issue of effectiveness here. One person may take one hour, another five hours to attain the standard. Most complex skills, however, cannot be measured so directly and interpersonal skills are particularly difficult to measure.
- A task is set and the trainee is observed throughout the task to see how he carries it out. This evaluates the method as well as the result and is much more useful. Results are only as good as the method used. If results are poor, you can analyse and evaluate the method to know what to change.

### Subjective evaluation

When the skills you are interested in are at the 'soft' end of the spectrum, and can only be assessed subjectively and qualitatively, for instance, leadership skills, then multiple description again becomes useful.

First, identify the key skills for assessment. What is most useful to assess? Then choose the best assessors. A multiple description by self, peer and manager is ideal.

Decide on the criteria for assessing the skill and make them as specific and clear as you can. Then design or choose the instrument for assessing. This can range from a simple questionnaire to actually using the skill under scrutiny. Have the different assessors pool their observations. You may want to use a weighted system. The descriptions do not have to agree. The more descriptions you get, the higher quality the information and the better chance of coming to a fair and accurate evaluation.

### Skill analysis

The NVQ approach is tailor made for evaluating more complex

skills. The skills are broken down into small components, each with an attached standard. The theory is that after achieving the standard for each, putting them together will give the whole integrated, complex skill.

When you use this approach of decomposing complex skills into their elements, however, you have to know when to stop, otherwise you could carry on dissecting to the point of confusion.

In Part Two, Before Training, we discussed learning by building up small chunks versus learning in large chunks at the unconscious level. Now we can integrate these two approaches, for how we learn a skill does not have to be the same as how we evaluate it. We can learn a complex skill in one piece and then evaluate its components. If we get the learning right, all the component elements will be there to evaluate by this method. So the evaluation stage is where the learner becomes conscious of all the subskills she has picked up unconsciously.

## Modelling projects

Whichever way you evaluate skills, you are likely to find an approximately normal distribution of capabilities – most people fall into the middle range, a few are top performers and a few are at the other end of the scale. The latter may do better if redeployed.

The top performers have skills and capabilities which are a potential gold mine in terms of developing organisational effectiveness and productivity. The problem is how to get at these riches. Now it is possible to model out from top performers exactly how they produce their outstanding results using NLP-based modelling techniques. You can then design training specifically to teach these effective strategies to the average performers to improve their results.

For example, we were called in by one of the well known car manufacturers in the UK who had reorganised their production into approximately 20 work teams, each with a team leader. Many team leaders were having problems, but three of them were superb. They were widely acknowledged to be the best. This kind of situation, where there are a few outstanding performers, is ideal for a modelling project to discover the differences that make a difference and then to make them available to everyone.

A typical sequence of events for this kind of work is as follows:

1. Preliminary interviews with the organisation to identify which set of competencies is most worth modelling, who the top performers are, how many people to model, what the budget is and to draw up an action plan.

2. Spend some time with each of the role-models, watching them in action in different contexts. Interview them to find out the beliefs, strategies, states and metaprograms they have about the skill that you are modelling from them. Interview their colleagues to get their descriptions.

3. Watch some average performers in the same contexts. Interview them to get the same information as you got from the top performers. Get the views of their colleagues too.

4. Make a contrastive analysis to find out what the top performers are doing that the average performers are not. Find out the critical differences between the top performers and the controls.

5. Test your results. If you can teach an average performer to get the same results as the top performers with your model, you know you have got the critical differences. If you cannot, you need to go back and refine your model.

6. Write up the full report to include the original brief, the methodology and the explicit model. This model covers the levels from identity, beliefs and capabilities through to mental strategies.

7. Design a training to teach the model to the average performers, in co-operation with the organisation's trainers. If all goes smoothly, train their trainers to run it and move on.

Steps 1 to 6 are likely to take somewhere in the order of 20 days' work, with step 7 taking perhaps half as long again.

These modelling and training packages are now widely used by many organisations in different countries.

Modelling can also be used to research important areas of interpersonal skills. For instance, Fiat became concerned about assuring that their future leaders were of the highest quality, since this was a critical part of their organisational development strategy. They called in NLP trainer and developer Robert Dilts to do a major research project using modelling to identify exactly the skills that good leaders use. One of his findings was a range of strategies for creating a shared culture.

Modelling without the training is also used in recruitment for particular tasks. Basically, you model the top performers and screen for similar skill patterns in recruits. In different ways NLP modelling is coming into its own in the nineties as a key technology of the learning organisation (see Business Consultancy Services).

---

## EVALUATING LEARNING

### *Key Points*

- Evidence for learning is a change in the way we think and act.
- Evaluation measures the results of learning, not the process.
- Learning can be knowledge, attitude and skills.

KNOWLEDGE
- Knowledge can be tested with multiple choice questionnaires, and gain ratios can be calculated to show how effective the training was in imparting what each trainee needed to learn.

ATTITUDE
- Attitudes are beliefs and values. Changes in beliefs do not necessarily mean a change in skill level, but may be necessary for a person to use the skill.
- Attitudes can be measured by a values questionnaire before and after the training and the difference can be evaluated.
- The best way to evaluate attitude is by change in behaviour.
- You can use behaviour scales to measure the strength and frequency of particular behaviour to evaluate change.
- A change in attitude will result in a change in the language a person uses, but not necessarily vice versa.

SKILLS
- There are two ways of measuring skills:
  set a task and measure results
  set a task and assess the method used to do it

- These two ways can be combined.
- The results can often be measured quantitatively.

EVALUATING BY MULTIPLE DESCRIPTION
- Soft skills, such as interpersonal skills, can be evaluated by multiple description.
- You can evaluate by multiple description by:
  having a number of assessors
  deciding on criteria for competent performance
  designing an instrument to assess the skill
  pooling the different evaluations by the assessors

S/NVQS
- The S/NVQ approach divides complex skills into small pieces and attaches standards to each piece. The complex skill is built piece by piece.
- Skills do not have to be learned in the same way as they are evaluated.

MODELLING
- In any skill assessment there will be top, average and poor performers.
- Modelling enables you to make explicit how top performers produce top results.
- You can then design training to pass these skills on to average performers.
- Modelling can be used for researching soft skills and for recruiting top performers.

# TRANSFER EVALUATION

By evaluating your trainings, you can make them more efficient. The next question is, how effective are they? How well do they transfer out to the workplace where managers and supervisors will be looking for improved performance? How well do they transfer out into the person's life, where he wants to make changes? A training may work brilliantly in the training room, but how can we ensure it transfers beyond those walls?

Much educational research makes it very clear that learning is state dependent and tends to be anchored to the place, situation and people present at the time. Interpersonal skills are easy to apply among friends in a supportive environment, with a good trainer to manage the process. On a wet Monday morning back at work, it is a different matter. Even the word 'work' can change someone's state of mind in our culture.

## LEARNING TRANSFER

There are three ways to think about learning transfer. One is to do all we can to prepare for the change in environment. Future pacing or mental rehearsal achieves this. Second, we need to be able to measure changes after the training to provide evidence of successful transfer. The third way is to provide the maximum support for trainees back in their personal or professional life.

### Future pace

Future pacing is mental rehearsal, imagining using the new skills in the place you want them. This is an essential part of any training programme and accomplishes three goals:

- It reminds trainees' that they will have to transfer the skills to another reality.
- It reinforces the learning through mental rehearsal.
- It acts as a safety net for problems.

Include possible difficulties and their solution in the future pace instructions by saying something like, 'As you imagine carrying out this skill back at your work, notice any factors that might make it difficult to do. As you notice them, begin to think what you can do to get round those problems and do it *now*.' You can also use the new behaviour generator as described on page 114.

This will bring out some anticipated problems and trainees can share solutions in a discussion group. The trainer can also tell stories of difficulties and how the heroes of those stories overcame them. A final session of pre-emptive dragon killing and fire fighting is a good preparation for going out into the world and doing battle.

Skills are much more likely to transfer from the training room if you can touch the levels of beliefs, values and identity in the trainees. The skills will then become part of the personality and be seen as valuable anywhere, for these levels are higher than the environmental level. The neurological levels integration exercise at the end of the last section (see page 191) will help here.

## Outcome setting

It is sometimes difficult for individuals on a public training course to evaluate how far it has helped them to make changes in their life. On a public course, few people go with any specific outcomes, while some go with such large, unrealistic outcomes such that they are bound to be disappointed. Disappointment, as they say, needs adequate planning. In the end, it is down to the individual's subjective feeling about the course and their (mostly unconscious) values of balancing time and money spent against results achieved.

There are ways trainers can encourage trainees to evaluate their own experience and make sure what they learn does transfer out into their life.

- Get everyone to set outcomes as one of the first priorities on the course.

- Encourage the trainees to separate these outcomes from their feelings about the course. They will enjoy it (you hope), yet you must be willing to court unpopularity in your attempts to help them get their outcomes. You may push people hard and perhaps seem unsympathetic in order to get change. So, although this book puts emphasis on training being fun, you may override this in the short term, for the trainees' long-term benefit.

- Outcome diaries are a good idea. It can be hard to keep track of outcomes consciously and easy to miss the fact that you achieved what you wanted. Once these diaries have been started, encourage trainees to review them, at least monthly.

- Tell trainees that others will react differently to them. This can be a valuable confirmation for them that there has been progress. If nothing changed in their life, that would be bad news indeed, so encourage them to look for differences.

- Remind trainees to watch for indirect consequences of their changes. Other people in their lives, especially their spouses, close friends and relations, have certain fixed expectations of them. Acting radically differently can upset their nearest and dearest. One move a trainer can make is to actually encourage people to *pretend* to be the same for a time and introduce the changes gradually. This is a nice move because it paces the change into their life, respects their relationships and puts them in control of the process of showing the changes.

- There may be other issues of ecology. There is a story of the time when John Grinder was teaching precision questioning skills, known as the Meta Model, for the first time in a Linguistics class at the University of California, Santa Cruz, in the early 1970s. This model is about asking very specific, sometimes challenging questions to get clear information. The next week most of the class came in looking extremely dejected. They had alienated their lovers and antagonised their friends by using the questions constantly. So supporting skills may be necessary for transfer of learning. In this case the skills had transferred all too well, but, lacking the supporting skills of rapport, had backfired. Without rapport the skills were too risky to use. The students also used them indiscriminately and too enthusiastically.

## Follow-up support

Follow-up after the training will help support the trainees. Keeping in touch with other trainees, practice groups and distance learning packages all help. In the NLP Practitioner trainings run by John Seymour Associates, trainees are strongly encouraged and helped to network and form practice groups. There is a newsletter every four months and an annual reunion to which trainees past and present are invited. A supportive network is important in keeping new skills alive in a neutral or unfriendly environment.

## TRANSFER TO THE ORGANISATION

The trainer is responsible for, and directly influences, only one part of the training cycle in an organisation. How well it transfers depends not only on the training, but also on how well the whole training cycle is handled:

### Selection of trainees

Organisations are looking for improved results. If the wrong people are selected for training, however well motivated they are and however brilliant the training, the *organisational* results will be disappointing. The trainer may get the blame. And yes, this is unfair. The more the trainer can be involved as a consultant in the whole training cycle, the more effective the results.

### Preparation of the trainees

Trainees need to be properly prepared and briefed, so they have reasonable expectations of the training. Pre-testing may need to be done, so changes can be evaluated afterwards.

### Motivation

Good preparation will ensure the trainees are motivated and see the training as valuable to themselves as well as the organisation they work for. Without motivation, there will be little learning and so little to bring back anyway.

### Course content

This is rather obvious, yet trainings do still trip up here. Check the competencies you are going to install are the ones that will make a difference. You can brilliantly install the wrong set of competencies in trainees. They then go back to work and find they are really good at just those skills that are not needed . . . Answer: be involved with the Training Needs Analysis at an early stage. Keep good lines of communication with the line managers and check that you are training what is required. If this analysis is mistaken, the skills you install will not get the required results. You may still get the blame . . . albeit unfairly.

**Measurement**

First make sure you have a measure of trainees' competence before training, otherwise you will not have a baseline from which to evaluate any changes. Know how trainees will be tested or appraised at the end of the training, before you start the training, so you can prepare them for the appraisal. You do not want trainees to get an unpleasant surprise on their return to work when they find out they are unprepared for the evaluation.

**Organisational system**

Finally, work factors beyond the trainees' control may make change impossible back at the workplace. Trainees may have an unsupportive line manager. More worrying still, the whole management system may unintentionally work against the changes. Any change in overall performance may be absorbed and lost by poor management practice down the line. Trainees may have the means and the capability but lack the chance to use what they know.

One of the challenges for the would-be learning organisation is how to create a culture in which effective learning can be recognised and valued. To do this, a trainer needs the skills of an internal consultant and change agent. This means integrating training more closely into organisational planning and the trainer working more closely with management. This move gets you two major steps forward. First, you get ready access to trainees where it matters, in their working environment. You can use this access to gather information for the Training Needs Analysis as well as to evaluate the transfer of learning. Second, and perhaps more important, you can form a co-operative partnership by involving managers in the process of designing and assessing improvements in effectiveness.

## Measuring performance

Performance is another difficult word to make sense of. It is usually defined as simply executing a task. We will take it to mean how an individual puts together their knowledge and skills to achieve their goals: a total measure of what they do.

Performance seems to consist of three main factors:

- The person must *want* to do the task. This is the area of motivation and values. The person needs to be drawn to do the task and feel it is important and valuable. If the task clashes with individual beliefs and values, the person will not be congruent and performance will suffer. This is the area of attitude and values training.

- The person must have a *chance* to do the task. If he does not get adequate opportunity, he is unlikely to get a good rating on performance.

- He must also know *how* to do it. This is dealt with by knowledge and skills training.

You need to measure performance in order to measure transfer. Performance is usually evaluated immediately after training and on a continuous basis by appraisal systems.

## Measuring transfer

Transfer of skills makes the jump from training efficiency to training effectiveness. If we can measure the changes in work performance after training, then we have supporting evidence for its effectiveness.

We can draw on the NVQ movement to assess competencies and their component skills. NVQ insists that competencies are assessed in the workplace or as close as possible to it. Whatever you are training, take a leaf from the NVQ book and hold the pre-training test and the post-training test in the workplace, so they compare like with like.

From Deming and the TQM movement we have another wealth of measuring and continuous improvement processes. Both manager and employee can be involved in designing ways and scales to measure performance back at work. The trainer can be involved as a consultant. The scales must assess whatever seem to be the most significant variables affecting overall job effectiveness. Remember the Pareto principle: 80 per cent of the results come from 20 per cent of the work. Target the important 20 per cent. You can do this by constructing so-called 'Pareto charts':

- Take the category that you are investigating, for example, customer complaints.
- Next count the number of instances of customer complaints in defined areas and plot a graph:
- Now take the category that has the most complaints and break it down again into categories with the associated figures:
- You can continue this process and pinpoint the important areas very quickly. (In Figure 4.4 component A is the clear culprit.)

Once you have decided what to measure, the next step is deciding how to measure it. You may be able to take hard, numerical measures or soft measures, depending on what you are measuring. A manager may be judged on the output of the department or on staff morale. A salesperson's performance is easily measured as volume of sales made, a production line worker's by the number of pieces produced per hour. You can use all the evaluation measures for learning described in the last section. You can also make up your own behavioural scales to suit the needs of the organisation you are working in.

## Transfer principles

- Make the training context as similar as possible to the working context. The amount of learning transfer is going to depend directly on how many crucial elements are the same in the job and the training situation. For example, psychomotor skills do transfer well, because the feedback given in training is essentially the same as the feedback that is given in the workplace. By contrast, communication skills do not transfer well because the feedback is artificial to the training situation. If the people in the training are not the same people that the trainee will be working with, this makes it doubly difficult.

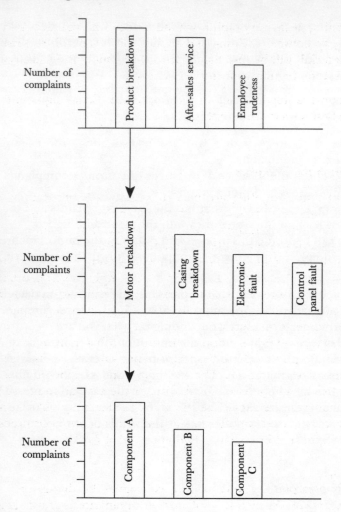

*Figure 4.4 Pareto charts*

- Encourage the trainees to set outcomes when they return to work. Make sure there are clear evidence, measures of progress and time-scales to achieve the outcomes. PC-based computer software is available to support this process (see Business Consultancy Services). The individual may use it at work to track outcomes. It can be linked both to specific training and to existing appraisal schemes.

- Trainees need to use the skills immediately. Memory and

learning decay very rapidly without review and practice. With a big gap between training and application it is hardly surprising that a skill will be lost. Safety procedures such as fire drills are best done regularly for this very reason.

- Support is needed back in the workplace. Coaching is one of the best ways to achieve this.

## Support in the workplace

Support and debriefing are needed at work for the training to transfer, otherwise a nasty vicious circle can operate. Individuals want training. Managers sometimes think that training is a necessary evil that has to be done and begrudge time away from the workplace. Once trainees return, however, it's time to get down to some 'real work'. Debriefing may simply consist of asking: 'Had a good time then?' Comparison with training in athletics shows how ridiculous this attitude is. Training is an integral part of improving performance.

When a person does not feel supported in his training and the manager does not believe training actually does much good, the training is less effective. The more training is marked out as different and separate from 'real work', the less it will transfer. The more managers are supportive, the more the learning will transfer. Ideally, off the job training is integrated into a continuous process that is supported by coaching and appraisal at work.

### Coaching

Coaching is guiding and helping colleagues by discussion and guided activity. As such it is valuable in organisations, quite apart from its function in transferring learning from training. It is one way the learning organisation continuously supports and improves the performance of the individuals who work in it. Coaching builds confidence as well as solving specific problems.

The interpersonal skills needed in coaching may not come easily and training in this area is an excellent investment. It has two main benefits: managers gain the skills to coach others and improve their performance; and coaching skills are also valuable interpersonal and managerial skills in their own right. More and more companies are investing in this sort of interpersonal skills training, and NLP skills are particularly useful and widely used in this area. This avoids the problems of the 'people principle' – managers are promoted to the level at which their people skills render them incompetent – the lesser known corollary of the 'Peter principle' – people are promoted to their level of incompetence.

Coaching needs good interpersonal skills such as gaining rapport, non-judgemental listening, asking useful questions and giving constructive feedback. These skills are particularly useful in a situation where an employee has failed in some task, for example, not completing a report on time. Feedback about poor performance is best done on a specific instance and made in the following terms. The coach states his own feelings or thoughts about the employee's behaviour, gives the reason and the consequences, and says what he would rather see. So in this example a coach might say: 'I notice you did not hand in the report on time this month. This made my work difficult without those figures and we could not complete the monthly sales figures on time. How can we make sure that next month's report gets in on time?' An example of inept feedback would be: 'Why do you always hand in your reports late?' To generalise and then blame, based on a specific instance, is particularly unhelpful and undermines future work as well as the relationship.

### Appraisal

Supporting and evaluating training can also be built into the appraisal process. In an appraisal, performance and outcomes can be reviewed and ways of measuring them agreed. Reverse appraisal is a growing practice in more enlightened companies. In a reverse appraisal, the person having their performance reviewed also gets to review the performance of their appraiser. Many companies have discovered that it is quite normal for managers to have an unrealistically high view of their interpersonal skills compared to the descriptions of those who report to them. Since the manager's people skills are very important, a reverse appraisal gives good feedback.

There is a second advantage to this practice: employees and managers at every level can look at outcomes and performance through several layers of management and see the degree of alignment (if any). Any wild mismatch will show up by comparing outcomes in the different management levels. Again, there is PC-based computer software to handle this process (see Business Consultancy Services). The very act of looking starts to make everyone aware of the systemic alignment in the organisation (or lack of it). Without alignment, everyone may be working very hard yet pulling in different directions, so the harder they work (because business is not going well), the more it pulls apart and the worse business gets. This is a good example of how treatment designed to fix the symptom actually makes it worse.

Mutual appraisal is one instance of systemic thinking in an organisation, which brings us neatly on to how training can be evaluated throughout the whole organisation.

## TRANSFER EVALUATION

### *Key Points*

- Trainings may be efficient, but are not always effective, because learning is lost when the trainee resumes normal life and work.
- Learning is state dependent, it becomes associated with the place it was acquired and the people who were there at the time.
- To deal with the problem of transfer, trainers need to:
    future pace it in the training
    be able to measure change to give supporting evidence for transfer
    provide maximum support for trainees after the training and encourage transfer by getting trainees to:
        set outcomes
        separate their feelings from their outcomes
        get multiple descriptions of changes from people in their life
        watch for the ecology of their changes
        ensure they have the supporting skills required
- How well learning transfers depends on the whole training cycle:
    the initial selection, preparation and motivation of trainees is important
    the Training Needs Analysis must be accurate
    trainees must be prepared for evaluation
    managers and the management system must be supportive

- As training is becoming more integrated into the organisation, the trainer's work broadens to include management consulting.
- Performance is a measure of motivation, opportunity and skill. It needs to be measured in some way for transfer evaluation both immediately after the training and in an ongoing appraisal.
- NVQ assesses competencies and component skills in the workplace.
- Behavioural scales can be made in consultation with management to evaluate key performance indicators and ways of measuring them. Key areas can be identified by such means as Pareto charts.
- Principles for successful transfer:
  make the training context as similar as possible to the working context
  encourage trainees in outcome setting when they return to work (this can be part of a formal appraisal process)
  trainees need to use the skills immediately
  provide support back at the workplace

COACHING

- Coaching is one way of providing support in the workplace.
- Coaching guides and supports colleagues and helps solve specific problems.
- Support for training and evaluating learning and transfer can also be built into the appraisal process.
- Mutual appraisal through different levels of management is one way of starting to look at systemic alignment in the organisation.

# 28

# EVALUATION IN THE ORGANISATION

If you think training is expensive – try ignorance.

*Anon*

Now we have reached the highest level of evaluation. The role of training in organisational change and development is a vast labyrinth. Our aim is to give a brief and practical thread as a guide.

## THE ORGANISATIONAL SYSTEM

Training courses train individuals, and individuals learn, grow and develop. A group is more than the sum of the individuals in it and the effectiveness of an organisation is more than the total effectiveness of each person in it. We have come full circle and need to think systemically. Organisations are complex systems; you cannot change them by simply changing the individuals in them. How can we look at training as part of the total system and start separating the effects of training from all the other changes that are happening?

Organisational systems share some common properties:

### Culture
This is embodied in the values and the mission statement of the organisation. It is a potent, though intangible aspect. To appreciate what a difference in culture can mean, think of IBM and then think of Apple computers. Or think of Virgin under Richard Branson and then think of the Disney empire. Culture answers the question, 'What is it like to work for this company?'

### Process
This is the production system and the goods and services it

supplies – anything from making microchips to running a rail network. The processes keep the organisation alive.

**Structure**
This is how all the parts fit together, what management systems there are and how they communicate.

There are also two other aspects on a different level. The first is how and what is measured both in the hard, numerical measurements and the soft, non-quantitative ones. Measurements seem so objective, but it all depends on your viewpoint. A million pounds may represent double the company's turnover or a tenth of it. What significance it has depends on the context it is in. One or two rude telephonists may lose a company dozens of orders. If you do not pay attention to these sorts of interpersonal skills, you will not notice their effect on the business.

Secondly, there is the overview or the *metaview*: how the organisation relates to the outside environment and other businesses, for example, co-operatively or competitively.

Training may be targeted at any of these organisational aspects. Most training goes for the process, to make the production more efficient or effective through increasing people's skills, although attitude training may seek to influence culture, usually unsuccessfully, as culture tends to arise as a by-product of the other aspects. It is very hard to influence directly.

The important point is that the training will fizzle or sizzle depending on all these aspects and changing one aspect on its own may not change the effectiveness of the whole organisation. The culture may stamp on the new process skills or the measurements set up may simply not detect any change, because they are not looking in the right place. Training needs strategic planning for the total effect of a training programme to exceed the sum of its parts.

Look at all the different aspects of the organisation to explore training effectiveness. Measurements of training effectiveness may be taken at the structure level. Here training can make a difference to communication between different parts of the organisation. Look at organisational culture too, and those intangibles such as staff morale, a feeling of belonging and commitment to the organisation. The level of staff motivation, job satisfaction and satisfaction with the system of rewards are all examples of these softer issues. They are not easy to measure directly, but what you can look at is the incidence of problems when staff morale is low:

- staff turnover (and therefore retraining and efficiency costs)
- absenteeism
- medical visits
- accident rates
- stoppages
- grievances
- official and unofficial complaints

All of these can be very costly if they happen consistently, so training in interpersonal skills can be an excellent investment.

In any complex system, trying to maximise only one part of the system stresses the other parts and the whole actually works less well. This simple piece of applied systems thinking may be the reason why businesses are less viable than we are. Three-quarters of businesses die in infancy and the others average 40 years. Keep the whole system in mind and think of profit as an evidence of success and not an outcome to be achieved at all costs.

## Cost analysis

With that caveat in mind, all organisations understand measurement by money. Many businessmen argue that the whole purpose of a business is to make money, perhaps not making the distinction between money as a by-product or as an end-product. So one way you can evaluate training is by cost analysis. Bear in mind that many organisations think of training as a cost that they cannot afford and forget the cost of ignorance. Training is in fact an investment they cannot not afford to make.

There are two ways of doing cost analysis on training. One is that given the organisational objectives, training is the most cost-effective way of achieving them of all possible choices. This is cost-effectiveness comparison. The second is to show that the increase in performance that training would bring is greater than the cost of the training. This is cost benefit analysis.

### Cost-effectiveness comparison

When you compare training costs with other methods, do a

thorough costing. The cost of training will minimally include:

• The cost of maintaining the training department.

• The cost of design. As a rule of thumb for training, allow seven days' design (research and development) for every one day delivered. With computer-based learning this ratio can reach 400:1.

• The cost of actually running the event: fees, expenses, accommodation, equipment, food.

• The cost of evaluation: follow-up interviews and questionnaires.

• The cost to the organisation of the trainees' attendance on the course rather than working.

## Cost benefit analysis

Studies from the TQM movement have shown that manufacturing businesses commonly have quality problems that are costing them about 25 per cent of gross turnover. If you think that is high, service businesses commonly have quality problems costing 35 per cent to 40 per cent of gross turnover. The organisations are typically unaware of these hidden costs and consider the situation normal. This is why there is gold in continuous improvement. You frame your training costs as investments that can show an impressive rate of return.

For example, some years ago, Girobank decided to improve quality at their main processing centre through 69 one-day quality awareness workshops. The follow-up studies showed an estimated £1,000,000 saving from an investment of £25,000 in training. This is an impressive return on investment.

Another option here is to look at value added to employees. After training they should perform better and be more valuable to the organisation. Think about it this way. Any group of employees will have different skill levels. Whatever the absolute levels, about 40 per cent will be near average, about 25 per cent will be below average and about 5 per cent pretty poor. Twenty-five per cent will be above average and 5 per cent really excellent. In other words, what is known as a normal distribution.

As we saw in the last chapter, this is fertile ground for a modelling project. An NLP consultant can set up a project to model the outstanding 5 per cent and then design a training course to transfer the expertise of that 5 per cent to the others. Modelling the top performers and teaching the skills in the workplace would take care of most of the transfer issues. Effectiveness can be evaluated using the measures that had already been used to decide who the top performers were.

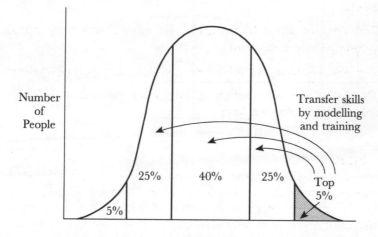

*Figure 4.5 Normal distribution curve of skills*

Motivation levels will follow a similar pattern, but you cannot assume the most skilled workers will be the most motivated. The very top group who are both highly motivated and highly skilled can be considered for promotion (after the modelling project). Those with low skills and low motivation can be considered for redeployment. Training either of these groups is a poor investment. For those who are poorly motivated yet have the skills, the best investment would be supervisory and coaching training for the next level of management. For the majority of average motivation and skill, training is a good option and added value can be calculated as a proportion of their salary.

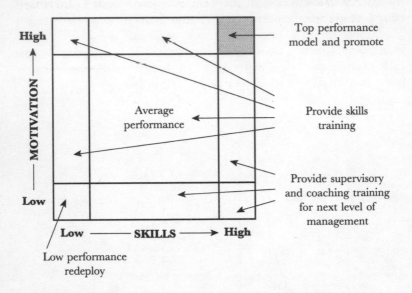

*Figure 4.6 Options for a group of different performance levels*

This sort of analysis is important for targeting training. If the training can provide an improvement in motivation and/or skills to a significant part of the workforce, it is going to make a difference to the organisation. Value added calculations can assess the value of soft benefits and prevent them from being ignored simply because they are hard to assess.

The other aspect of systems is that there may be a time lag between cause and effect. The training investment is made up front, while the benefits will typically accumulate over a number of years with the kind of investment payback curve shown in Figure 4.7.

All good training will produce some benefit. The trainer's job is to target the area of most benefit and present it to the managers in a clear way. This analysis must include:

- the benefit
- the cost
- the cost of alternatives

The benefit may be in terms of increased profit, either by

increasing efficiency (same performance, lower cost) or increased effectiveness (better performance, same cost).

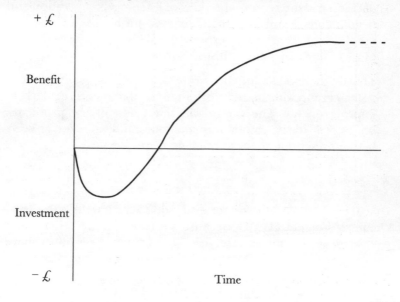

*Figure 4.7 Investment payback curve*

## TEAM DEVELOPMENT

The team is the intermediate step between individual and organisation. By tracking only individual performance, you will miss out on group performance in different parts of the organisation. Team building is an important part of the training function. There are three main approaches:

- First, you can increase the awareness of group dynamics and team roles. Teams need balance – for example, a team of very creative people may plan unrealistically without someone to keep their feet on the ground. Belbin (1981) describes useful models of roles to balance a team (see Bibliography).

- Secondly, interpersonal skills training may improve communication and co-operation in teams. The more complex the task, the more important the relationships within the group.

Simple puzzles require only that the individuals in the team be competent, polite and organised. Problems like strategic decision making require the skills of listening, co-operation and negotiation. Employee management problems will further require high levels of interpersonal skills, thinking skills and those of disclosing and utilising feelings.

• Thirdly, there is the 'quality circle' approach. A quality circle is a small group with shared work interests that meets regularly to improve quality. The group will select and define problems, brainstorm ideas, gather information and search for answers before presenting them to management.

## Quality

One of the best places to go for evaluation instruments is the Total Quality Movement (TQM), because it is based on the belief that if you want to be more effective at anything, you must have appropriate measures of performance in order to know if you are improving it.

It's worth thinking about the word 'quality' a little more deeply. It can be a descriptive adjective, for example a quality car. When it is used as a noun it is abstract, you cannot hold it in your hand. What do you have to do to get quality? What is the hidden verb? It has to be 'assessing', 'qualify' or 'quantify'. Now we have several more questions:

• Who is assessing? (subject)
• What is being assessed? (object)
• What are the criteria being applied?
• What are the threshold values for the criteria? (A threshold is a standard that must be met without exception. Otherwise it is a guideline.)

An example would be a quality racing car (object) for a driver (subject) for whom top speed (criteria) must be more than 150 mph (threshold). In a service industry like the Post Office, an example would be a first-class letter delivery service for the customer (subject) delivering the letter (object) on the next day (threshold).

In quality measurements, the customers are the sole setters and assessors of quality. They set the criteria and the threshold value. Every quality programme stresses this and goes to great pains to find out what the customer wants. Market positioning is about installing criteria and thresholds in the target market. The organisation knows if it has got it right by customer response: do they come back for more? The meaning of organisational action is determined by the response it gets from the customer.

Traditional organisations match specifications and try to get the same standard. The TQM approach seeks continuous improvement by looking for difference. It looks for what is wrong in order to improve it and is not content to do what it has always done. It is more future oriented than traditional approaches. The organisation is only as effective as its weakest part.

Organisations often use *benchmarking*: a process of comparing your performance with the market leaders in your field. Here you use your best competitors as your yardstick. Quality becomes a measure of organisational effectiveness. If training can improve the quality of the product, whether it be machine tools or customer service, by the customer's criteria and threshold, as measured by the customer, then it more than justifies the investment in it.

You will have noticed that the TQM thinking has some overlaps with NVQ. Both specify quality. The NVQ structure has a Lead Body (subject) that makes the measurements of training (object). It has a five-part structure of levels of competence (criteria). It measures competencies to defined standards (thresholds).

Just as the NVQ approach does not tell you *how* to reach the standards, so TQM does not spell out *how* the trainer can make a difference. NLP does precisely this.

Knowing *what* to target needs applied systems thinking.

## QUALITY TRAINING

The recurring theme of this book is that training is customer driven. Training is not something you do to a group, it is a two-way process, a mutual interaction. At its best, you cannot tell who is leading and who is following. At the organisational level, your customer is the organisation. Trainers have to come up with a language, structure and content of a first-class specification for training and then communicate it. In the actual delivery, your customer is the group. Find out customer criteria, standards and success measurement and meet them. That is the secret of successful training. Simple, isn't it?

We started this book with the changes in organisations and how this influences training, and we have come full circle. There is a dance between training and organisational development. Sometimes one leads, sometimes the other. Leading will always work if you lead where the other party wants to go, otherwise it is called 'pulling'. The learning organisation creates the type of training that will create it. The values of the learning organisation and the training that creates it – learning, empowerment, and self-development – are worth working for. Especially as it becomes more satisfying to do so.

NVQ competency-based approaches give us a way of thinking about skills that we train and skills that we use. NLP gives us the means to develop them. The learning organisation gives us the context and values. Quality is the target, people are the focus, and the challenge to you, the trainer and developer, is to thrive on these opportunities. Few are as privileged.

We began this book with the quotation:

May you live in interesting times.

You do. This was understood as a curse. Now, it may be a blessing in disguise . . .

---

## EVALUATION IN THE ORGANISATION

### *Key Points*

- Organisational evaluation must address two problems:
    organisations are complex systems and more than the sum of individual performance
    how to separate the effects of the training from all the other processes
- There are three main parts to an organisational system:
    culture: corporate values
    process: production of goods and services
    structure: management systems and communications
- There is also the measurement aspect: what and how things are measured; and the metaview: how the business relates to other organisations.

- Training may target any one of these aspects to increase organisational effectiveness. Usually it is process.
- Look at all the different aspects of the organisation to evaluate training effectiveness.
- There are two ways to evaluate by cost analysis:
     show that given the organisational objectives, training is the most cost-effective way of achieving them of all the possible choices (cost-effectiveness comparisons)
     show the increase in performance that training would bring is greater than the cost of the training (cost benefit analysis)
- Cost benefit analysis can use resulting improvement in quality and value added to employees in evaluating the training.
- The trainer can present an analysis detailing:
     a measurable benefit in efficiency and/or effectiveness
     the cost
     the cost of alternatives
- Team building is a connection between individual and organisation.
- Training can increase awareness of group dynamics and team roles.
- Interpersonal skills training can improve communication and co-operation.
- Quality circles are small groups with shared work interests that meet regularly to improve quality and plan action.
- TQM is based on the belief that if you want to be more effective at anything, you must have appropriate measures of performance.
- Quality is an abstract noun deriving from the verb 'to qualify' or 'measure'.
- In quality measurements, the customers are the sole setters and assessors of quality. They set the criteria and the threshold value.
- Quality can be a measure of organisational effectiveness. If training can improve the quality of the product, measured by the customer's criteria and threshold, then it justifies the investment.
- NLP and systemic thinking are tools to improve quality.
- Organisations are trainers' customers. Trainers need to discover and meet their standards, criteria and the way they measure and meet them.
- The learning organisation creates the training that will create it through values of empowerment and learning.

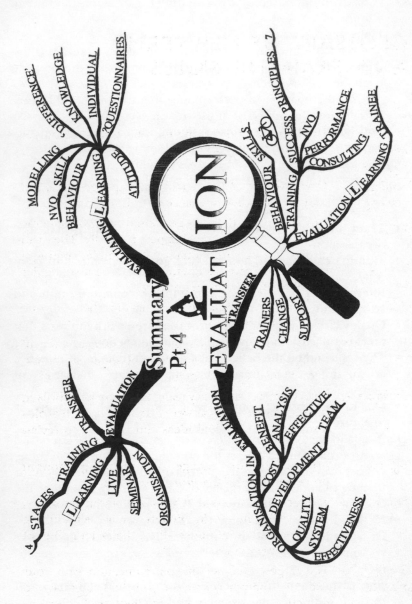

ION

Summary Pt 4

**EVALUAT ION**

**EVALUATING Learning**

MODELLING

'DIFFERENCE'

KNOWLEDGE

INDIVIDUAL

NVO SKILL

BEHAVIOUR

ATTITUDE

?QUESTIONNAIRES

**SUCCESS PRINCIPLES 7**

BEHAVIOUR SKILLS

TRAINING

NVO

PERFORMANCE

CONSULTING

**EVALUATION Learning TRAINEE**

**TRANSFER**

TRAINERS

CHANGE

SUPPORT

**4 STAGES TRAINING TRANSFER**

**Learning EVALUATION**

LIVE

SEMINAR

ORGANISATION

**EVALUATION**

ORGANISATION IN

COST BENEFIT ANALYSIS

DEVELOPMENT

EFFECTIVE

TEAM

QUALITY

SYSTEM

EFFECTIVENESS

# GLOSSARY OF NLP TERMS AND TRAINING SKILLS

*Accessing audience resources*  Drawing out and making use of trainees' resources and learning states.

*Analogue marking*  Using your voice tone, body language, gestures, etc. to mark out some key piece of training material.

*Anchor*  Any stimulus that is associated with a specific response. Anchors can happen naturally. They can also be set up intentionally for example, ringing a bell to get a group's attention or using a particular place to stand for taking questions.

*Anchoring*  The process of creating an association between one thing and another.

*'As if' frame*  Using guessing, imagining or pretending as a way of doing something that you have not done before. Ask, 'How would it be if I could . . . ?'

*Backtracking*  A very precise summary using the same key words in the same voice tones as were originally used. It avoids distorting the original ideas and is useful to review key points.

*Behaviour*  Any activity we engage in, including thought processes. One of the *neurological levels*.

*Beliefs*  The generalisations that we make about ourselves, others and the world. Beliefs act as self-fulfilling prophecies that influence all our behaviour. One of the *neurological levels*.

*Body language*  The largest channel of communication with your audience (55 per cent). Use your body language to influence the group and notice theirs as feedback as the training progresses.

*Calibrating*     Accurately recognising another person's or a group's state by reading non-verbal signals. For example, calibrating to high quality attention so that you can recognise it when you have it from a group.

*Choreography*    Systematically using different places in your training area for different kinds of training behaviour. For example, standing or sitting in a different position for delivering input, setting up an exercise, taking and answering questions, recounting stories, etc. This sets up spatial anchors for the group.

*Chunking*        Changing perceptions by moving up or down levels. Chunking up is going up and looking at a level that includes what you are studying. For example, looking at the intention behind a question chunks up from that question. Chunking down is going down a level to look at a more specific example or part of what you are studying. For example, the first step in formulating an outcome is to phrase it in the positive.

*Coaching*        Knowing when and how to intervene in a process to
*skill*           enable learning. Often using questions to shift someone's attention in such a way that the desired change in behaviour happens of its own accord.

*Congruence*      Consistent alignment and fitting together of different parts: i) personal congruence – alignment of beliefs, values, skills and actions; being in rapport with oneself; ii) messenger–message congruence – when the trainer is an embodiment and model of the skills or values she is training; iii) alignment congruence – when all parts of your communication – words, voice and body language – give the same message.

*Conscious*       The third stage of the learning cycle in which full
*competence*      conscious attention is still needed to carry out an activity. The skill is not yet fully integrated and habitual.

*Conscious*       The second stage of the learning cycle in which
*incompetence*    conscious attention is on the task and the results are variable. Although uncomfortable, this stage is when

the rate of learning is greatest.

*Conscious mind*   The part of our mind that is in present moment awareness. It can only pay attention to a few variables at once and does not see longer term or deeper consequences.

*Content*   The words that you say, as distinct from the way that you say them.

*Control frame*   Setting a limit on the scope or time of an activity, for example, processing an exercise.

*Covert*   Subtle or out of conscious awareness.

*Credibility*   Your standing with the group, the degree to which they see you as sincere, competent and congruent. Establishing your credibility helps establish a positive expectation set that will increase learning for the group. Sometimes you need to disclose your qualifications as an authority on the subject.

*Demonstration*   Giving a model of the activity the group will be doing. A clean demonstration provides a clear model and is one of the most important influences on how well the activity is carried out.

*Design*   The structure, process and content of a training, determined to achieve the training outcomes.

*Dovetailing outcomes*   The process of fitting together different outcomes to create the best win-win situation. This is the basis of agreements and negotiations. Part of the trainer's job is to dovetail different outcomes in the training.

*Downtime*   This is when you attend to your own thoughts and feelings. Downtime is useful after training to process, relax and care for yourself.

*Eliciting*   The skill of drawing out behaviour from others, such as comments, questions, outcomes, states and skills. Can be done verbally or non-verbally, covertly or overtly.

*Embedded commands*   This is what you do when you *mark out certain phrases* that could stand on their own as commands, *by changing your voice tone* or gesturing *so that they* don't *get it* consciously, only *unconsciously*.

*Environment*   The physical context you create for learning, for

|  | example the room, furniture arrangement, materials, handouts, visual aids and equipment. |
| *Exercises* | Structured activities with an outcome; the heart of experiential training. Good exercises create a context where learning is easy. The stages of an exercise are: design, setting up, demonstrating, coaching and processing. |
| *Experiential training* | Creating learning through experience. We learn skills best by doing, because this involves both conscious and unconscious mind. Cognitive knowledge involves only the conscious mind and a good memory. |
| *Feedback* | The responses you get from your actions. You need the sensory acuity to notice them and then the flexibility to adjust your actions to keep on course for your outcomes. |
| *Filters* | See *perceptual filters*. |
| *First position* | Experiencing the world from your own point of view and being in touch with your own reality. One of the three main perceptual positions, the others being second position and third or metaposition. Together these give a multiple description. |
| *Framing* | Instructions on how to understand and interpret the material that follows, what to pay attention to and what to disregard. An example would be setting an outcome frame and looking at each part of the training to see how it contributes to achieving your outcomes. See also *reframing* and *outframing*. |
| *Future pacing* | Mentally rehearsing new skills, knowledge or attitudes in an imaginary future where they will be needed. Essential to transfer learning outside the training room. |
| *Identity* | Self-image or self-concept. Who people take themselves to be. One of the *neurological levels*. |
| *Incongruence* | Contradiction or conflict between parts of yourself, beliefs, values or actions. May be sequential – one action followed by another that contradicts it – or simultaneous – positive words expressed with a doubtful voice tone. |

| | |
|---|---|
| *Integrity* | Congruence and honesty. Personal integrity and ethical actions are necessary for a high level of training skill. NLP skills will backfire unpleasantly without them. |
| *Intention* | The purpose or desired outcome of any behaviour. |
| *Internal representations* | All our thoughts and feelings. The mental pictures, sounds and feelings we remember and create. |
| *Intervention* | Interrupting an interaction to change the outcome. Effective intervention means knowing when to (sensory acuity) and how to (behavioural flexibility). Aim to get the biggest gain from the smallest intervention. |
| *Language* | Although the smallest channel of communication in presentations at seven per cent, language is still critically important. Consists of statements or questions which can be very specific (Meta Model) or artfully vague (Milton Model). |
| *Layout* | The way you structure the training environment (e.g. arranging seats in rows or in a circle). Layout will give a metamessage about the training. |
| *Leading* | Changing what you do with enough rapport so the other person or group goes with you. |
| *Learning* | The process of getting knowledge, skills, experience or values by study, experience or training. |
| *Learning cycle* | Stages of learning to build habitual skills – unconscious competence, then conscious incompetence, then conscious competence and finally unconscious competence. |
| *Learning strategies* | Sequences of images, sounds and feelings that lead to learning. From a training viewpoint, ensure that you provide a mix of seeing, hearing and doing to cater for all strategies. |
| *Learning styles* | Different preferred ways of learning. There are many different models, including different senses, metaprograms or concept-structure-use. A key skill is to cover all styles, rather than teach to your own preferred and unconscious style. Also, the group may have an overall preference. |

| | |
|---|---|
| *Linking* | This is making explicit the connections between the different parts of the training as you move from one to the next, to provide continuity for the trainees. |
| *Matching* | Adopting some aspects of another person's communication style for the purpose of building rapport. For example, matching their posture. Matching is not mimicry, which is conscious, exact copying of another person's behaviour. |
| *Meta* | Existing at a different level to something else. Derived from the Greek, meaning 'over and beyond'. |
| *Metacognition* | Having the knowledge about a skill to not only do it well, but be able to explain how you do it well. Being able to take a detached view of your skills. |
| *Metacomment* | To make a comment about a process that is happening, for example, *you are reading this explanation*. In training it helps to mark these out spatially. |
| *Metamessage* | Literally a message about a message. Spelling iz verry importent in thys Glosserie. The metamessage of that sentence is not the same as its message. Your non-verbal behaviour is constantly giving the group metamessages about you and the material. |
| *Meta Model* | A powerful set of language patterns and questions from NLP that links language with sensory experience. Key questions to clarify and specify meaning. |
| *Metaphor* | Indirect communication by a story or figure of speech implying a comparison. In NLP 'metaphor' covers similes, parables and allegories. |
| *Metaposition* | The third perceptual position, the detached and benign observer of self and others. |
| *Metaprograms* | Habitual and systematic filters we put on our experience, typically unconscious. For example, being motivated by moving towards rewards, rather than away from unpleasant consequences. Awareness of these patterns can make training easier and more effective. |

| | |
|---|---|
| *Milton Model* | From NLP, the inverse of the Meta Model, using artfully vague language patterns, so people can make just that specific meaning from their own experience that is the most useful for them. |
| *Mismatching* | Adopting different patterns of behaviour to another person for the purpose of redirecting a meeting or conversation. |
| *Modelling* | Either acting as a behavioural model for others, as when doing demonstrations, or the process of making explicit the sequences of thoughts and behaviour that enable someone to perform a skill or task. Modelling is the basis of both NLP and accelerated learning. |
| *Multiple description* | Taking different viewpoints to gather as much information as possible about a person or situation. For example, looking at training from your own viewpoint, the trainees' viewpoint and the organisational viewpoint, or first, second and metaposition. |
| *Multitracking* | The skill of attending to many different things at once – for example, in taking a question, you assess what the questioner actually want from you (second position), the time available, group interest levels, a number of different answers and what the group would get from each one – before opening your mouth! |
| *Negotiation* | The skill of trading off differences to reach a win-win agreement for both parties. |
| *Neuro-Linguistic Programming* | The study of excellence and a model of how individuals structure their experience. |
| *Neurological levels* | Also known as the logical levels of experience: environment, behaviour, capability, belief, identity and spiritual. |
| *New behaviour generator* | A simple and effective technique for the mental rehearsal of new skills and behaviour or for making changes in existing behaviour. |
| *Open frame* | An opportunity for trainees to raise any comments or questions about the material that interests them. |

| | |
|---|---|
| *Outcome* | A goal or objective that meets the following conditions: it is stated in the positive, specifies the person's own part in achieving it and the resources they have to do so, is specific enough to have sensory-based evidence and has been checked for unforeseen consequences. |
| *Outframing* | Setting a frame that excludes possible objections. |
| *Pacing* | Joining others in their reality and building rapport before starting to lead somewhere different. You can pace at any level from behaviour to values and beliefs. |
| *Pattern interruption* | Any intervention designed to stop ongoing behaviour . . . k$yr per centbnf&pd@lfd . . . so that you can lead somewhere more useful. |
| *Perceptual filters* | The world is always richer than our experience of it. Our perceptual filters determine what we notice and what we delete. You can develop filters for all the patterns in this glossary. For example, the emotional state of a group, etc. |
| *Perceptual position* | The viewpoint we are aware of at any moment can be our own (first position), someone else's (second position), or an objective and benevolent observer's (third position). |
| *Physiology* | Concerning the body, rather than the mind. Develop the skill of calibrating to subtle shifts in physiology if you want to know what is going on for others. |
| *Positive intention* | The positive purpose underlying any 'difficult' behaviour, what it gets for the person who does it that is important to him. Finding it gives you the key to how to respond effectively. |
| *Presupposition* | Something that has to be taken for granted for a behaviour or statement to make sense. |
| *Process and content* | Content is what is done, whereas process is about how it is done. For example, *what* you say is content and *how* you say it is process. We often get stuck by noticing only content. While training, keep most of your attention at the level of process. |
| *Processing exercises* | A comments and questions session after an exercise, to bring out the different learning points. |

| | |
|---|---|
| *Questions* | Do questions represent the intersection of language and learning? Can you elicit questions, frame questions, outframe questions, utilise questions and answer them by asking another question? How much do you think the quality of the questions you ask yourself determines the quality of results you create? |
| *Quotes pattern* | We have heard this defined as, 'A linguistic pattern in which your message is expressed as if by someone else.' |
| *Rapport* | The process of building and maintaining a relationship of mutual trust and understanding. The ability to elicit useful responses from others. Often operates at the levels of words, actions, values and beliefs. |
| *Recovery strategy* | A way of feeling resourceful and generating new choices when you feel stuck or under pressure. |
| *Reframing* | Changing the way of understanding a statement or behaviour to give it another meaning. |
| *Relevancy challenge* | Asking how a specific statement or behaviour is helping to achieve an agreed outcome. |
| *Representation systems* | How we code information in our minds in one or more of the sensory channels: visual, auditory, kinesthetic (movement and emotions), olfactory (smell), gustatory (taste) and vestibular (balance). Using our senses internally. |
| *Resistance* | A block to understanding or acting. Any resistance only exists by virtue of a continued push in the opposite direction. So in training, the useful question to ask is, 'What am I doing that is contributing to this person's resistance?' |
| *Resource anchoring* | A simple process for bringing resourceful states into the present moment whenever they are needed. |
| *Resourceful states* | A combination of thoughts, feelings and physiology that makes any task easier and more enjoyable. |
| *Second position* | Seeing the world from another person's point of view and so understanding their reality. One of three *perceptual positions*. |

| | |
|---|---|
| *Sensory acuity* | Training your senses to notice finer and more useful distinctions in the world. An important part of learning to read body language. |
| *Sensory-based description* | Description in terms of what a person would see and hear and feel, rather than interpretation and hallucination of what you think is happening. |
| *Sensory channels* | Our six senses as channels of communication with the world: sight, hearing, touch, smell, taste and balance. See *representation systems*. |
| *Setting up exercises* | Introducing an exercise in such a way that people want to do it and are clear about what, why and how they will be doing it. |
| *Skill* | Consistent and effective action or thinking that achieves the desired outcome and is backed by empowering beliefs. |
| *Softeners* | Lessening the impact of a direct question or statement by using a soft voice tone or preamble such as 'Would you be willing to tell me X?' rather than, 'Tell me X.' |
| *Spatial marking* | Consistently using different areas of space for different actions to associate location with action. See *choreography*. |
| *State* | Shorthand for physiological state, which is like a snapshot of the total neurology: the mental, emotional and physical experience. Managing one's own and the trainees' states is probably the single most important training skill. |
| *Submodalities* | The qualities of mental pictures, sounds and feelings, for example, pictures may be large or small, moving or still, in colour or black and white. |
| *Systemic* | To do with systems, looking at relationships and consequences over time and space rather than linear cause and effect. |
| *Third position* | See *metaposition*. |
| *Time frame management* | Using time to the greatest advantage in a training, so activities are not unnecessarily curtailed or lengthened. |

| | |
|---|---|
| *Tonal marking* | Using your voice to *mark out* certain words as being significant. |
| *Tracking* | Paying attention to particular aspects of the training. Can be done consciously or, with practice, unconsciously. |
| *Trance* | An altered state with an inward focus of attention. |
| *Unconscious competence* | The fourth stage of the learning cycle in which the skill has been fully integrated and is habitual. |
| *Unconscious incompetence* | The first stage of the learning cycle in which we are unaware of a skill. |
| *Unconscious mind* | Our unconscious mind consists of everything to do with our inner reality that we are unaware of in the present moment. |
| *Uptime* | A state in which your attention is mainly external, and you feel very alert and resourceful. |
| *Utilisation* | The skill of being able to turn any behaviour or eventuality to further your training outcomes. |
| *Values* | Those things that are important to us. They drive our actions. |
| *Voice quality* | The second most important channel of communication and influence in presentations. Research suggests it is 38 per cent of the total impact of the communication. |

# S/NVQ AND TRAINING

The system of National Vocational Qualifications (NVQ) and Scottish Vocational Qualifications (SVQ) is a set of competency-based standards to facilitate more effective skills learning in all major industries.

During the 1980s it became clear that in the UK the existing vocational education and training system could not meet employers' demands for a skilled workforce. Existing assessment methods were biased towards testing knowledge, while employers wanted competent *application* of skills and knowledge.

In 1986 the government set up the National Council for Vocational Qualifications. Its task was to reform vocational qualifications by defining competence and its accompanying standards for a wide variety of professions. 'Industrial Lead Bodies' were created for this purpose for different sectors of industry and commerce. Each Industrial Lead Body developed the standards of occupational competence for its own industry.

The National Council for Vocational Qualifications is the overall accrediting body and awards National Vocational Qualifications (NVQs) to individuals who meet these standards. In Scotland there is the Scottish Vocational Education Council (SCOTVEC).

The Industry Lead Bodies take occupational skills and break them down into small elements, providing a logical and sequential map. A trainer can look at the skills in finer and finer detail, and see the standards of competence required and the criteria by which they will be judged.

### The Training and Development Lead Body (TDLB)

The TDLB sets national standards and administers NVQs for trainers. It was set up in 1989 to define standards and work out vocational qualifications for those in the training and development field – full- and part-time trainers, supervisors and line managers. The standards are meant to define more than existing practice, they are intended as a pointer towards best practice. The standards are also a help in establishing goals in trainer training and in measuring the effectiveness of existing training materials.

### Training standards

The national standards for training and development are set out in a structured hierarchy. At the top is the key purpose of training:

> To develop human potential to assist organisations and individuals to achieve their objectives.

This key purpose divides into five areas of competence that closely follow the training cycle:

- Diagnosis: to identify training and development needs.
- The planning and design of training.
- The delivery of training, the providing of learning opportunities and resources.
- To evaluate the effectiveness of training and development.
- To support advances in training and development.

Each of these five areas is divided into two sub-components. For example, diagnosis is divided into identifying organisational requirements and identifying the learning needs of individuals and groups. Each of these 10 sub-components is further analysed into a number of *elements of competence*.

Standards are made of three pieces:

> **Elements of competence.** These are the outcomes a competent person is expected to achieve.
> **Performance criteria.** This is the evidence by which you would judge a competent performance.
> **Range of applications.** This is the type of resource, location, time, etc., in which the element is to be achieved.

As an example, the third area, C, delivery of training, divides into two elements of competence:

C1    To obtain and allocate resources to deliver training and development plans.

C2    To provide learning opportunities and support to enable individuals and groups achieve objectives.

These two divide into 10 units, C11–C28, as shown opposite.

The units C11–C28 in turn are divided into 31 standards, each with assessment criteria and range statements.

It is clear that NVQ standards focus down to a considerable degree. There are 126 elements in total: a menu that can be sampled to define different training work. They can be used not only to structure vocational qualifications, but also as a basis for job descriptions and to develop training programmes. When the standards are used as a basis for vocational qualifications, they are grouped into larger units of competence to reflect employment needs. At the moment there are five levels of qualification.

## Standards as a map

Standards are a map of training and development. They are useful because they focus on performance, with evidence for what constitutes a competent performance. An individual who achieves the standards by meeting the criteria obtains the appropriate level of NVQ. These levels form the basis of a career structure, depending on the particular employer.

The rapid growth of the NVQ system has implications for employers and trainers alike. Employers have the opportunity to influence and establish agreed standards of performance for the workforce in their industries. Performance assessment happens in the workplace, making the Training Needs Analysis more effective. With better targeted training and development of the workforce, investment in training is more attractive. Trainers will have clearer goals to achieve, defined by competencies in the workplace.

*National standards for training and development*
*Area C: Provide learning opportunities, resources and support*

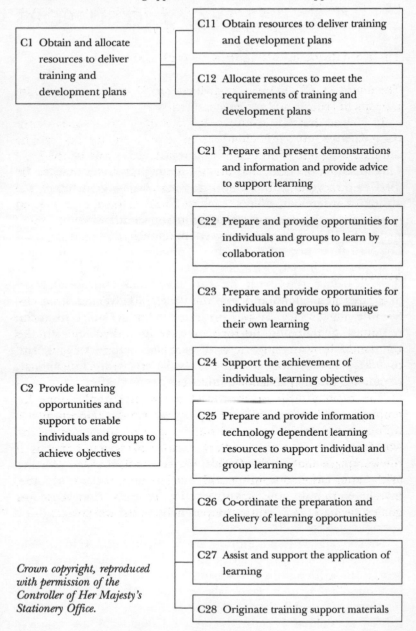

C1 Obtain and allocate resources to deliver training and development plans

C11 Obtain resources to deliver training and development plans

C12 Allocate resources to meet the requirements of training and development plans

C2 Provide learning opportunities and support to enable individuals and groups to achieve objectives

C21 Prepare and present demonstrations and information and provide advice to support learning

C22 Prepare and provide opportunities for individuals and groups to learn by collaboration

C23 Prepare and provide opportunities for individuals and groups to manage their own learning

C24 Support the achievement of individuals, learning objectives

C25 Prepare and provide information technology dependent learning resources to support individual and group learning

C26 Co-ordinate the preparation and delivery of learning opportunities

C27 Assist and support the application of learning

C28 Originate training support materials

# TRAINING SUPPORT

## *Using different resources*

This appendix is a brief look at the learning resources that can be used to complement live training. Some learning materials are obvious and familiar, others, such as forms of computer assisted learning, are newer and more of an unknown quantity.

These different resources present material in different ways and how well they succeed depends to some extent on the learning strategies of the user. A trainer has at least three advantages over these learning resources: he can use them appropriately to maximise their effects and minimise their disadvantages; he can teach learning to learn skills, so trainees can get more from the resources anyway; and he is responsive and flexible, with the human skills of rapport and sensitive support, and the presentation skills to make the material engaging, fun and an adventure. Many of these resources can be used after training to effectively transfer the learning back to the workplace. They are a reference and a resource for the trainee outside the training room.

### Books

Books are cheap and available on any subject, but all the motivation has to be provided by the user. Books are not interactive, they do not respond to what the reader does. They are limited to the written word and still images, and are not good for learning physical skills.

Booklets and written handouts are useful on a course to provide a record that the trainees can take away and think over. The greater the writing skills of the trainer, the more useful the books, handouts and written materials generally. Writing clearly and simply is another skill for the competent trainer. The quality of the written material is part of the general quality of the training (which is why we have included an appendix on writing training materials, see page 273).

## Audiotapes

The spoken word carries more information and has more impact than the written word. This is reflected in research that shows we remember twice as much of the material we hear than the material we read. However, audiotapes are slow and most people read quicker than the tape speed.

## Visual material

Charts, diagrams, overhead transparencies, three-dimensional models and slides, although static, can hold and transfer a great deal of information very quickly, and are already well integrated into training. In training, a picture is worth a lot more than a thousand words and a video is worth tens of thousands.

Videotapes can have much more impact, and their range and quality have grown enormously. There are companies that are major training video providers and many companies make videos in-house.

## Computer-based training

Many training tools are computer based and growing in sophistication. We will sketch some current possibilities. The field is developing very quickly. It is satisfying to equip people for change using the very technology that is generating the changes.

Computer assisted learning (CAL) has featured in education and training for some time, the flight simulator being a classic example. Most applications are for the ubiquitous PC. As the new technology and the consequent training grows, attention has broadened to explore how the computer itself can be used to train the user to operate it. Interactive help can be embedded in the programs or put on extra software support. Interactive video (IV) and interactive multimedia combine the advantages of computer-based training with video pictures and sound. Expert systems have a knowledge base and a set of rules on how to use it and are useful for diagnosis, evaluation and decision making.

Software for generative learning is starting to become available, and both authors are involved in different projects in this field.

### Neural networks

Neural network computing is beginning to produce systems that can learn and respond to feedback. By contrast, conventional computers have to be programmed with an explicit step-by-step series of instructions that the computer always follows.

Neural computing gives the possibilities of intelligent programs that can monitor the learner's responses and direct her to the relevant information. The program can also explain the reasoning behind the steps. It acts as an intelligent expert system. A number of universities as well as businesses are researching these possibilities.

The future of computer assisted learning is probably what is being called an Electronic Performance Support System, where employees would have immediate individualised on-line access to a full range of information, guidance, advice, data and assistance, allowing them to perform their work more efficiently with a minimum of distraction. They would literally have the information 'at their fingertips'. This would probably work like a organisational bulletin board. There are already international networked bulletin boards, such as Compuserve, that allow users to access information on almost any topic, including NLP.

Virtual reality is already with us and is a computer simulation that you are actually inside, like a flight simulator, that encompasses all or nearly all your senses. This is done at the moment through special gloves and headsets. The whole field opens up a future prospect of virtual training and virtual learning in sophisticated interactive simulations.

Like a car engine, computers are useless by themselves, they need a user and an interface to do anything in the world. Technology is only as smart as the people who build it and use it.

### Recall of material

All these resources for training give information and stimulating ideas for the learner. Books give only words and recall is at its lowest when words alone are presented. Recall is better when words are linked to a sound track, but the learner still has to visualise. Television, video or film, where there are pictures and sound, give even better recall. Recall and learning are greatest in direct experience and this is the domain of experiential training.

# WRITING SKILLS FOR
# WRITTEN TRAINING MATERIAL

Good handouts and written material enhance the training course and give a metamessage about the whole training. These are what trainees will take away with them and show to others. You will want to make sure they are representative of the quality of your training. These guidelines apply to writing simulations, support material and exercises for computer screens or paper.

- First be clear about your outcomes. What are your outcomes for the material? What do you want the trainees to get from it? For example:

    revision of key points
    extra support material
    reference lists
    resources
    instructions
    homework
    documented examples

- There are some useful guidelines for your writing:
    a) Use different sensory words – visual, auditory and feeling – so the reader can see, hear and get a grasp of what you are saying.
    b) Questions are useful to engage the reader, aren't they?
    c) Write so the reader has a sense of a real person writing.
    d) Talk to the reader as an equal, explain rather than lecture.
    e) Use the second person when you write. If I use the first person I tend to set myself up as an authority, haven't I?

- Make it visually interesting as well as informational.

- Write clearly and simply, unless you deliberately want to be ambiguous to leave open different possibilities.

- Use simple punctuation.

- Be grammatically correct when you write, bearing in mind general usage. Poor grammar and punctuation give a negative message about the material.

- If you use instructions, frame them positively, i.e. explain what to do, not what not to do. For example, 'Do not agree a referral until you have the customer's name' is expressed negatively. 'Obtain the customer's name before referring them' is more positive and also clearer.

- Use examples wherever possible.

- If the material is long (more than 1,000 words), state at the beginning what it contains and have a summary at the end.

If you want an idea of how clearly you are writing, then you can apply the aptly named 'Fog Index'.

To work out the Fog Index of any piece of writing proceed as follows:

- Firstly, take a section of between 100 and 300 words.
- Count the average number of words per sentence. Call this number 'A'.
- There are some exceptions which you do not count:
  a) Do not count proper names (in other words, any nouns starting with a capital letter).
  b) Count compound (hyphenated) words as one word if each part has two syllables or fewer.
- Next, count the number of words of three syllables or more per 100 words. Call this number 'B'. Leave out words that achieve three syllables by changing the part of speech (e.g. verb tenses or plurals). For example, 'anchoring' would not count, as its third syllable is due only to its verb tense.

The Fog Index = Average number of words per sentence added to the number of words of three syllables or more per 100 words, multiplied by two fifths.

Fog Index: A + B x 0.4

Reasonably clear writing has a Fog Index of between 9 and 12. Aim for an index between 7 and 10.

For example, this Appendix has 572 words and 47 sentences. An average of just over 12 words per sentence.

It has 54 words of three syllables or more.

Fog Index is 12 + 10 multiplied by 0.4 = 8.8.

Read your material the day after you compose it from the trainees' point of view. Is it clear? Does it achieve your outcomes? Revise it until you are satisfied.

## United Kingdom

For further information about:

### NLP

*Joseph O'Connor*
*John Seymour Associates*
See pp. 286, 288.

### Training

*The Institute of Training and*
*Development (ITD)*
Marlow House
Institute Road
Marlow
Buckinghamshire
SL7 1BD
Phone: 0628 890123
Fax: 0628 890208

### TQM and Deming

*British Deming Association*
2 Castle Street
Salisbury
Wiltshire
SP1 1BB

Phone: 0722 412138

## NVQ and SVQ

Details of NVQ structure:
*The Employment Department*
Moorfoot
Sheffield S1 4PQ

also
*National Standards for Training and*
*Development*
*Crown Copyright 1992*
Available from:
Cambertown Ltd
Commercial Road
Gold Thorp Industrial Estate
Gold Thorp
Nr Rotherham
S63 9BL

## United States of America

For further information about
training, contact:

*The American Association for Training*
*and Development (ASTD)*
1630 Duke Street
PO Box 1443
Alexandria
Virginia 22313

Phone: 703 683 8100

# BIBLIOGRAPHY

Alexander, F. M., *The Use of Self* (Centerline Press, 1986).

Andreas, Steve and Connirae, *Heart of the Mind* (Real People Press, 1989).

Bandler, Richard and Grinder, John, *Frogs into Princes* (Real People Press, 1979).

Bateson, Gregory, *Steps to an Ecology of Mind* (Ballantine, 1972).

Beer, Stafford, *Diagnosing the System* (Wiley, 1985).

Belbin, R., *Management Teams: Why They Succeed or Fail* (Heinemann, 1981).

Bendell, Kelly, Merry and Simms, *Quality Measuring and Monitoring* (Random House, 1993).

Bentley, Trevor, *The Business of Training* (McGraw-Hill, 1991).

Blanchard, Kenneth and Johnson, Spencer, *One Minute Manager* (Fontana, 1983).

Bond, Tim, *Games for Social and Life Skills* (Stanley Thornes, 1990).

Bramley, Peter, *Evaluating Training Effectiveness* (McGraw Hill, 1991).

Brandes, Donna and Phillips, Howard, *The Gamester's Handbook* (Stanley Thornes, 1977).

Brandes, Donna, *Gamester's Handbook 2* (Stanley Thornes, 1982).

Brittan, A. and Maynard, M., *Sexism, Racism and Oppression* (Blackwell, 1984).

Buzan, Tony, *Use Both Sides of your Brain* (E. P. Dutton, 1985).

—, *The Mind Map Book: Radiant Thinking* (BBC Publications, 1993).

Checkland, Peter, *Soft Systems Methodology* (John Wiley, 1989).

Cooper, Susan and Heenan, Cathy, *Preparing, Designing, Leading Workshops* (Van Nostrand Reinhold, 1980).

Covey, Stephen, *Seven Habits of Highly Effective People* (Simon and

Schuster, 1989).

Decker, Bert, *You've Got to be Believed to be Heard* (St Martin's Press, 1992).

Deming, Dr W., *Out of the Crisis* (Cambridge University Press, 1988).

Dilts, Robert and Epstein, Todd, *NLP in Training Groups* (Dynamic Learning Publications, 1989).

Dilts, Robert, *The Spelling Strategy* (Dynamic Learning Publications, 1989).

—, *Changing Belief Systems with NLP* (Meta Publications, 1990).

Fletcher, Shirley, *NVQs Standards and Competence* (Kogan Page, 1991).

Eitington, Julius, *The Winning Trainer* (Gulf, 1984).

Gallwey, T., *The Inner Game of Tennis* (Random House, 1974).

Gelb, Michael, *Present Yourself* (Aurum Press, 1988).

Handy, Charles, *The Age of Unreason* (Business Books, 1989).

Heron, John, *The Facilitators Handbook* (Kogan Page, 1989).

Ishikawa, K., *Quality Circles Activities* (Union of Japanese Scientists and Engineers, 1968).

Karasik, Paul, *How to Make it Big in the Seminar Business* (McGraw-Hill, 1992).

Kolb, D., *Experiential Learning* (Prentice-Hall, 1984).

Kubistant, T., *Performing your Best* (Human Kinetics, 1986).

Laborde, Genie, *Influencing with Integrity* (Syntony Publishing Company, 1984).

Leeds, Dorothy, *Power Speak* (Piatkus, 1988).

Leigh, David, *A Practical Approach to Group Training* (Kogan Page, 1991).

Maslow, Abraham, *Towards a Psychology of Being* (Van Nostrand, 1968).

Mehrabian, A., *Silent Messages* (Wadsworth, 1971).

— and Ferris, R., 'Inference of Attitudes from Non-Verbal Communication in Two Channels' in *Journal of Counselling Psychology* Vol. 31, 1967.

Minsky, Marvin, *The Society of Mind* (Simon and Shuster, 1988).

Mintzberg, Henry, *Mintzberg on Management* (Free Press, 1989).

Munson, Laurence, *How to Conduct Training Seminars* (McGraw-

Hill, 1984).

National Standards for Training and Development, *Crown Copyright 1992* (available from Cambertown Ltd, Commercial Road, Gold Thorp Industrial Estate, Gold Thorp, Nr Rotherham, S63 9BL).

Neave, Henry, *The Deming Dimension* (SPC Press, 1990).

O'Connor, Joseph, *Not Pulling Strings* (Lambent Books, 1987).

— and Seymour, John, *Introducing Neuro Linguistic Programming* (Aquarian, 1993).

Oliver, M., *The Politics of Disablement* (Macmillan, 1990).

Parsloe, Eric, *Coaching, Mentoring and Assessing* (Kogan Page, 1992).

Peters, T. and Waterman, R., *In Search of Excellence* (Harper and Row, 1982).

Peters, Tom, *Liberation Management* (Macmillan, 1992).

Phillips, Keri and Shaw, Patricia, *A Consultancy Approach for Trainers* (Gower, 1989).

Pimental, Ken and Teixeira, Kevin, *Virtual Reality* (McGraw-Hill, 1993).

Pont, Tony, *Developing Effective Training Skills* (McGraw-Hill, 1991).

Powell, L. S., *Guide to the Use of Visual Aids* (BACIE, 1978).

Rackham, N. and Morgan, T., *Behavioural Analysis in Training* (McGraw-Hill, 1977).

Rogers, Carl, *Freedom to Learn* (Merrill, 1983).

Robbins, Anthony, *Unlimited Power* (Simon and Schuster, 1986).

—, *Awaken the Giant Within* (Simon and Schuster, 1992).

Scannell, Edward and Newstrom, John, *More Games Trainers Play* (McGraw-Hill, 1980).

Semler, Ricardo, *Maverick!* (Century, 1993).

Senge, Peter, *The Fifth Discipline* (Century, 1990).

Skinner, B. F., *Beyond Freedom and Dignity* (Knopf, 1971).

Stewart, A. and V., *Business Applications of Repertory Grids* (McGraw-Hill, 1981).

Thompson, Neil, *Anti-discriminatory Practice* (Macmillan, 1993).

Tracey, Brian, *Maximum Achievement* (Simon and Schuster, 1993).

Truelove, Steve (Ed.), *Handbook of Training and Development* (Blackwell, 1992).

Items with * are listed in the glossary.
The main reference page number is in bold type.

# ABOUT THE AUTHORS AND BUSINESS CONSULTANCY SERVICES

## JOSEPH O'CONNOR

Joseph O'Connor is an author, trainer, consultant and software designer. Joseph trained in NLP with John Grinder and Robert Dilts. He trains NLP directly and uses NLP in his training and consultancy work internationally. He has a BSc degree, is a Licentiate of the Royal College of Music and a qualified teacher. His involvement in music and the arts has resulted in modelling projects in the areas of the theatre and music. He has also modelled excellent tennis players, and is interested in the link between coaching skills in sport and business.

Joseph is fascinated by individual learning and how this links to organisational learning, and is working to bring together ideas of NLP, generative psychology and computer software to combine leading communications skills with advances in technology. He works with an international team designing and producing software and training users.

After writing *Introducing Neuro-Linguistic Programming* and *Training with NLP* with John Seymour, his next book is *Successful Selling with NLP*, to be published in 1995.

### Business consulting and training
Joseph works as a trainer and consultant for organisations, offering:
- Practical applications of NLP in business
- Communications and coaching skills
- Trainer training
- Courses tailored to organisation needs

### Modelling projects
- Identifying and modelling top performers in any field, finding

the patterns that make them excel, and designing training to pass on these skills to others.

## Software: products, design and consultancy

Joseph is part of an international team that designs and produces generative psychological software for organisational and individual development. This software is currently being used in over 60 companies world-wide.

Available at present:

- *Objectives*

  This program helps you to develop, refine and analyse your business decisions and objectives, individually and in groups. It is used to explore the consequences of your objectives, and to break them down into a series of achievable steps, clarifying roles and responsibilities to make an action plan.

- *Values*

  This program is used to explore individual and organisational values, and to define and understand group values in team-building exercises.

- *Working Styles*

  This software allows you to find out your preferred styles of working, to mange your work towards your natural strengths, and work co-operatively with others.

- *Business Objective Review*

  A program in three stages

    Deciding and specifying objectives

    Reviewing progress.

    Final review and completion.

  The program enables users to look at objectives through several layers of management and see the degree of alignment in the system.

All programs work on any IBM compatible PC with Windows 3.1. All programs have user definable help screens and can be tailored to the user. They are used together with live training and also to transfer training back to the organisation.

Contact Joseph O'Connor
c/o Lambent Training
4 Coombe Gardens
New Malden
Surrey
KT3 4AA
UK
Phone: 081 715 2560
Fax:    081 715 2560
E-mail: *lament @ well.sf.ca.us*

## JOHN SEYMOUR

John Seymour is a consultant, trainer and author. He founded John Seymour Associates, the longest established NLP training organisation in the UK, to provide NLP skills training for personal and organisational development. John is one of Britain's most experienced NLP trainers and works internationally. He provides in-house consulting and training for organisations large and small, including both the health and education services at national level. He is co-author with Joseph O'Connor, of Britain's best selling NLP book, *Introducing Neuro-Linguistic Programming* which has been translated into many languages. John's main interests are in personal development, systems thinking and learning organisation. He lives in the Bristol area with his life partner Annie. John has two postgraduate diplomas in Education and one in Applied Humanistic Psychology. He did his original NLP training with John Grinder and later with Richard Bandler. He is a Fellow of, and a Certified NLP Trainer with, the North American Association for NLP (previously the International Association for NLP). He also serves on the advisory board of the international NLP journal *NLP World*.

## JOHN SEYMOUR ASSOCIATES (JSA)

Founded by John Seymour in 1985, JSA is a team of NLP trainers, coaches and staff dedicated to helping people and organisations to learn and develop themselves. At the time of going to press, JSA offer the following:

## NLP training for the public

- Britain's longest established NLP training provider.
- *NLP Practitioner Training*: fully recognised, top quality trainings held in Britain and abroad.
- NLP Training Skills for Trainers: especially for trainers, presenters and teachers who wish to greatly enhance their effectiveness.

For inclusion on our mailing list, and free brochure listing our current programmes, please write or phone.

## JSA business consulting services

- *NLP Skills Training*, tailor-made to suit specific requirements.
- *Modelling Projects* on high-performers, and designing training to pass on these skills to others.
- *Training of Trainers* to greatly enhance their effectiveness.
- *Personal Consulting* John also works as a personal consultant to heads of organisations.

If you would like to know more, please phone us.

## Generative psychological software

In connection with John Hollis (Hollis Research), John Seymour is currently generating an entirely new and unique concept in software, which could be thought of as 'mindware' instead of software!

*Results Accelerator* acts as your personal coach to improve the results you produce. It interacts with you conversationally, using your own language, to help your get clear on ways forward for personal or organisational projects. The software runs on Microsoft MS-Dos version 3.1 or later, Mircrosoft Windows version 3.0 or later in standard or enhanced mode. It also runs on IBM OS2.

John Seymour and John Hollis together provide a *consultancy service* specialising in innovative interactive software, tailored to meet the needs for continuous improvement in learning organisations. Please phone if you want to know more about how this can help you.

## Hardware

Also in connection with Hollis Research, we distribute their portable, galvanic skin-response *Biofeedback meter – GSR1*. The GSR1 has multiple uses and can be used with the Results

Accelerator. It is invaluable for monitoring personal stress levels and helps the user learn less stressful responses to given situations (useful for high blood pressure problems). About the size of a personal stereo, this model is particularly accurate, sensitive and cost effective. Please contact us for a leaflet.

**Books**
Mail order books:
*   *Introducing Neuro Linguistic Programming* by Joseph O'Connor and John Seymour
*   *Training with NLP* by Joseph O'Connor and John Seymour

John Seymour Associates
TWNLP
17 Boyce Drive
Bristol BS2 9XQ
UK

Before August 1994 please phone us on 0272 557827
After August 1994:
Phone: 0117 955 7827; for international calls dial 44 117 955 7827
Fax:    0117 941 3004; for international calls dial 44 117 941 3004